CANYON, MOUNTAIN, CLOUD

Canyon, Mountain, Cloud

Absence and Longing in American Parks

TYRA A. OLSTAD

Oregon State University Press   Corvallis

Library of Congress Cataloging-in-Publication Data

Names: Olstad, Tyra, author.
Title: Canyon, mountain, cloud : absence and longing in American parks /
    Tyra A. Olstad.
Description: Corvallis : Oregon State University Press, 2021. | Includes
    bibliographical references and index.
Identifiers: LCCN 2020057155 | ISBN 9780870711022 (trade paperback) |
    ISBN 9780870711046 (ebook)
Subjects: LCSH: Parks—United States. | National parks and reserves—
    United States.
Classification: LCC SB482.A4 O48 2021 | DDC 363.68097—dc23
LC record available at https://lccn.loc.gov/2020057155

♾ This paper meets the requirements of ANSI/NISO Z39.48-1992
    (Permanence of Paper).

The quote on the following page is an excerpt from Han Shan's "The gorge is
long . . .," translated by J. P. Seaton, in *The Poetry of Zen*, edited by Sam Hamill
and J. P. Seaton. Translation copyright © 2004 by J. P. Seaton. Reprinted by
arrangement with The Permissions Company, LLC, on behalf of Shambhala
Publications Inc., www.shambhala.com.

First published in 2021 by Oregon State University Press
Printed in the United States of America

Oregon State University Press
121 The Valley Library
Corvallis OR 97331-4501
541-737-3166 • fax 541-737-3170
www.osupress.oregonstate.edu

Who's ready to leap free of the world's traces:
come sit with me among white clouds?

—Han Shan

Contents

Preface ix

PART I   WHERE DRAGONS AND STARS WANDER
Black Canyon of the Gunnison National Park, Colorado

    1   Canyon 3

    2   Fossil 25

    3   Bobcat 39

    4   Self... 57

PART II   QUESTIONS CLOUD-HIDDEN PEAKS POSE
Denali National Park and Preserve, Alaska

    5   Scenery and Wild Life Therein 61

    6   Mountain 81

    7   Fang 89

    8   Self 109

PART III SKY, AND I INVITE CLEAR WIND FOR COMPANY
Adirondack Forest Preserve, New York

    9   Steward 127

    10 Skylight.. 167

    11 "Wild"... 187

    12 Interim (*Black Canyon of the
          Gunnison National Park, Colorado*) 199

    13 Self 207

Epilogue: Mountains the Gate, Rivers the Door (*Arctic Alaska*) 225

Acknowledgments 245

Notes 247

References 253

Index 263

Preface

I am part canyon, part mountain, part cloud. I am rivers and lakes and the sky overhead. I am sunburned and rain drenched, scoured by ice and smoothed by the wind: anorthosite, sandstone, pre-Cambrian gneiss. I am tundra and forest, desert and bog. Raven, caribou, and lithe, tawny cougar, glancing over my shoulder as I pad off on big, silent paws.

We are each an amalgam of our experiences: places we've been, places we've dreamed, memories real and imagined. Every time we venture forth, we have the potential to learn, to grow, to let some conspiracy of landscape and circumstance rewire our synapses and change our sense of self. Especially when visiting big, wild places— places where, as Gary Snyder puts it, "All the junk that goes with being human / Drops away, hard rock wavers"[1]—we can rethink *who* we are in the context of *where* we are. Officially designated "wildernesses" or not, areas governed by natural ecological processes and dominated by non-human species offer opportunities for recalibration. Recreation, yes, in the sense of re-creation. Re-search. Reconnection with what it means to be human—alive in a sometimes magnificent, sometimes terrifying, ancient, ever changing, endlessly fascinating world.

But some landscapes resonate more loudly, some circumstances cut more deeply. No matter our beliefs, expectations, or desires, we can't ever really know if or how a wild place will change us until we're there, living it. In some cases, the best we can do may be, again in the words of Gary Snyder, to "learn the terrain, nod to all the plants and animals and birds, ford the streams and cross the ridges, and tell a good story when we get back home."[2] In others, as Barry Lopez urged, we can try "to sense the range and variety of [the land's] expression—its weather and colors and animals . . . to preserve some of the mystery within it as a kind of wisdom to be experienced, not questioned."[3] Then, in rare and precious instances, "the land gets inside of us; and we must decide one way or another what this means, what we will do about it."[4] (The part titles in this book, which strive to capture the magic found in some places—and inside ourselves as a result—are fragments of classical Chinese poetry, translated by David Hinton.[5])

I have become part canyon, part mountain, part cloud: Black Canyon of the Gunnison, Colorado; Denali, Alaska; the Adirondack High Peaks, New York; with a touch of Arctic Alaska stirred in. How does it change a person, to spend time upon the rocks, by the waters, in the sky?

PART I

Where Dragons and Stars Wander

BLACK CANYON OF THE GUNNISON
NATIONAL PARK, COLORADO

Dawn, Chasm View. Sunlight reverberating between canyon walls, water cutting far below.

CHAPTER 1

Canyon

Come dawn, the sky barely lightened to a thick, sleety gray. Normally, I would have slowed to appreciate the scene: ragged blanket of clouds sweeping low across a sea of sagebrush; wind tearing tatters of moisture from the air and scooping up swirls of dust and debris; lonely highway cutting south, away from Wyoming and the place I'd called home for a year. Spectacularly empty, desolately expansive—my kind of landscape.

This morning, though, I had more to think about than the view. Foremost: how to navigate surprisingly and almost impassably large patches of ice and piles of snow. Minnie's Gap near Flaming Gorge boasted drifts up to three feet deep. Hoping that I wouldn't end up stranded—car stuck in a snowbank; me freezing in an attempt to walk fifty-odd miles back to Rock Springs—I rammed my poor little low-clearance front-wheel-drive sedan into the drifts, clambering and skidding on through. Mile after mile of howling wind and swirling flurries, headlights barely keeping the pressing grayness at bay. When my car finally crested over to the leeward side of the pass, I felt a surge of relief, followed by a wave of sorrow. So this was how I'd go—cloddishly, onward at any cost.

Onward. As I descended from the Uinta Mountains onto the Colorado Plateau, the snow turned to steady rain. The midmorning sky grew even darker. New concern: the rhythmic thwap of the windshield wipers began lulling me to sleep. *Drive!* I told myself, taking deep breaths and shaking my eyes open. *Drink more coffee! Don't leave so darn early!* Thwap! the wipers agreed, Thwap! Thwap!

I also struggled to keep my attention on the road, away from whirling doubts: *Why am I leaving? Where am I going? What, exactly, do I think I'm doing?* Objective answers aside—my seasonal position at Fossil Butte National Monument had ended, and I was aiming for western

Colorado to start a new job—I didn't understand my motivations or desires. I'd been happy in Wyoming, coaxing fifty-two-million-year-old fossil fish out of a paleontological quarry all summer and then, once autumn and winter rolled in, helping with interpretation and outreach. The seasons had been rich with sage-scented storms, bugling elk, blazing aspen, and, best of all, endless miles of sparkling white snow. All winter, I'd scribed ski tracks across freshly snow-swept ridges, squinting into sunshine during the day and gasping at the icy beauty of the moon and Milky Way at night. Living at the monument's bunkhouse, ten miles west of the town of Kemmerer ("Fossil Fish Capital of the World"), I went days at a time without seeing or speaking with anyone except the snowshoe hares huddled at my doorstep and the coyotes howling from the ridges. Wind, solitude, and empty white expanses had scoured my soul into something elemental. Fundamentally me.

Offered the opportunity to stay for another season in the quarry, though, I'd balked at the idea of trying to rival or repeat past experiences. What if the summer wasn't as interesting a second time around? What if I tarnished happy memories? What if I missed out on something even bigger, more beautiful, more wild? What if he—the biology technician with whom I'd spent the previous season climbing and hiking and falling in love—chose not to return? What if he did?

To Colorado, then—more work as a paleontological technician for the National Park Service (NPS), but with different duties than the meticulous quarrying at Fossil Butte. As suggested in the job announcement and corroborated during the interview, I'd spend most of my time in remote backcountry and wilderness areas in Black Canyon of the Gunnison National Park and Curecanti National Recreation Area, assessing the condition of all documented fossil localities and surveying Late Jurassic and Early Cretaceous geologic formations for new discoveries. ("Please find a dinosaur track," my soon-to-be-supervisor implored, half-jokingly, half-longingly.)

Although Curecanti hosts the headquarters for the jointly managed NPS units, I'd be based out of Black Canyon, along with a few other resource science and stewardship personnel and interpretation rangers. I'd never been to the park. In fact, I'd passed by it the previous autumn without bothering to stop. The bio tech and I had been on our way back to Fossil Butte after a monthlong post–field season road trip throughout the Southwest. Late one afternoon, we followed Highway 50 west through Curecanti—along the sunlit shores of Blue Mesa Reservoir, past eroding pinnacles of sandstone and breccia, through groves of golden aspen and valleys filled with saltbush and sage—toward Black Canyon. When we neared the brown road sign announcing the turn up to the park, he said to skip it—"Not really worth it just to drive in." We continued on, northward, back to Wyoming—the drive I was now making in reverse, alone.

The place must be something special, though? It is, after all, a national park. A place of superlatives: tallest cliff in Colorado, falling 2,250 sheer feet; narrowest canyon in the country, contracting to a width of only forty feet; one of the fastest river descents on the continent, dropping thirty-four feet per mile; some of the oldest exposed rock on the planet, dating back 1.7 *billion* years. Judging from descriptions in brochures and on websites, the place is what its name suggests: a chasm so narrow and deep that it captures light and emanates shadow, a Black Canyon.

By the time I'd driven over winding mountain passes and through traffic-clogged cities (really, Grand Junction?), followed signs east out of Montrose, taken that previously foregone turn at the brown sign, wound up the access road, and pulled into the visitor center parking lot, I couldn't have cared less what the canyon's dimensions were or why the place was a park. I was exhausted. Disoriented, distressed, wracked with self-doubt. I got out of my car, stiff from sitting, and shuffled to the obligatory overlook, hoping the view would revive or at least reassure me.

"The impressive effect of the scene reduces us to inadequate adjectives," US Representative Scott McInnis attested to his fellow congressmen at the ceremony marking Black Canyon's upgrade from monument to park status in 1999: "gorgeous, awesome, spectacular."[1] My first impression was a bit more prosaic: deep, dark, and craggy. Cold. Far below, the Gunnison River frothed with recent snowmelt. Billows of mist swirled and seethed, engulfing needles of gneiss in their featureless embrace. Clouds sagged with the thickest, wettest gray of late afternoon, or maybe it just felt that way. A distinctly uninviting chill permeated the place. "The gorge is long," I could have summarized, using the words of ninth-century Chinese poet Han Shan (Cold Mountain), "Rocks, and rocks and rocks, jut up."[2]

Retreating to the warmth of the visitor center, I stared at the displays until my new supervisor arrived. I'd soon come to recognize him as one of the kindest, most affable people I've ever had the joy of knowing, but at first, I struggled to just pay attention during his brief orientation to park offices and housing. By the time he showed me to my quarters in the park bunkhouse, dusk had descended and rain was turning back into snow. I didn't feel like unpacking, nor was I hungry for dinner. I tried calling the bio tech, but my phone had no reception. Grayness giving way to the true darkness of night, I fell into a murky sleep, chasm pulling at my dreams.

I am a plains person. I like my skies wide and my horizons distant. I like to see storms building and watch hawks soaring, smell sage baking and hear coyote singing, taste wind whirling and feel space, always space, more space, I *need* space, out on the plains.

Black Canyon is entirely un-plains-like. In addition to the verticality of the canyon itself, the park is hemmed in by series of ridges and, beyond them, snow-capped peaks. Worse yet, a century's worth of fire suppression has allowed thickets of Gambel ("scrub") oak and serviceberry to proliferate. In places, the brush is so thick that it's nearly impossible to see, much less move, farther than a few feet. Such tangles would discourage even the hardiest of woods lovers. To a plains person, they're downright preposterous.

Waking early on the morning after my arrival, I stepped out of the bunkhouse aiming to figure out where and what I'd gotten myself into. The air was fresh with the scent of newly fallen snow, the world quiet under an inch of white. Scrub oak crowded the edges of the staff parking lot, bleak tangled brown. With a slight rustle, four deer materialized from the brush. They froze, considered whether I was cause for concern, then went back to browsing. I continued onto and along the main road, treading carefully on ice-glazed pavement, listening for other signs of life. I'd intended to walk down to the first scenic overlook, but after a long, slippery half mile, I still hadn't seen the canyon. Hadn't seen anything but the deer. Couldn't see anything. Just trees, branches, clawing at me, a claustrophobe. Where was the *sky*?

People don't go to Black Canyon to see the sky. They go to see a geologic wonder, a curiosity, a freak of nature unrivaled, according to the NPS brochure, for its "narrow opening, sheer walls, and startling depths."[3] They go to see the Chinese Dragons' silica-rich slithers and the Kneeling Camel's schisty lumps, maybe hike S.O.B. Draw down to the Gunnison River or rope in and climb up Chasm Wall. Those who study the park map may note a significant amount of acreage above the canyon rim—much of it designated wilderness—but it's difficult to access and seemingly unremarkable (unless you too are a fossil nut who looks at the interbedded sandstones and mudstones of the Morrison Formation and dreams of dinosaurs). No, the vast majority of visitors do what they do in every park: drive the road and pause at designated viewpoints; perhaps walk some of the trails, perhaps listen to a ranger talk; learn a few facts, maybe foster a sense of appreciation; snap a few photographs, make a few memories; then leave.

I'd committed to a full field season, nearly five months. I was stuck.

When I told friends and family that I'd be spending the summer at Black Canyon, they marveled, "Another park! You get to live and work in a *national park!*" Unstated but implied was how lucky I was to stay in such a wild, scenic place. National parks must, by virtue of their being national parks, be wild and scenic. Designated scenic; destined to stay wild. Ripe with opportunities for enjoyment, unimpaired.

I've been fortunate to have had opportunities to live and work at several parks and public lands: Petrified Forest and Badlands National Parks, Fossil Butte National Monument, and Tongass National Forest. Outside of work, I've visited a hundred-odd NPS units (national parks, monuments, preserves, historic sites, seashores, lakeshores, rivers, and recreation areas), plus several dozen each of US Forest Service (USFS) national forests and grasslands, Fish and Wildlife Service (FWS) refuges, and Bureau of Land Management (BLM) conservation areas and checkerboard range. Wilderness areas, primitive areas; backcountry, frontcountry. State parks, county parks, city parks. Few forgettable, some memorable. Most pretty, some beautiful.

What makes a place beautiful? What keeps it wild?

Generations of artists, philosophers, geographers, economists, ecologists, engineers, land managers, and people generally in pursuit of meaning and inspiration have asked these questions and come up with countless answers. In *The Experience of Landscape*, geographer Jay Appleton—one of the first scholars to wonder, "What do we like about landscape and why do we like it?"[4]—pursues the hypothesis that aesthetic appreciation is related to "environmental conditions favourable to biological survival."[5] By this logic, we like to see landscapes that contain bodies of water, lush vegetation, and abundant wildlife because they fulfill our biological needs (what's come to be called "habitat theory"). Moreover, out of our instinct to be predator and not prey, we like to be able to view these scenes from vantages that afford the "ability to see without being seen" ("prospect-refuge theory")[6].

Meanwhile, psychologist Stephen Kaplan focuses on the cognitive dimensions of landscapes—how our brains process what we're viewing. His research subjects reliably express preference for images of landscapes with a touch of what he codes as "Complexity" and "Mystery," girded by comforting "Coherence" and "Legibility."[7] In other words, we enjoy scenes that capture our attention, pique our interest, and offer balance between the unknown and the knowable. Landscape architects adopt many of the same ideas, using formal principles of design to create interesting yet navigable settings that are part wilderness, part garden.[8] Public land managers, in turn, evaluate "visual resources"—landforms, vegetation, water, and cultural modifications—and rate "scenic quality" based on the main design elements of form, line, color, and texture.[9] At the National Conference on Applied Techniques for Analysis and Management of the Visual Resource in 1979, the BLM's chief landscape architect crowed, "What had been considered extremely subjective (aesthetic judgment, particularly in the landscape) was found to have identifiable consistent qualities [such as visual variety and harmony] which can be described and measured."[10] ("What is a scenic resource? Who decides that a location has quality and on what basis? Of what value is a scenic resource?" artist Alan Gussow challenged bureaucrats at the same conference.[11] "There are no quantitative criteria," he tried to insist.[12])

A decade earlier, Luna Leopold—son of the famous ecologist and writer Aldo—made a "quantitative comparison of some aesthetic factors among rivers," with the ambitious goals to "eliminate personal subjectivity in landscape analysis" and better inform land management.[13] After developing a rubric for "uniqueness ratios for aesthetic factors" based on physical features (such as valley height versus width, river pattern, and flow velocity), biologic and water quality (turbidity, algae, land flora), and human use and interest (accessibility, historic features, artificial control, pollution, and vistas), he tested it by evaluating several sites in Idaho.[14] He then compared top-ranked Hells Canyon to several national park landscapes, chosen on the basis of "the assumption that national park status is a formal recognition of exceptional aesthetic quality."[15] While some of his premises are debatable—Are braided channels objectively more beautiful than meanders? Why do cattails outrank water lilies? *Is* national park status a recognition of exceptional aesthetic quality?—his conclusion feels right: the Grand Canyon edges out Hells Canyon in both "Valley Character" and "River Character," and both exceed the aesthetics of valleys in Yellowstone. (At the visual resource conference, Gussow quoted mountaineer Willi Unsoeld: "'When I stand at the rim of the Grand Canyon, I ask: what is the value involved here to a human being? I'm not satisfied that it is just a pretty view.'"[16])

Had Leopold included Black Canyon in his analysis, it would have rivaled if not superseded Hells: steep gorge under distant mountains; powerful river; no sign of human impact (provided onlookers are unaware of three dams upstream). It has spectacular views. From Tomichi Point—the first overlook along the Rim Drive, the one I was aiming for and didn't quite reach that first morning—visitors gaze into a nearly 2,000-foot-deep abyss (shallow, compared with the 2,700-foot drop-off of Warner Point at the end of the road). Walls of dark, twisted rock jut skyward. A few foolhardy junipers and Douglas firs cling to ledges. There is a distant but audible roar of water. Far below, the Gunnison River rages through the same channel it began cutting two million years ago, when it meandered through soft volcanic debris; by the time it reached the hard Precambrian bedrock, it was so entrenched in its route that it had no choice but to keep cutting down. Upstream from Tomichi, this section of canyon twists on a north–south axis, so in the early mornings and late afternoons, sunlight illuminates one wall and leaves the other in full shadow; promontory after promontory fades into the distance behind diagonal shafts of light. After a soaking rain or on warm mornings, the gorge belches mist. How to quantify those qualities?

Aside from Leopold, few scholars have tried to understand the unique aesthetic of canyons. Meanwhile, other landscapes have been thoroughly dissected. Mountains are often seen as sacred—avenues to the sky and links to the gods, "mountain as center, heaven, source of

Sunrise view from alongside a gnarled old juniper on the Rim Rock Trail, light spilling into the snow-laced chasm.

water, place of the dead, and so forth."[17] Pastures signify the Arcadian ideal. Cities represent human ingenuity and industry. Even factories and highways are valued as the vernacular—manifestations of sociocultural development and emblems of everyday life. Researchers evaluate people's responses to forests and fields, seashores and waterfalls, slums and Superfund sites, but canyons are overlooked (pun intended) as uncommon and aberrant.

An important distinction: aesthetically and geomorphologically, canyons are different from valleys. Broad V- or U-shaped valleys open to the sky and act as part of rolling landscapes—pleasant undulations that add variation to the view; necessary absences to counter the gentle presence of hills. Vertical-walled chasms that incise down instead of out seem inverted and unbalanced. When water wears rock away too quickly to give other erosional forces time to catch up, it cuts an almost indecent peek into a planet we prefer to think of as solid. Like caves or caverns, canyons are remarkable for what they're not—for an abrupt lack of rock. The word "canyon" itself comes from a Spanish word for "tube"—something hollow, empty. "Chasm" from Greek for "yawning hollow, gulf"—disruptive, impenetrable.

Same view, different weather. Visual resource rubrics don't account for clouds.

The deeper a canyon, the greater the absence. It fills with winds, which flow erratically between pockets of air pressure. It distorts sounds, muffling some noises and amplifying others. Above all, it swallows light. "Gorge" is from French, "to swallow." Gorge, chasm, canyon: soul-sucking emptiness.

Living on the thin skin of this earth, we rarely have reason to think of what's underneath our feet—the soil horizons, the bedrock, the continental crust that is to the planet the thickness of a shell to an egg. Canyons enable us to look down into the lithosphere and back through layers of time. Fascinating to some, frightening to others. If mountains are the abodes of gods, then canyons must be the realm of the devil, "Hells Canyon" redundant. Deep, dark, otherworldly places where the light doesn't shine. Places in which one can become trapped. Places to avoid, to curse. Certainly not places to celebrate.

Downstream of Black Canyon of the Gunnison, the Grand Canyon of the Colorado River is a notable exception to negative stereotypes. Quite the opposite: studies on landscape aesthetics and scenic value cite the Grand Canyon as an exemplar of magnificent, awe-inspiring natural beauty. In the very first sentence of his discussion of humans' "strong liking for scenic nature," philosopher Robert Fudge equates "the popularity of the Grand Canyon" to that of the Cliffs of Dover and the Matterhorn—"parts of nature that are visually striking and that we would most expect to find captured in photographs."[18] Similarly, another philosopher of aesthetics, Yuriko Saito, groups "the grandiose splendor of the Grand Canyon" alongside Yellowstone and Mt. Rainier.[19]

In *How the Canyon Became Grand*, environmental historian Stephen Pyne explains that the wide, deep chasm was once viewed as a "wasteland."[20] It only became a "national emblem" when Americans developed a taste for Romantic, sublime scenery in the late nineteenth to early twentieth centuries. The first European American to see the Grand Canyon from within—Joseph Christmas Ives of the US Army Corps of Topographical Engineers, exploring in 1857–58—conceded the scenery was "astounding" but also "terrifying" and "altogether valueless."[21] After surviving two expeditions through the "granite prison" in 1869 and 1872, John Wesley Powell—the first person known to have traversed the length of the landmark by boat—wrote more favorably of the Grand Canyon for a tourism brochure: "The traveler on the brink looks from afar and is overwhelmed with the sublimity of massive forms . . . the traveler among the gorges stands in the presence of awful mysteries—profound, solemn and gloomy."[22] Clarence Dutton, a geologist who joined Powell's second expedition, viewed the canyon with such otherworldly awe that he filled it with toponyms evoking Hindu deities—Vishnu's Throne, Brahma Temple, Shiva Butte; the Creator, the Sustainer, the Destroyer. In his history of the landform, Dutton also veered from strict scientific analysis to characterize the Grand Canyon as "the sublimest thing on earth."[23]

The superlatives continue. Celebrating the Grand Canyon's "wonderful grandeur, the sublimity, the great loneliness and beauty" during a visit in 1903, President Theodore Roosevelt insisted that "in that canyon Arizona has a natural wonder which, so far as I know, is in kind absolutely unparalleled through the rest of the world."[24] With perhaps his highest praise of all, John Muir opined that the Grand Canyon, with its "stupendous scenery," was one of the "few big places beyond man's power to spoil"—an honor it shares with only the "ocean, [and] the two icy ends of the globe."[25] Continuing with characteristically purple prose, Muir described the canyon as

> a gigantic sunken landscape of the wildest, most multitudinous features, and those features, sharp and angular, [form] a spiry, jagged, gloriously colored mountain range countersunk in a level gray plain. . . . [S]ide canyons, gorges, alcoves, cloisters, and amphitheaters of vast sweep and depth, carved in its magnificent walls; [a] throng of great architectural rocks . . . resembling castles, cathedrals, temples, and palaces, towered and spired and painted, some of them nearly a mile high, yet beneath one's feet.[26]

Notably, Muir himself recognized that his words barely "give any idea of the impression of wild, primeval beauty and power one receives in merely gazing from its brink."[27]

"Sublime," as defined by seventeenth-century English essayist Joseph Addison (writing of the Alps' snow-draped spires), is the feeling of "an agreeable kind of horror." A transcendence of primeval beauty and power and fear. The ratios of horror to agreeability and fear to beauty vary depending on whether a person is looking into versus being *in* a canyon. To some people, a canyon's narrowing walls might afford a sense of familiarity—an ability to touch the rock, to be embraced by the land. For example, Barry Lopez describes his experience rafting down the Grand Canyon: "I had entered a private place in the earth. I had seen exposed nearly its oldest part. I had lost my sense of urgency, rekindled a sense of what people were . . . and a sense of our endless struggle as a species to understand time and to estimate the consequences of our acts."[28] To others, being in a canyon triggers alarm—the feeling that the earth could at any moment change its mind, that the cliffs might collapse or close back together. Mere mortals oughtn't be below the horizon, where flesh and bone are no match for the weight of the rock, the air, all of that empty space.

The Grand Canyon ranks as what psychologist Thomas Herzog calls a "Spacious Canyon"—intriguingly textured and agreeably vast, expanding both horizontally and vertically. It fits the aesthetic criteria of Appleton, Kaplan, and landscape designers. Black Canyon, meanwhile, is the epitome of a "Narrow Canyon," so much so that Herzog used photographs of it to analyze research subjects' reactions to its illegibly and hideously deep profile. In his "Cognitive Analysis of Preference for Natural Environments," Herzog finds that compared to other scenery—deserts, snowy mountains, smaller mountains, and spacious canyons—Black Canyon ranks as the least preferred, especially in terms of spaciousness, texture, and identifiability.[29] "The Narrow Canyons category seems to be an exception to the general rule that for natural environments mystery enhances preference," Herzog muses, attributing the dislike to "the feeling of danger or insecurity" created by the canyon's steep walls and secretive depths.[30] Shudder, to imagine a chasm so dark, so deep—what dragons lurk in its shadows?

Then there is the river. In their discussion of values and perceptions of water, Shmuel Burmil, Terry Daniel, and John Hetherington celebrate the many roles that water plays in arid landscapes, from "life sustaining and practical aspects" to pure aesthetics—the "beneficial psychophysiological effects" of watching light reflected off a pool's surface or listening to the soothing sound of cascades.[31] Water's erosional force has both practical and metaphorical significance, they note: "Where water meets the most resistance it works the hardest. The harder the material, the narrower the area carved. The larger the vertical height differences and the shorter the horizontal distance between the point of origin and the point of termination, the greater the carving forces of water."[32]

River versus rock, height versus width: the Gunnison is liquid power; Black Canyon pure resistance. Looking down from the canyon's rim and especially standing by the river's banks, it's impossible not to subscribe to a sense of "fluvialism"—the idea that, through the course of almost unimaginably long spans of geologic time, "rivers shaped the land, not merely the landscape its rivers."[33]

Unfortunately for Black Canyon, research by Thomas Brown and Terry Daniel into perceived scenic beauty of "Wild and Scenic Rivers" finds a parabolic relationship between stream flow rate and aesthetic attraction: test subjects rated Colorado's Cache La Poudre more beautiful when it had more water flowing through it, but only up to about 1,500 cubic feet per second (cfs).[34] Beyond that, high discharge was less and less attractive, to the point where people preferred looking at a nearly dry bed more than seeing water flowing at 2,500 cfs. Mean

High? Check. Narrow? Check. Wild river, undeveloped nature (at least as seen from park overlooks), fits most of Luna Leopold's "objective" criteria to rank as a unique and aesthetically pleasing canyon.

daily flows of the Gunnison through Black Canyon exceed 3,000 cfs throughout the late spring and summer months, with occasional flooding approaching 8,000 cfs, and in June 1921 reaching 19,000 cfs.[35] Terrifying. Repulsive.

But Brown and Daniel's study (and much research into landscape aesthetics) is based on photographic interpretations. Had subjects been questioned while standing by the rivers—breathing in the scent of life, feeling the cold spray, and above all *hearing* the soothing babble or thunderous roar—their aesthetic experiences would have been quite different. Would people find the Gunnison's power exhilarating or frightening? Its foaming, snarling, silt-laden waters animated or possessed?

River, canyon, space: I didn't know what to make of Black Canyon, or even where to begin. Especially when compared with the open, spare lines of plains horizons, there's too much to see, think, and believe. John Muir may have loved multitudinous sharp features and throngs of rocks, but I like simplicity. What was I supposed to make of all of the distractions? The color of shadow in the depths, the play of light along the rim. Distant roar of rapids. Warmth of rising thermals, coolness of swirling mist. Human history, natural ecosystems, the paleontological legacy that had brought me there. How to fit into such a landscape?

In the first few weeks at Black Canyon, I walked from my quarters to Tomichi Point before and after work each morning and evening, trying to learn the place's shapes and moods. I drove the Rim Drive twice—first with a map, stopping to read the signs at every point, then again with my supervisor, who filled in details about the topography and toponymy. (Warner Point? Named for a local minister who promoted access to and preservation of the canyon in the 1920s and '30s. Sunset Point? The best place from which to watch sunset.) We spent a day visiting the more remote, more dramatic, and less frequented North Rim—only a thousand feet from the south as the raven flies but, for earthbound travelers, an eighty-mile, two-and-a-half-hour-long drive away. (Kneeling Camel View? Sort of looks like a camel, if you think zoomorphically and squint. Grizzly Ridge? No idea. Only black bears here.)

I hiked all of the maintained trails—along the canyon's rim, through the scrub oak, out to every overlook. After a few repetitions, I began forming mental maps, marking this tree *here*, that bump *there*; a twist in the road, a straightaway; one particular grouse who flapped and boomed at me every morning, suspicious of the interloper tromping past his patch of brush.

As soon as the lingering snow and ice began to melt into navigable pools, I decided it was time to try following the primitive Gunnison Route—access to one of only a handful of hikeable ravines—down into the chasm itself. "Towering walls and the overpowering rush of the Gunnison River dominate existence in the inner canyon," the NPS rhapsodizes on their website; "Joining this scene yourself can be the trip of a lifetime." ("Routes are difficult to follow," officials add, warning that "only individuals in excellent physical condition should attempt these hikes. Hikers are expected to find their own way and to be prepared for self-rescue." Oh, and "poison ivy is nearly impossible to avoid."[36])

Early one Saturday, I tossed food and water into a backpack, filed for a wilderness permit, laced up my boots, and set off, switchbacking down the established Oak Flat Trail to the start of the Primitive Route, thinking, *This is it! This will be the transformative experience!* Rather than continuing to pace the canyon's edge, looking out and wondering what it is about the place that people find so breathtaking—The depth? The darkness?—I would get to know it firsthand, from within. What had Powell written of the Grand Canyon—from within, the traveler is in the "presence of awful mysteries—profound"?[37]

As soon as I turned into the designated wilderness, I had to stop worrying about philosophical or psychological interpretations of aesthetics and instead concentrate on where I was putting my feet. The "route" is not a single, well-defined trail but a semi-identifiable path that braids through vegetation and bifurcates around boulders, little more than steep mud and unconsolidated talus. Skins of ice in shadow. My mittened hands stuck to frost-coated surfaces. Rocks skidded out from underfoot, bouncing down tens or hundreds of yards, crashes echoing and amplified as the canyon got steeper. More than once, I cliffed out and had to backtrack to find an alternative way. Attention thus engaged, I barely noticed as the strip of blue sky overhead narrowed and the vein of green-brown water below thundered ever more loudly.

After one mile, eighteen hundred feet of elevation, and two very anxious hours, I stood at the edge of the roiling river, marveling at the height of the gorge. Sunlight spread down the cliffs and spilled into crevices, adding color and dimension to what had seemed like monolithic walls. Schist, gneiss, and pegmatite glinted and writhed. Immense ponderosa pines filled the air with their butterscotch scent. Bear tracks ambled along the shore, and birdcalls echoed over the water. Had I allowed myself to linger, surely I would have been enchanted by the solitude, the sunshine, the wonder. Utter wildness, a different world than the pavement-and-overlook one above the rim.

But I did not stay to ponder the place. All too aware that I had to climb eighteen hundred feet back *up* a wall of mud and scree, I couldn't relax and settle in. I was anxious to get going. Snap a photo, splash water on my face, then turn right back around and begin the ascent.

Although physically more strenuous, going up proved easier and slightly faster. I had more control facing the rocks and roots. Plus, I was now in known terrain—remembered twists served as markers by which I could gauge progress. (*Ah, that rock pile. Not long now . . .*) An hour

Inner canyon, both literal and metaphorical. "Young clear-voiced dragons in these / gorges howl. Fresh scales born of rock, / . . . Ageless teeth / cry a fury of cliffs, cascades gnawing / through these three gorges, gorges / full of jostling and snarling, snarling" —Meng Chiao (translation by David Hinton 2005, 144).

and a half later, I stood on the deck of the visitor center, looking down into the chasm I'd just conquered. "With newfound appreciation," I was supposed to think, or "triumphantly," but it didn't feel that way. "Conquered" wasn't even the right word. Quivering quadriceps aside, I was no different. I had hoped—so much, maybe too much—to delve into the depths and emerge with enlightened appreciation for the canyon's scale and grandeur. Greater awareness of the rock's age and the river's power. Understanding, maybe intimacy. But, if anything, the canyon felt smaller. Duller. Knowable.

My mistake: I had, in the words of Barry Lopez, "come to the canyon with expectations."[38] Lopez had experienced a raw freedom on his float trip through the Grand Canyon—a "radical change of proportion" during which what he and others "had come to see or do fell away. We found ourselves at each turn with what we had not imagined."[39] But I had had no revelation. No radical change, no profound mysteries. After weeks of exploring, I was still unawed, uninspired, puzzled. What makes *this* a national park? Why do people come *here* to ogle the natural wonders? What do we seek in parks and what do we find?

Clambering back up the Gunnison Route felt like fighting the earth to get back to the sky.

Four centuries ago, while Spaniards were questing for cities of gold in present-day New Mexico, and before British and French settlers began turning the dense woodlands and rocky soils of eastern North America into farms and towns, Ute people came to what is now Black Canyon of the Gunnison National Park to hunt, collect chert and knap lithics, gather piñon nuts, and perhaps hold ceremonies, mostly on the northern ridges. They had little reason to venture below the canyon's rim—the terrain was too precipitous, the environment too harsh, and the inner gorge lacked any worthwhile resources.[40]

As Euro-American mountain men began seeking animal furs and adventure in Colorado in the early nineteenth century, trappers "discovered" the Gunnison River.[41] The waterway wasn't officially documented until 1853, though, when Captain John Williams Gunnison of the US Army Corps of Topographical Engineers reported "a stream embedded in [a] narrow and sinuous canyon"—the river that now bears his name.[42] To Gunnison and his men, the canyon was a barrier to westward progress—something to note, then laboriously navigate around. Finding the high, steep walls equally "impenetrable" decades later, surveyors from the Denver and Rio Grande Railroad discontinued plans to lay track through the chasm, deeming the very idea "impossible."[43]

In 1901, hydrologist and engineer Abraham Lincoln Fellows and superintendent of the Montrose Electric Light and Power Company and eager town advocate Will Torrence became the first men to raft through the "ominous and foreboding gorge."[44] Their purpose was to gather topographic information to determine the feasibility of building a tunnel to divert water from the Gunnison toward thirsty high-desert crops in the Uncompahgre Valley—an ambitious endeavor they concluded was both worthwhile and practicable. Construction of a 5.8-mile-long tunnel through the 2,000-foot-high Gunnison Uplift began in 1905 and was completed in 1909. This monumental achievement was so emblematic of American can-do spirit that President William Howard Taft joined the dedication ceremony.[45] More than a century later, farmers in the Uncompahgre Valley—one of Colorado's prime agricultural regions— still rely on irrigation water from the Gunnison Tunnel.

While the city and farms of Montrose flourished in the early twentieth century, Black Canyon itself was mostly ignored. Lacking any resources and prohibiting travel both east–west and north–south, the roughly twelve-mile-long stretch making up the deepest and narrowest parts of the chasm seemed, by all accounts, nothing but a nuisance. That was, until Americans developed a taste for sublime scenery and nature-based tourism. As with the Grand Canyon, emergence of a Romantic aesthetic engendered appreciation for wild, craggy, "useless" but breathtaking landscapes. Almost as soon as members of the 1920s Montrose Lions Club (including Reverend Mark Warner, eponym of Warner Point) learned that "there was a canyon up there that was worth seeing and a road should be built so people could get to it,"[46] they rallied to design and construct Black Canyon Scenic Drive, "mak[ing the beautiful scenery] more accessible to the general public," as Montrose County Commissioner John Howell explained at the dedication ceremony.[47] Within two years, hundreds of people, including a representative from the NPS, had made the steep, winding trip up to the top of Vernal Mesa to gaze at "one of the most spectacular gorges of the United States."[48] Based on the enthusiastic support of local and state groups—and after some last-minute finagling and funding to reimburse the Ute Nation for 17,019 acres of ancestral land, fulfilling the nearly forgotten Treaty of 1888—President Herbert Hoover used the power granted by the Antiquities Act to designate Black Canyon a national monument in 1933, "for the preservation of the spectacular gorges and additional features of scenic, scientific and educational interest."[49]

"The Black Canyon of the Gunnison has always held a strange fascination for those who had the privilege of peering into its awful depths," Reverend Warner celebrated, writing for the *Montrose Daily Press* in 1934, "But this fascination . . . is greatly intensified for those who are privileged to traverse the rough river bed, and view the rugged canyon walls from below . . . One will never have seen the Black Canyon in its more majestic and thrilling aspects until he sees it from the bottom." Majestic and thrilling! Fascinating and fearsome! Um, steep. Still just deep, dark, and craggy. "Rocks, and rocks and rocks jut up."[50] Even after I'd looked up at the old, jagged cliffs from the river's edge, I couldn't find it as fascinating as I was supposed to, nor could I find the place as meaningful as I wanted to. What was wrong?

"What begins as an undifferentiated space becomes place as we get to know it better and endow it with value," humanistic geographer Yi-Fu Tuan writes in his seminal *Space and Place: The Perspective of Experience*.[51] Simply naming a location or putting an identifying mark on a map distinguishes a place as a *place*—more meaningful than otherwise anonymous landforms or unimportant geographic features. In turn, names and labels shape our perceptions. "Black Canyon" implies a dark, narrow hollow carved out of the earth. First intentionally and now subconsciously, "Gunnison" privileges the history of nineteenth-century Euro-Americans over the earlier presence of the Ute.

It's possible to know and value places without ever visiting them in person. In fact, this is how we experience much of the globe. Few people get to go to Venice and Venezuela, Ulan Bataar and Antarctica, but most of us have basic understandings of where they are and what they're like thanks to educational curricula and popular media—atlases and encyclopedias; literature, art, film, photography; the power of the Internet. Before I'd ever even seen the Black Canyon of the Gunnison, I'd formed a suite of impressions about and assigned a set of values to it. Mostly hazy, questionable meanings based on incomplete secondhand knowledge (the NPS website, Wikipedia, and the bio tech's "not really worth it just to drive in") and my own existing personal biases (national park—an American crown jewel), but a sense of place nonetheless.

Geographers and philosophers love to debate "sense of place." How do people perceive and understand geographic localities? How does "sense of place" reflect and shape our relationships with our environment? What is "place," anyway, and are "senses" more physical or psychological? Phenomenologists interpret the phrase literally, describing a sense of place as a "conscious cognition of direct experience"[52]—the world as filtered through sight, sound, smell, touch, taste, and proprioception.[53] (Edmunds Bunkše puts it succinctly: "feeling is believing."[54]) But, environmental psychologists argue, our brains always kick in, weaving sensory input into an ever evolving fabric of personal knowledge, beliefs, and values. Don't forget the sociocultural and political influences, sociologists and anthropologists add, so we're left with the seemingly simple concept of "place" as a complicated tangle of personal and societal processes and practices, layered on the biogeophysical world.[55] To use geographer Cary de Wit's definition:

> sense of place [is] . . . the experience of place in all its dimensions: physical, social, psychological, intellectual, and emotional. It includes the symbolic meaning of place and the beliefs, perceptions, and attitudes held toward a place . . . who and what people in a place conceive themselves to be as a consequence of that place.[56]

Or to invoke Barry Lopez's poetic explanation:

> The mind, full of curiosity and analysis, disassembles a landscape and then reassembles the pieces—the nod of a flower, the color of the night sky, the murmur of an animal—trying to fathom its geography. At the same time the mind is trying to find its place within the land, to discover a way to dispel its own estrangement.[57]

It's not just a question of "What is Black Canyon?" but "Who am *I*, when hiking into, sitting with, or contemplating Black Canyon?"

While "sense of place" is technically a neutral term—individuals form impressions about locations, sometimes liking them, sometimes hating them, sometimes not caring much either way—it is "often associated with an emotional or affective bond."[58] A combination of the Greek roots for "place" (*topos*) and "love of" (*philia*), the term *topophilia* (title of another of Yi-Fu Tuan's influential works) refers to the pleasure, joy, or fondness a person may feel for a location.[59] When experienced strongly enough, this fondness can develop from mere preference into more meaningful, bonding "place attachment"—loving "thoughts, feelings, memories, and interpretations" that a person associates with a place.[60] Place attachment, in turn, may intensify into full-fledged "place identity," wherein an individual's understanding of self becomes rooted in or contingent upon their geography.

To some degree, all people experience and acknowledge place identity. In asking the ubiquitous icebreaker "Where are you from?" we presume to learn something about who a person is—their language, their cuisine, their topographic or climatic comforts, their hometown sports teams—based on their geographic past. Most telling, perhaps, is a response that begins, "Well, I was born and raised in x, but really feel at home in y," or "I can't help but visit z every year—I just love it there." In saying something as seemingly simple as "My family has a camp in the Catskills" or "I left my heart in San Francisco," people are sharing intimate details about their lives and selves.

When I say, "I am a plains person," I mean that the sweeping emptiness of wide skies and distant horizons are what Tuan would call my "geographic double—the objective correlative of the sort of human being I am when the shallow, social layers are stripped away."[61] It doesn't matter that I'm a tall, bony, blonde-haired, brown-eyed woman, raised in a typical middle-class, two-parents-one-sister-a-dog-and-two-cats family in a quiet semirural corner of western New York, formally educated in anthropology, earth sciences, and Russian language and literature at a college in New Hampshire, subsequently employed as a seasonal park ranger between semesters and years of graduate school in Wyoming and Kansas, where I studied geography and taught yoga. No, what matters is that in my early twenties, I discovered the great sweeping semidesert sagebrush steppe of northeastern Arizona and for the first time in my life felt I was *home*. Alive. Truly, fully *me*. Peel back my skin, and you'll find sage-studded ravines and snow-swept ridges. Peer into my soul, and you'll see quiet sunrises and towering thunderstorms. Heart of pronghorn and rattlesnakes, blood of black-footed ferrets and meadowlarks. Spine of a juniper gnarling out of a sandstone ledge. I need space, I breathe space, I *am* space, out on the plains.

In leaving Wyoming, I'd left my self.

And the bio tech—I'd left the place I'd shared with him, a brown-eyed, brown-haired, brown-bearded rock climber who rode a motor-cycle and traveled the world; who was kind, responsible, and quick to smile; and who was the first and only person who accepted me, sandstone and sagebrush and all. For what, labyrinths of scrub oak? A distant roar of rapids? This deep, dark chasm with its scenic overlooks and its convoluted old rock? In search of new wilderness and a dinosaur track. Out of fear and stubbornness and an unquenchable thirst for more.

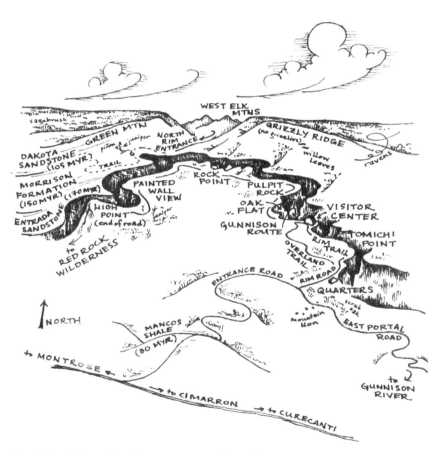

Map of Black Canyon. South entrance seven miles up from Highway 50, seven miles from Tomichi Point to High Point, five miles and two-thousand-plus feet of elevation loss on East Portal to the River, North Rim a two-and-a-half-hour drive from the South Rim, though only a stone's throw away.

CHAPTER 2

Fossil

A few days after I hiked the Gunnison Route and only a few weeks after I'd moved to Colorado, I went back to Wyoming. Not for good—just for a weekend. Paleontologists and fossil preparators from institutions and public land management units around the country were gathering in Kemmerer for the Fossil Preparation and Collections Symposium and the Conference on Fossil Resources. I'd spent much of the preceding winter helping plan the events, so I was eager to see them through. (Not to mention it was an excuse to return to the land of sage and sky.)

To get to Kemmerer in time, I left Black Canyon long before sunrise. The descent from park headquarters was familiar—by then, I'd wound down and back up past the pine-filled sandstone ridges, across the irrigated green bench of Bostwick Park, and through the heaving twists of shale out to the flat relief of Highway 50 at least a dozen times—but the drive was more serene in the early morning darkness, crisp edge to the air and moon shadows sharp across the landscape. (Or maybe it was just the anticipation.) Montrose was pleasantly deserted, streetlamps illuminating the roads just for me. Rolling into Grand Junction, I was so enchanted by the sky glowing beyond the sleeping giant of Grand Mesa that I failed to register warning messages flickering on my dashboard. Twenty-something miles north of Loma, my car died, leaving me just enough inertia to roll onto the shoulder. By the time I'd walked into cell signal range ("I'm past mile marker 20, by a grove of cottonwoods. Oh, a coyote!" I distinctly remember telling the AAA representative, unsure which details were most important), waited for a tow truck, waited for a garage to open, and waited for them to install a replacement alternator, it was early afternoon. The symposium had started, three hundred miles and two mountain passes away.

In hindsight, it would have saved me a fair amount of angst to realize then that the trip back and forth between Fossil Butte and Black
Canyon would never go smoothly.

Although I missed the first day's events, the remainder of the
weekend proved successful. Fossil preparators (experts who work in a
laboratory, using dental picks, small air-compression tools, and chemical solutions to painstakingly remove matrix from around delicate
specimens or to make molds and casts of significant items) and collections specialists (those who develop systems for accessible, long-term
storage and display of fossils) shared their techniques and tips. Of more
direct relevance to my work, paleontologists discussed new discoveries, historical trends, monitoring methods, and the implications of the
federal Paleontological Resources Preservation Act (part of the Omni-
bus Public Land Management Act of 2009), which requires federal land
management agencies to develop comprehensive regulations for the
inventory, monitoring, collection, curation, protection, research, and
educational uses of fossil resources on public lands.

Paleontological resources have been documented in more than
250 different units within the NPS alone, though only a few parks and
monuments were designated specifically to protect fossil resources.
(Fossil Butte is among these exceptions.) Because most parks are
better known for their scenery, ecosystems, cultural significance, or
historic legacy, only a handful of units have trained paleontologists—
or geologists, even—on their staff. This means that research into and
protection of fossils has often depended on outside interest or non-
continuous seasonal staffing, and it hasn't always been carried out in
a systematic manner.

At Black Canyon and Curecanti, park personnel weren't even looking for, much less protecting, fossils until the mid-1990s, when paleontologists from the Perot Museum of Nature and Science in Dallas
and other institutions undertook a survey of all NPS units containing
outcrops of the fossil-rich Morrison Formation—a rock layer that contains an impressive wealth of dinosaurs and other Jurassic life-forms,
most famously exposed in Dinosaur National Monument on the border
between Colorado and Utah.[1] Initially, researchers focused on sandstone and mudstone cliffs in Curecanti, where they discovered "a wealth
of paleontological finds, including crayfish burrows, termite nests,

unionid clam burrows, root casts, and a sauropod dinosaur."[2] They returned to conduct more complete excavations, uncovering additional bones, teeth, shells, and ichnofossils (tracks, burrows, and other fossilized traces of ancient lifeforms' activities). In the early 2000s, Curecanti hired a seasonal technician to begin surveying all potentially fossiliferous geologic formations, including the Late Jurassic Morrison (about 150 million years old); the younger Early Late Cretaceous Dakota Sandstone, which is elsewhere known to contain dinosaur bones and tracks and leaf impressions (about 105 million years old); and, above that, the Late Cretaceous Mancos Shale, which is most famous for its plesiosaurs but more commonly contains marine molluscs (about 80 million years old). During two seasons, the technician expanded the taxonomic and geographic scope of known fossils to include petrified wood and specimens on Black Canyon's North Rim.[3] Even so, it wasn't until 2005 that the NPS began systematically documenting all localities, assessing the condition of known resources, and surveying for new finds.[4] I was there to continue that work.

By the time the conferences in Wyoming had wrapped up, I was eager to start surveying in earnest. Dinosaur bones! Mollusc shells! Any number of plants! It didn't hurt to know that the biology technician would soon be visiting Colorado. He'd surprised me by showing up at Fossil Butte on the second day of the conferences, getting there before his summer position restarted so that he could drop off gear, and also see me for the first time in months. (Yes, he'd decided to return to Wyoming for another season.) As I was getting ready to begin my drive south, he asked if I'd join him on a trip to Buena Vista over Memorial Day weekend. Of course! As with the previous summer and fall, I would have gone with him anywhere. The return to Black Canyon—three weeks of fossil hunting followed by a weekend with him—no longer seemed intolerable.

Understandably, most visitors to Black Canyon and Curecanti spend their time observing the chasm and recreating on the reservoir, not traipsing about distant ridges, hidden arroyos, and sagebrush flats on the uplands. But the park contains 30,750 acres (15,599 of which are designated wilderness), and the recreation area totals 43,095 acres. There's plenty to explore beyond the main attractions.

Work didn't take me into the canyon itself, whose ancient, meta-morphic rock is too altered by heat and pressure to contain traces of life, but it did entail exploring the remote, rugged backcountry: along the bluffs above Blue Mesa Reservoir in Curecanti; around to Grizzly Ridge and Green Mountain on Black Canyon's North Rim; and, my favorite, over to Red Rocks Wilderness in the park's far southeastern corner. Some days—days spent driving dusty access roads, scrambling through juniper forests, and winding up sandy draws, forever studying rock—I could even forget the canyon was there.

Red Rocks is an aptly named uplift of colorful Mesozoic strata, where cliffs of durable Dakota sandstone cap rainbow-hued Morrison mudstones and sandstones, gypsum-rich layers of Wanakah limestone, and, in a few locations, ledges of deep-pink Entrada sandstone (the same formation out of which the arches of Arches National Park are carved). The about 170-million-year-old Entrada sits directly atop the dark, deformed Precambrian rock of the inner Black Canyon, marking a geologic nonconformity—millions of years of missing time during which new layers weren't deposited or were eroded away from atop the metamorphic underbelly.

To stand on that nonconformity requires a drive from Montrose north and east onto the questionable dirt roads of the BLM's Gunnison Gorge National Conservation Area, a hike across part of Gunnison Gorge to reach the NPS wilderness boundary, then a much longer hike around or over a juniper-studded soaring fin of sandstone, through branching drainages and over sheer ledges, up tight arroyos, and back down to the edge of the canyon—a few miles as the raven flies but an arduous ten- or twelve-mile trek on foot, not counting detours to sur-vey promising outcrops. No trails, no guidebooks, no reason to be out there but for scientific surveys and the sheer beauty of it all.

During my first forays to Red Rocks, I worked alongside a BLM intern who was hired to look for fossils in Gunnison Gorge. Because both of us were new to the area, our supervisors felt that it would be safer and more productive for us to learn our way around the terrain as a team. We coordinated schedules, packed up our rock hammers and put on our cowboy hats, steered a government vehicle down the winding, potholed dirt roads, and set off hiking, eyes scanning promising rock faces and minds trying to reconcile the busy topographic and geologic

Deep in the Red Rocks Wilderness, overlooking the twisted geography of the Gunnison Gorge National Conservation Area—a view that can't be seen just by stepping out of a car or following a premade trail. Cliffs of Precambrian rock rise above the Gunnison River. Sitting atop the nonconformity, bottom up: Entrada Sandstone, Wanakah Limestone, Morrison Formation (Dakota Sandstone not visible). Long, flat Grand Mesa fifty-odd miles to the north.

maps with the even busier real world. On our first day out, we skirted a ridge, dropped into a canyon (what would become for me one of the central features of Red Rocks—a drainage cutting through the heart of the Morrison Formation), then followed a narrow, winding arroyo up through layers of limestone. Along the way, we were convinced that we were seeing tracks in every erosional feature, coproliths (fossilized feces) in every mineral deposit. Barely an hour in, we discovered a huge slab of sandstone at the bottom of a drainage, perfectly tilted for its ripple-marked surface to catch edges of sunlight. Surely, if the motion of water on an ancient shoreline could be so perfectly preserved, we exclaimed with glee, there must be all sorts of other bits of geologic history waiting to be found.

But we soon reined in expectations, realizing just how long it takes to hike a mile, how many areas are eroded or overgrown, and how frequently we'd encounter impassable cliffs. The Wanakah Formation, we learned, is not only friable but relatively fossil-poor. The Dakota is rich with plant material such as petrified wood and root casts, but better to skim through en route to the real mystery: the Morrison, its tangle of arroyos and ledges most likely to harbor significant secrets. Over in Curecanti, the most exciting materials—Sauropod limbs and vertebrae! Crocodilian teeth!—were found in exposures of the Morrison, now well surveyed.[5] But—expectations lifting—the Morrison-rich drainages in the Red Rocks area and on the steep slopes of Black Canyon's North Rim were practically unknown.

The thrill of paleontology is in the discovery—that moment when you turn a corner or peer under a rock, an odd color or shape catches your eye, and you know with a joyous jolt that you're seeing *something*, something that's not part of regular mineral deposition or crystallization but rather holds signs of ancient life; that moment when you realize what a fossil is and what it means. But most of the work is an exercise in patience, attention to detail, and moderation of disappointment. For every find, there are hours, days, weeks even, of fruitless searching, false steps, hard hiking, and wasted diversions. (Though, in a place like Red Rocks, there are side compensations: bright views across the ridges and arroyos; eating lunch in the sunshine amid the sweet scent of baking junipers; a slot canyon here, an amphitheater there, the skull and antlers of a mule deer bleached ghostly white by the sun.)

When a specimen is discovered, the initial excitement gives way to a sense of duty. Finds must be meticulously documented. If left in the field, specimens must be periodically revisited and assessed to see how they're holding up to weather and other damaging forces; if collected, there are even more steps in the accession process—careful cleaning, preservation, labeling, and housing, maybe display. To contribute to meaningful research, each fossil must be identified, analyzed, and correlated with stratigraphic layers and other fossils in the same and nearby formations and time periods. It's precise, exhausting work, punctuated by moments of sheer exhilaration.

Surveying is full of drama, but the more prosaic duty of locality assessment—revisiting places where fossils had previously been found to see what condition they're in and to look for other resources in the vicinity—is equally if not more important. I focused on assessments at the beginning of the season, in part to train my eye to know what to look for and in part because many of the fossils at Curecanti are located at or just below the average shoreline of Blue Mesa Reservoir. It was crucial to reach them in early spring, before mountain snowmelt filled in and submerged the sites.

The reservoir—the largest body of water in Colorado, fourteen times the volume of the state's largest natural lake—was created in 1966, when Blue Mesa Dam was built to hold back the waters of the Gunnison River. The nearly four-hundred-foot-high dam was authorized under the Colorado River Storage Project Act of 1956, long before researchers recognized the presence and significance of the paleontological resources it would flood. While local residents and visitors enjoy the reservoir's practical and recreational opportunities—water storage, hydroelectric power, and fishing and boating amid towering, colorful scenery—its seasonally fluctuating water levels continually reveal, re-inundate, and erode nearshore fossils, making some more visible or accessible, and putting others out of reach or destroying them altogether.

I visited most of the shoreline sites in late April and early May, while aspen were beginning to bud and stiff winds swept across the cold water. Right away, I realized that the recreation area has a different feel from the national park next door, stemming from its different enabling legislation and thus different management strategies. While Black Canyon was established "for the preservation of its spectacular gorges and additional features of scenic, scientific, and educational interest," with recreational opportunities and wilderness of additional benefit, the main intended use of Curecanti is "for general purposes of public outdoor recreation."[6] No matter how far I hiked, I could still hear the traffic from Highway 50 whizzing by. Moreover, there were always boats on the water—people out sailing, motorboating, fishing. The presence of so many other people made me feel somewhat conspicuous, poking around cliffs, rock hammer in hand.

One of my first days out on the northern shoreline, I dutifully set out to find a locality in the Mancos Shale below the Dillon Pinnacles (craggy breccia remnants of Tertiary volcanism), about seven hundred feet above the surface of the water. This trip required following a maintained trail for a couple of miles, then branching off through the brush to reach and skirt the shoreline; positioning myself below the locality as best I could, clambering up a series of Morrison mudstone slopes and sandstone ledges, and finding a scalable route through a thick layer of Dakota bluffs; finally, perching in the crumbly, yellow-gray shales of the Mancos long enough to document a few fish scales and shells. Only after completing the task did I realize that I was stuck—couldn't downclimb the bluffs, and, looking up, couldn't navigate the increasingly steep and crumbly Mancos. No way to go but sideways, following a bighorn sheep trail that skirted ledges and zigzagged through gullies toward the safety of a flattish slump. I began shuffling gingerly along the narrow path, leaning into the slope and digging my rock hammer into the soft shale more for reassurance than safety. Heart pounding and legs shaking, I was so focused on not falling that I didn't notice a skiff parked in the water below until I heard someone's voice drift up: "Whoa, that's not a sheep! That's a *person!*"

A few weeks later, I hiked out to a locality in the far southern part of the recreation area. Having not factored in rising water levels on the reservoir, I had to make much-longer-than-anticipated detours around now-flooded drainages, then wasted hours slogging through entirely un-fossiliferous shrublands. With a mile left to the locality and at least one more hill to ascend, I began to hear strange sounds. Were those *bells*? And *baa*-ing? Curious, I went up and over the rise—yes, a flock of sheep. Not bighorn—domestic, at least a hundred of them, with a couple of dogs and a man on horseback watching over them. The dogs didn't seem to mind my presence, and the sheepherder just tilted his hat to me, so I went around the flock and continued on to the locality— a few bone fragments tumbling out of a small gully. The sheepherder must have wondered what I was doing, stopping in the middle of the shrubs to stare at my feet, set down my pack and crawl around, photograph a few rocks, measure off what must have looked like a regular old patch of dirt and brush, then erase my boot tracks, turn around and leave. But when I passed by him, he didn't ask any questions—merely tipped his hat again.

Curecanti was like that: unexpected, a little odd. Managed alongside a national park but a working landscape and a designated recreation area. Aesthetically lovely but artificial. Had the dam never been built and reservoir never been filled, it would have been just another dusty valley, unlikely to be entrusted to the care of the Park Service. (And, in turn, unlikely to be surveyed for fossils. Had the dam not been built, I wouldn't have been hired, and I wouldn't have ever been there, scraping at rocks halfway up a mesa, contemplating the meaning of the place.)

Following bighorn sheep trails along [very, very steep] cliffs of sandstone and mudstone above Curecanti Reservoir, in search of fossils.

Philosopher Allen Carlson recognizes the aesthetic experience as a conjunction of emotion-based "noncognitive" responses to and knowledge-based "cognitive" interpretations of the environment.[7] We look at scenes and judge their beauty based on our preferences for certain surficial properties. If we approach scenes knowing something of their natural or human history—it's a park; it's a reservoir—our initial reactions are colored by this knowledge. In turn, our perceptions evolve as we learn and experience more. The noncognitive can never quite be divorced from the cognitive. In fact, Carlson insists, to truly experience a landscape and form a relationship of "self to setting" rather than merely "traveler to scene," appreciation of the natural environment requires "knowledge and intelligence [to] transform raw experience by making it determinate, harmonious, and meaningful."[8]

Yi-Fu Tuan agrees: "The aesthetic response depends on, and can perhaps be endlessly extended by, association, memory, and knowledge."[9] For weeks, I'd been striving to extend my aesthetic response. Knowledge:

geology, ecology, history, I wanted to learn it all. Memory: day after day, week after week, I was out on the land. Association: I enjoyed the remote, rugged Red Rocks, but I couldn't stop comparing the chasm to wide open ridges, just as I couldn't forget that the reservoir used to be a river. Couldn't stop aching for low grasses, huge skies, more time with the bio tech, an eight-hour drive away.

Over a long, sunny Memorial Day weekend, I joined the bio tech on a trip to Buena Vista. We climbed granite slabs, camped by the Arkansas River, emptied a growler from the local brewery, and ate a carton of ice cream, laughing as we raced to spoon it out before it melted. Two weeks later, we met in Moab, Utah, to repeat the same experiences in a different setting: sandstone cliffs, Colorado River, no beer. We made plans for a Fourth of July trip to Yellowstone, then Kemmerer's annual bluegrass festival in August. Maybe, just maybe, we could rekindle the relationship we'd started the previous summer?

Back at Black Canyon, the North Rim is more isolated and thus less visited. It also feels wilder, perhaps because the dirt road creeps right along the canyon's precipitous rim, perhaps because it also features sandstone ridges that rise several hundred feet above the inner gorge, perhaps because the south-facing wall is much steeper (thanks to increased sun exposure, which in turn decreases the amount of wintertime ice and slows freeze-thaw erosion; the river incises, and the rest of the rock remains). As with the South Rim, numerous overlooks and short trails afford views of the chasm. The North Rim boasts a longer trail, though—a three-and-a-half-mile footpath that winds out to Exclamation Point ("What a view!") then switchbacks up a long ridge called Green Mountain (which is neither a single mountain nor very green, though it does boast stately piñons and junipers on its steeper slopes and obnoxious thickets of scrub oak everywhere else).

"Those continuing to Green Mountain will be rewarded by panoramic vistas," the park's website promises.[10] The "aerial perspective of Black Canyon" reveals its geographic context: the canyon is a deep sliver gouged out of a large Mesa Inclinado tableland, which tilts toward the west-southwest and is ringed by the long rise of Grand Mesa to the north, the volcanic spires of the West Elks to the east, and the jagged snowcapped peaks of the San Juans to the south. The western horizon arcs away to the low, dusty mass of the Uncompahgre Plateau, with irrigation-fed fields and the towns of Montrose, Delta, and Grand Junction tucked in the valleys.

Geologic maps show tantalizing exposures of the Morrison Formation on the far northwestern slopes of Green Mountain, miles from the maintained trail, but little paleontological work had been done there owing to its general inaccessibility and steepness. Of course, I was eager to survey it. (*Dinosaurs!* anticipated my paleontology technician brain. *Mountain lions!* dreamed my explorer heart.) Before making the long trek out, though, I figured I ought to revisit localities on the more accessible eastern Green Mountain as well as on Grizzly Ridge—another high, flat landform stretching above the canyon, on the other side of the entrance road from Green Mountain. Several shallow drainages cut into each ridge's sandstone caps, revealing permineralized wood fragments, casts of roots and branches, and traces of invertebrate burrows and tracks—peeks back to "a time [during the Early Cretaceous] when rivers and swamps deposited sand, mud, and decaying plant material along a tropical marine shoreline."[11]

These fossils and the layers in which they're found are just as exciting as dinosaur bones, for they allow paleontologists to understand ancient ecosystems, reconstruct continental configurations, and generally piece together the grand history of the earth. But many of the fossils on Green Mountain and Grizzly Ridge are too small or fragmented to be identifiable and too dispersed to be contextualized. If anything, they merely gave me the excuse and impetus to scratch through scrub oak, meander between sun-scented junipers, clamber over conglomerate outcrops, poke at boulders with a rock hammer, watch cloud puffs float over Black Canyon's abyss, and enjoy being in places to which few people have reason to go. The ridges aren't classified wilderness. In fact, they can be ascended within an hour or two and are mostly visible from the park road. But I never saw a boot print, much less crossed paths with another person; they *feel* remote.

One day, early June, I had just tucked into the cool embrace of a juniper to eat lunch, halfway up Grizzly Ridge, when a conspiracy of ravens burst out from behind the horizon and filled the sky overhead. They swirled and soared, rising like a flight of bats or a murmuration

Pegmatite stripes of Painted Wall, barely visible from high on Grizzly Ridge.

of starlings, but bigger and noisier. Cackles filled the air—were they laughing at me? They *were* laughing at me—and feathers drifted down like huge, black snowflakes. After a good twenty minutes, they caught a breeze or tired of taunting me, so they circled away, following the canyon westward until they disappeared over its darkness, the ridge reverberating with their absence.

Another day, a couple of weeks later, I was so focused on the rocks at my feet that I failed to pay attention as a strong wind stirred and shadows began to block the hot sun. It wasn't until I heard a grumble of thunder and felt the air cool with the scent of rain that I looked up to see a gathering storm. Too far from the road to make it safely to my work truck, I tucked my pack (and metal hammer) under a tree, then crouched in a clearing and hoped the lightning would stay in the sky. Clouds darkened. Ozone crackled. Fat raindrops splatted down, then poured all at once. Within minutes, I was soaked to the skin. Rivulets flowed through the dirt. Everything reeked of rain. Then, just as quickly as it came, the storm moved on, trailing tendrils of virga. The sun reappeared; the ground began to steam. And, as if reminding me to look up every once in a while, a brilliant rainbow blazed over Black Canyon.

Near the end of the month, when I was fairly accustomed to the work and terrain and not anticipating any more surprises, I was traversing the uppermost ledges of Grizzly Ridge, dutifully searching for an outcrop that, according to the records, boasted a few ichnofossils (in this case, indentations left behind by clams resting on Cretaceous river or seabeds). A rock caught my eye: impressions of long, simple, willow-like leaves embossed on a smooth, creamy surface, traces of some of the earliest of angiosperms, clear as if just yesterday they'd fallen from a *Salix* shrub onto soft mud. Astonishing, the confluence of factors that had to have occurred for me find such delicate fossils! The thin leaves must have flowed down a small stream and come to rest on a silty shoreline, then been entombed in mud before decaying. The silt hardened and was buried under other layers of sediment, including those left as the massive Western Interior Seaway filled in the center of the North American continent in the Middle to Late Cretaceous, about 115 to 66 million years ago. Then the area was uplifted, exposing overlying strata to the forces of erosion. Over millions of years, everything else was carried away—any layers above, all of the rocks that made up the edges of the canyon and ridge cut by the Gunnison. Now the most miraculous part: at the very moment that the leaf impressions were exposed but had not yet eroded away—a narrow window of perhaps ten or twenty years in the span of millions—I happened to be tromping around that exact spot—within a few feet, out of tens of thousands of acres—glanced in the right direction while the sun was at the right angle, was not distracted by birds or storms, and knew what I was looking at. Fieldwork like this is less a matter of systematic sampling than an informed search for serendipity. (And odds. For every new locality I found, surely hundreds or thousands sit undiscovered.)

Only one other find rivaled that of the early-willow leaf impressions. Mid-July, I dedicated a day to exploring the cliffs that tower over Highway 50 near park headquarters in Curecanti. I poked around the unconsolidated dirt and loose rubble alongside the road (or, rather, slipped and slid, relying on my trusty rock hammer to self-arrest) while trucks and RVs whizzed by below. Several outcrops of Morrison looked promising but didn't even boast ripple marks. As the sun got higher and hotter, I ducked into a shady arroyo and continued to poke around, enjoying the aroma of piñons and the relative coolness and quietude, away from the road. Late morning, I found some large tree molds but otherwise passed through hundreds of feet of rock deposited over tens of millions of years of time without incident. I'd intended to return to the road via the opposite side of the arroyo, but upon seeing loose pebbles and shrubs (that is, no intact rock) on the northeast-facing slope, I decided to stay to the southwest, hugging a layer of beautifully cross-bedded Dakota sandstone. Unfortunately, this outcrop seemed to be devoid of anything but a few concretions. After an hour of fruitless peering under ledges and turning over slabs, I called it quits and began to descend for the day; the tree molds were a decent enough find. Reaching out a hand to steady myself through a steep section, though, I happened to glance at the cliff next to me: fifteen vertical feet of rough-grained, cream-colored sandstone, and there, suspended at the bottom, was a perfect cross section of a pine cone. Or I should say an inverse pine cone—instead of any organic or mineralized matter, it was a collection of neatly arranged gaps, the shape of scales that had curled out and up from a central core seventy-odd million years ago. The organic matter had long ago rotted away, leaving this cast—hardened sand filled between where pine cone scales had been—as the only testament to its existence. Again, how improbable! Out of tens of thousands of acres and tens of millions of years, I happened to be in the exact spot at the exact time to put my hand out and find this echo of life, recognizable only for the shape of its empty spaces.

CHAPTER 3

Bobcat

I needed that pine cone. I found it just after a trip to Yellowstone with the biology technician, during which everything began to fall apart.

The Fourth of July weekend began scenically but not smoothly, with that long and unfortunate drive from Black Canyon to Fossil Butte. Having left fairly late after work, I was so disconcerted by the traffic in Grand Junction that I didn't want to stop for gas. The "empty" light flashed on in the same stretch north of Loma where the alternator had died a month earlier. Weighing the remoteness of the road against my better judgment, the pull of Wyoming won out and I continued onward, anxiety building with every mile up to Douglas Pass and continuing as I coasted down through narrow, winding valleys, tank empty, emptier. Again, a huge wave of relief, this time when I just barely managed to roll into a gas station in the town of Rangely. Luck seemed on my side. After that, the drive was buoyed by an edge of euphoria, all positivity and possibility—I was on my way back to Wyoming! To visit the bio tech! As the sun slipped below the horizon near Dinosaur, Colorado, it sent shadows flaring across the plains; one of the most beautiful sunsets I've ever seen. A thunderstorm left Vernal, Utah, freshly washed; I rolled down my windows and steeped in the scent of rain-soaked sage. Switch-backing up into the Uintas, I had the road to myself, headlights shining across bogs and into birch groves. Somewhere between Flaming Gorge and Mountain View, I pulled over and got out to marvel at the night sky—the darkness, the stars, so many stars. And me, there, standing out on the plains, a warm sage-scented breeze rising gently off the earth, universe twinkling overhead. *Four whole days* with the bio tech!

He was waiting for me when I pulled into Fossil Butte, just after midnight. Home, like I'd never left. Like he'd never left and come back for another season. The next morning, we made pancakes and sat on the porch sipping coffee, staring across the familiar sweeping steppe, lingering a little later than intended. By the time we were finally on the road, heading north, it was well after noon. Stops for gas, for groceries, and for information at the visitor center for Grand Teton delayed us even further. Five or six hours later, we were outside Jackson, looking for a turn onto a Forest Service road that would take us to what were supposed to be charming campsites near a small lake. We eventually found the correct road but encountered a sign announcing seasonal closures: lingering snowdrifts made the drive impassable. With late afternoon tilting toward early evening and without having made any backup plans, we parked below the sign and hiked camping gear up to the lake, stubbornly post-holing through the snow for the final half mile.

Oh, but it was worth it. No one else was there—even in the Greater Yellowstone region on a busy holiday weekend, we had the lakeshore to ourselves. (And to mosquitoes. Lots of mosquitoes.) Although I soon became cold and he kept swatting at bugs, such temporary discomforts were forgettable. All that mattered was that we were together. Sparkling water, shining rock, soft patches of moss illuminated by sunlight cutting diagonally through the pines. Magical.

After a failed attempt to smoke the mosquitoes away with a campfire, we pitched the tent and dove in. Midsummer light lingered in the sky. We talked and talked and tried playing cards but eventually just lay there, listening to insects hum in the pale, piney air.

"I wish we could see where we are." I couldn't help but disturb the stillness. "I have no idea where this place is in relation to anything else." The geographer in me always likes to know the general lay of the land— the names of the peaks and the routes of the rivers; the distance to or from the nearest town—but with all of the turns and the rush and the roadblock, I'd gotten fairly disoriented. I also thought that the place was so eerily beautiful—clear mountain lake rimmed with tall trees, snowdrifts still shimmering at the beginning of July—that it couldn't quite be real. I wanted to see a little red dot blinking away on a GPS to let me know that we truly were somewhere in northwestern Wyoming and hadn't instead blundered into an enchanted corner of another world.

"Why aren't there any ducks here?" I again broke the silence, after a long pause. I felt like we should have been able to hear ducks' soft quacking, or hawks' sharp ptchoos. I would even have taken the raucous honks of a goose. I wanted a loon or two to call out across the glistening blue water. Not just birds—where were the moose? The elk? The bears? Why weren't all of the animals in the forest snuffling and gliding down to the water's edge, right there, then? A quotation from Rick Bass's *Book of Yaak* tickled the back of my memory—something about dusk and water and wildlife—but I couldn't quite remember the words or the meaning, just the feeling of land coming to life.

> No one can say for sure when a place becomes your home, or when a fit is achieved, or peace, any more than one can say when a river best fits the valley through which it cuts. It flows and changes, shifts—cuts deep in some places, fills in in others. It transports sediment, logs and lives. It makes music in the day and in the night. Animals come down out of the mountains at dusk to stand at the river's edge and drink. In the dimness, as light fails, the animals sometimes cross the river, wading or swimming.[1]

That's what I meant to ask, that's what I wanted to know: Where were all the wild beasts? Who were we, in relation to this world? Was it just us and this place; was this all that mattered? "I love you," I meant to tell him. But instead, a question about ducks.

"I don't know," he paused, as if pondering a reasonable answer. He was usually good at coming up with explanations for my absurd questions, or at least tolerating my incessant exclamations, my frequent non sequiturs and leaps of imagination. For this one, though, he didn't have a response. There was no response. There was nothing to say. With the stars ready to shimmer and moon about to rise, bobcats and wolves somewhere out there at the edge of night, we lay and listened to wavelets lap ducklessly against the shore.

Morning dawned cold and mosquito-free, bright daylight breaking the enchantment of the lake. We fired up a camp stove, ate the usual oatmeal, packed up and trudged back down to the car, then were off to play tourist in Yellowstone. True to form, we didn't have any plans, so we opted to hit the highlights: Old Faithful, of course, amid a gaggle of onlookers; a few other geysers and fumaroles; then Yellowstone Falls, also with a crowd, always with a crowd, Yellowstone. Too much traffic on the roads, rest facilities too far between, hot springs too far away. Blazing sunlight. We ran out of water and had a late lunch the first day; I got cranky. The second day, he was disappointed to find the mud volcano less dramatic than he'd remembered from a childhood visit. Camera-toting visitors harassed bison and elk on the roadsides. We disagreed about which trails to take and got lost, ending up wading across a meadow full of bison chips on the first day and sliding down sand dunes the next. A year earlier, we would have laughed at our misadventures, but this weekend, we (or, more accurately, I—my over-thinking, my oversensitivity) were on edge. We had such precious little time together. I wanted every minute to be perfect. Instead, so much sitting in the hot car. So many mosquitoes. So much for America's crown jewel.

Sociologists, economists, planners, and psychologists in the field of recreation and leisure studies strive to understand what inspires people to travel to certain locations, what people hope to learn or find, and how (in the interest of resort managers, marketing agents, guides, local store owners and restauranteurs, and others dependent on the tourism industry) to ensure that visitors have a good time and want to return. What are tourists' motivations, demands, and expectations? What improves tourist satisfaction, in terms of pre-trip planning, the actual experience, and post-trip recollection?

According to Yellowstone's most recent visitor use survey, most people go to the park to view geysers (conserved thanks to the Yellow-stone National Park Protection Act of 1872), to view the scenery and wildlife therein (conserved thanks to the NPS Organic Act of 1916), and to "experience a wild place" and "hear . . . the sounds of nature/ quiet" (partially protected by subsequent legislation and regulation, such as the Wilderness Act of 1964 and more recent standards for aircraft and motorized winter recreational vehicles).[2] Though more than half of visitors complain of traffic, difficulty parking, others "act-ing unsafe" around wildlife and thermal features, and generally "too many people in the park," seventy-nine to eight-five percent report that their visit met their expectations. The most common grievance is that people "wanted to see more wildlife." (One percent also say they were "underwhelmed by Old Faithful."[3]) (Underwhelmed by Old Faithful!)

Had the bio tech and I been asked to answer survey questions, we would have reported similar desires: we too wanted to view the scenery and wildlife, as we always sought wild places. We muttered about traffic, inappropriate behavior, and overcrowding. Old Faithful was duly impressive, though, and I was content to not encounter a grizzly. Of course there were crowds; it was the Fourth of July. There was nothing objectively dissatisfying about the destination, no reason to think the trip had been anything but a resounding success.

But I hadn't gone to Yellowstone to ogle the geologic wonders or the wildlife. I would just as readily have camped in downtown Manhattan if it meant getting to spend time with the biology technician. The park was just a setting, the vacation an excuse. Place dependency.

Our third morning, after packing up from a different campsite along the Forest Service road (we'd opted not to post-hole to the lake again), we went for a hike in Grand Teton National Park. Surely, a nice, long walk in fresh mountain air among relatively fewer people would make us feel better? I don't know which trail we chose—a steep one, up to a lake— and it doesn't really matter. As soon as we were at the trailhead, he was off, bounding along while I plodded far behind, catching up at the lake hours later, then again at the car. Lost in thought, I saw nothing of the land around me. I think there was a forest, then a series of big boulders, a meadow? It might have begun to rain. I'm pretty sure it rained.

The only thing I fully remember from that day was the drive back to Fossil Butte across the great gray expanse of western Wyoming. It was beautiful—the sagebrush steppe, yawning beneath a low dark sky. Beautiful, too—the huge sky, hovering over the flat, dusky earth. Intolerable, that beauty; unfathomable, that space; impossible, that I had to stay in that stifling car, sitting together in aching silence, watching the scenery roll by. I wanted to leap out and run away, off into a landscape whose stark splendor should have brought me joy and instead crushed me with its emptiness.

For the first time, my plains failed me. Open sky, wide earth—I needed more.

Something deeper.

Back at Black Canyon (I somehow managed to make the long drive home, even though the radio broke and I had to pass the miles and hours with nothing to listen to but the self-pitying thoughts echoing in my head), I began to take longer walks. More frequent walks. Before work every morning and after dinner every evening, an extra mile, then two, three. I wanted to walk—*needed* to walk—more than to eat or sleep. Footsteps on pavement, footsteps on dirt; eyes and ears open, any little miracle—please?

One morning, a member of the maintenance staff told me he'd seen a bobcat along East Portal Road, just past where it splits off of the main Rim Drive. A *bobcat*! I'd seen photos and tracks, but I had never met a wild cat before. With their secretive, solitary nature, they'd taken on special significance in my mind—a more elusive spirit of wildness than conspicuous bears and ubiquitous coyotes. As Gary Snyder noted in *Practice of the Wild*,

> There are more things in the mind, in the imagination, than "you" can keep track of—thoughts, memories, images, angers, delights, rise unbidden. The depths of mind, the unconscious, are our inner wilderness areas, and that is where a bobcat is right now . . . I do not mean personal bobcats in personal psyches, but the bobcat that roams from dream to dream.[4]

Years earlier, when working at Badlands National Park, I'd gotten into the habit of walking to Cliff Shelf Nature Trail every day at dawn, hoping to glimpse a bobcat I'd been told haunted that area. All in vain; that wildness remained in my mind, in my dreams. As soon as I learned of the bobcat at Black Canyon, I adopted the same strategy, lurking along East Portal Road at daybreak, waiting for the cat to appear or the sun to rise, whichever came first. (The sun.)

Before switchbacking down to the river and Gunnison Tunnel, East Portal Road climbs away from the park entrance booth—a slight elevation gain, only a hundred feet or so, but enough to rise out of the scrub oak and afford a full view: Coffee Pot Hill to the southeast, Grizzly Ridge to the northeast, Grand Mesa far to the north-northwest, edge of the canyon below—a gash, yawning as though the mesa had split apart, river lost in the depths. Each morning, I walked up and watched as the canyon grew dimmer while the sky got brighter, anticipation building. Not without warning but a surprise nonetheless, the sun would shoot out from behind Grizzly Ridge, blinding me and casting everything else in shades of purple blue black. Every morning, week after week, the air filled with color and light, the canyon radiated darkness, and the bobcat prowled through a corner of my awareness, surely somewhere just out of sight.

For a bit of variety (and with the recognition that my bobcat quest was a bit quixotic), in the evenings, I walked to the visitor center and from there wound around Oak Flat Loop. Aptly named in that it's a loop and passes through gnarled patches of Gambel oak, though not very flat, the trail boasts colorful wildflowers, groves of rustling aspen, and a soothing, needle-soft stretch of Douglas fir. The true highlights are unexpected glimpses of the canyon, though. Descending counterclockwise from the visitor center, a half-mile-long stretch of switchbacks and trees emerges onto an outcrop overlooking the ravine, bare boulders jutting into space. After another mile of trees and a gradual ascent, the trail turns back toward the visitor center, passes through the firs, and, for those who know to look carefully, veers off onto a slight social trail for a view straight down Black Canyon, rock walls perfectly framing the ribbon of water.

These vistas aren't exactly secrets. The NPS trail guide even advertises "a rock outcrop, a pleasant location where you can relax and enjoy the view" and "another unmarked overlook offering spectacular views downstream."[5] But by early evening, while most visitors are either gathering at Sunset View or on their way out of the park, I had them all to myself. I could sit at the rock outcrop or, better yet, the unmarked overlook for as long as I wanted, listening to the whispers of leaves and wingbeats of wrens. Always, the distant roar of the river—water through rock, over rock, against rock, ever deeper.

On clear days, the last of the sun's light shone in a narrowing strip on the canyon's upper edge, blazing brightly as if fighting the shadows rising from the inner gorge until giving up and turning its warm gaze on Green Mountain, pausing, then lifting from there, too, and fading up through the sky. On overcast days, the sky and land underneath simply got dimmer, a nearly imperceptible transition from gray to darker gray to dark to canyon black. Increasingly, I lost track of time and had to stumble back up the trail and along the road back to quarters in the gathering night, accompanied by emerging planets and the brightest of stars. Every now and then, a serendipitous mix of sinking sun and falling rain sent rainbows arcing across the evening air. Not just through

Sunrise, Tomichi Point. "Canyons gathering . . . lull, the inner" —Hsieh Ling-yün (translation by David Hinton 2012, 192).

the sky, like normal rainbows in normal places, and not even the full horizon-to-horizon semicircles I'd loved to see out on the plains—these rainbows curved from the mesa above, out, and over open space, then dove down into the canyon, light leaping into the earth.

Ah, Black Canyon, I began to understand. It isn't that the chasm dominates or distracts from the landscape—I could still appreciate the great dome of the sky and the crinkled surface underneath it. Rather, the canyon offers an entirely new dimension. Furiously eating away at the uplifted sandstone, mudstone, and gneiss, the Gunnison River had opened a dragon space between 1.7-billion-year-old walls of continental crust. Sitting or walking along the edge and peering down in, I could perch somewhere between rock and air and churning water, sometime between the Precambrian and now.

Of course, few people can step out their front door and hope to see a bobcat; even fewer get to stay in a park for days, weeks, months, until they begin to figure out what the place means. According to a visitor use study conducted in 2010, seventy percent of survey respondents were visiting Black Canyon for the first time.[6] They stayed, on average, for less than a day (a mere four hours, for day-use-only visitors), fitting the stop into a larger vacation. (Black Canyon was "one of several destinations" for two-thirds of visitor groups. Another fifth "indicated that the park was not a planned destination." Only thirteen percent planned it as the primary goal.) "General sightseeing" ranked as both the most common and the most important activity, done by eighty-seven percent of visitors. While forty percent took day hikes, barely three percent ventured into the inner canyon. One percent were there for rock climbing.[7]

That's what had brought the biology technician to Black Canyon the spring before we met—climbing. He and a friend followed one of the North Rim's primitive routes down to the river, then ascended straight up the cliffs, alternately climbing and belaying. Was all their attention focused on finding scalable stretches, feeling for little lips of rock that could serve as toe- and handholds, or did they appreciate the aesthetic of the gneiss, listen to the echoes off the walls? Were they accompanied by swallows? Ravens? Black bears have been spotted scaling the canyon's ravines—did they encounter claw marks? I never thought to ask.

Conversely, what is the park like for the twenty-seven percent of visitors who have physical constraints that confine them to the visitor center and overlooks? What do they observe that others might miss? And for the twenty-four percent who are trammeled by a "lack of time," what meaning do they find? "Not really worth it just to drive in," the bio tech had told me. I'd interpreted this as "not that spectacular," but maybe he'd meant, "Only go if you're planning to climb," "You have to do more than stop at the overlooks," or "There's more to the place than scenery." Did he realize that, when I ended up working there, it would take me weeks to learn the shapes and names of the topographic features; months to traverse the backcountry ridges, canyons, and cliffs; day after day, daybreak into night, before I finally began to appreciate Black Canyon?

The world is rich with beautiful and unique places. It would be impossible to see them all. But if people are going to take the trouble to swing by Black Canyon, then surely they need at least a full day, preferably two or more, to soak in the scenery and see some of the wildlife therein—enough time to slow down and stop, to let the landscape awe, and change, and cut.

Maybe not. Even with such short stops, ninety percent of visitor groups rated the "overall quality of facilities, services, and recreational opportunities" at Black Canyon as "very good" or "good." Asked what aspect of the park's story they might share with family and friends (in other words, what makes the place special), visitors spoke of the beautiful views and canyon's remarkable depth, narrowness, and sheerness. Geological history and the power of the river also ranked highly, or, at least, above the "[orientation] film in [the] visitor center." Maybe that's all that most of us want, need, or expect—a smooth road and superlative scenery? Bonus for those who catch a "great sunset" or "lightning storm," or witnessed general "awesomeness."[8]

"All this is yours. Come here frequently," Reverend Warner encouraged early visitors to Black Canyon. "Enjoy the beautiful things of the out of doors. Look into the eternal depths and upon the painted walls of this wonderful work of nature's art."[9]

He also insisted that something about the place—the way the canyon catches light and casts shadows, the way it mixes colors and lines and textures in interesting and aesthetically stunning combinations; something about its breathtaking dimensions, the narrowness of the span, the age of the rock; something about the smell of the air or sound of the water, the unfathomable *wildness* of it all—would change you, would crack to the core of who you are. "Look into the eternal depths," he vowed, "And you will go back to your homes and your daily tasks with a nobler attitude toward life."[10]

Writing of the Inner Gorge of the Grand Canyon, Barry Lopez would agree: "I do not know, really, how we will survive without places like [this] to visit. Once in a lifetime, even, is enough."[11] Wild places change us, make us who we are.

On our road trip the previous fall (the one on which we'd chosen not to turn into Black Canyon), the bio tech and I made whirlwind visits to dozens of other national parks, monuments, and forests—Saguaro to White Sands, Casa Grande to Carlsbad, Big Bend to Bandelier. We only spent a few hours at some—long enough to stop by a visitor center, maybe take a short tour. At others, we opted for longer stays—showing

Unmarked ledge, a long bushwhack from the road. Would it have afforded a nobler outlook on life if I'd merely driven up to it or if I'd seen it from a trail or from behind the safety of a railing? (No.) Would I have ever had the chance to see it—or Red Rocks, or Green Mountain, or any of the spectacular sunrises, sunsets, or thunderstorms—if I'd only been able to spend a few hours at the park? (No.) Unlike love-at-first-sight plains places, it took time for me to see more than just the pretty view here.

off my favorite petroglyph panel at Petrified Forest; summiting Guadalupe Peak through thick fog; attempting to backpack Big Bend's grueling Outer Mountain Loop from the Chisos Mountains down to the Chihuahuan Desert and back up again.

I remember all of them. The colors of the sky at Saguaro, the warm grit underfoot at White Sands, the maelstrom of bats rising out of Carlsbad Caverns and whirling off into the night (one of the most spectacular natural wonders I've ever witnessed). Debating whether to detour to Fort Bowie. Fearing that we'd wash away in a cloudburst outside Guadalupe. Day two of the backpack at Big Bend: straggling into the designated campsite well behind the bio tech, arms covered in blood, skin slashed open by the piercing thorns of cacti and ocotillo that I'd been too exhausted to bother trying to avoid. (He'd wanted to do the longest, most grueling loop, of course, and I hadn't wanted to say no, even if it meant being miserable. I hadn't anticipated the thorns.)

Day three: looking at the ascent back up into the Chisos and finally admitting that I'd never make it, saying I couldn't keep up with him, wouldn't ever be strong or fit enough to keep up with him, just leave me there in the desert. (No matter how disappointed he was, he was willing to scrap the rest of the hike. Patiently, kindly, he coaxed me to the nearest road and we left Big Bend.)

Aspen blazing with the brilliance of early autumn as we drove through Curecanti, and again as we followed steep dirt roads onto Grand Mesa hours later, back seat full of fresh peaches we'd purchased at a fruit stand outside Orchard City. Pitching the tent in a palace of golden leaves and burrowing in for a near-freezing night. Sitting in silence for most of the drive back to Fossil Butte the next day, watching the dusty miles of Wyoming's Red Desert roll by and growing ever more aware that our trip was ending; he'd be picking up his things and leaving, maybe not coming back. Questions about what to do and where to go from there remaining unasked under the huge, pale Wyoming skies.

As with all travels, my memories of these places are marked by the circumstances when I happened to be there. Surely, Guadalupe isn't always shrouded in mist. Probably, I'd have liked Ironwood if I hadn't been tense from traffic in Phoenix. Possibly, I wouldn't have found Carson National Forest as charming if we hadn't shared a jug of wine and slept under a blanket of stars. I'll forever hate Big Bend. Like them or not, these places are all now imbued with personal meaning. Even with the brief and somewhat haphazard travel style, and despite—or more so, because of—the tangle of emotions I experienced day by day, hour by hour, I remember each location vividly. It was worth it to visit every one. Those memories, those places are part of who I am.

The bio tech came to visit Black Canyon in late July. Rather than head off for some other destination, we chose to stay in the park for the first time. I told him I was tired of traveling, but what I really meant was: I want to share this place with you. I think I'm starting to like it here, and I want you to like it, too. (I want you to still like *me*.)

We walked a few of the short trails and checked out a good bouldering area, but the main excursion was a hike down to the river via a semi-secret, little-used side canyon, recommended by a ranger. (Yet another perk of living and working in a park is learning about the out-of-the-way places that are as good if not better than those listed in the guidebooks or drawn on the maps.) Once we fought through the top stretch, all raspberry bushes and poison ivy, it wasn't hard to find the way—the only option got narrower and narrower, hemmed in by increasingly taller cliffs, tilting down steeper scree. Down, down. Colder, louder, the roar of the river pounded back at us from every direction. Sound and shadow everywhere. If the ranger hadn't said that the route went to the bottom, I would have sworn it would taper off and trap us; we'd end up wedged between the walls. Rock, all rock, tight mineral glint.

Without warning, we were through the geologic portal, standing at the river. Roar of rapids. Smell of fresh, cool water. Shaft of sunlight pouring onto the bright foam and reverberating off the flood-smoothed boulders, blinding our shadow-tuned eyes. Impossible, that the light could make it all the way down to the bottom of the canyon. Unbelievable, that we were there at just the right moment to see it, to feel it, air lifting with its warmth. As with the lake outside Jackson, I had the feeling that we'd left civilization behind and crossed into a placeless place—a bright, elemental utopia of water, rock, and sun. If only we could stay there forever.

Barry Lopez knows: "The living of life, any life, involves great and private pain, much of which we share with no one. In such places as the Inner Gorge [of the Grand Canyon] the pain trails away from us . . . You can hear your heart beat. That comes first."[12]

But of course the world kept whirling. The sun disappeared beyond the canyon's rim, and the space filled with shadows. Cold. The bio tech seemed to like the canyon fine, but no more so than any other place. The river kept roiling, abrading into the rock. Heartbeats drowned out by the roar of the rapids, there was nowhere to go but back up, back to the surface earth, back to our regular lives and a relationship in which we'd become strangers. Or perhaps we'd always been strangers. Back to Lopez's "great and private pain."

The next work week, I finally made it out to the western slopes of Green Mountain, in the far northwestern corner of the park. It took a long drive around to the North Rim and a hour bumping down an array of braided BLM roads, then a couple of hot, dusty miles on foot through that delightful scrub oak before I dropped off the plateau into

Brief moment of liquid sunlight, pure joy, before darkness returns, two thousand feet into the earth.

a landscape unlike anything else I'd seen: a giant, bowl-shaped valley rimmed by hundred-foot slopes, ribboned with storm-scoured stream-beds, and textured with a surprisingly verdant piñon and juniper forest. I'd stepped from high desert shrub-steppe into a hidden jungle, a lost world. Cretaceous Park. The rock looked right: judging from the miles of sandstone cliffs and mudstone slides—Morrison almost all the way down to the rim of the canyon—*this* must be where the dinosaurs had been hiding all along.

Thus engaged, I spent the full day zigzagging up and down steep slopes, peering under ledges, turning over slabs, lingering at conglomerates, and tracking loose float back to its source. Just me and all of those acres; even the ravens couldn't be bothered to fly this far out. Although the tree canopy provided welcome shade and roots served as hand- and footholds, I still managed to get a wicked sunburn and scrape up my palms and knees—hazards and badges of honor from happy hours spent scrambling around south-facing cliffs, attention focused entirely on fossils. It wasn't until long after I'd reluctantly called it a day, made the slog back to the truck, and driven most of the way home, exhausted and exhilarated, that I realized that I hadn't thought about the bio tech all day.

I also finished up my semi-systematic survey of the Red Rocks Wilderness: another long hike up and around the tilted ridge of Dakota sandstone, along miles of ravine-laced Morrison mudstone, down crumbly gypsum-filled slopes of Wanakah limestone, and finally to a distant exposure of Entrada sandstone that had been taunting me all summer. Elsewhere, the Entrada boasts impressive dinosaur track sites (including one in Grand Staircase-Escalante National Monument that includes trail drag marks). I was still hoping to make the first track discovery in Black Canyon, but it wouldn't be here—wind and water had scoured the sandstone into a sweeping amphitheater of smoothed, friable rock. Hot and gritty. If there had been a series of sauropod-stomped indentations here once upon a time, they'd have quickly eroded into unidentifiable bumps. Although a paleontological disappointment, the hike was a resounding success. The location was spectacular—a touch of Utah's red rock country, à la Arches, hidden in Colorado. Unlike Arches, though, I had the place to myself—no other people for miles, and who knows how long it had been or would be before anyone else ever stepped foot there. What reason was there to make such an arduous trek to such an odd corner of the park? No trails, no dots on a map, not a word about it in brochures. For that afternoon, all of that beauty, that wildness was mine to enjoy and absorb, mine alone.

Yes, I decided as I made it back to the truck and began the drive home, thoroughly exhausted and happy again. *Yes. I like it here, Black Canyon.*

One seemingly unremarkable day, early August, I headed out on my usual morning walk—East Portal Road, short climb to the crest, wait for sunrise. Rounding the corner from the entrance booth, I glanced up and was startled to see I wasn't alone. No more than forty yards ahead, strolling away from me, right down the middle of the pavement: the bobcat! I'd been hoping to see it for so long that I didn't dream that I ever actually would. The bobcat! It seemed to notice me at the same time I noticed it. (I may have gasped. I probably gasped.) The bobcat! It paused to look back, glancing at me over its tawny shoulder. Its fierce golden eyes met mine for an eternal moment—all the wildness of the world in that gaze, pure power and grace—then it broke contact and calmly veered off into the brush, giving a last flick of its long, thick, black-tipped tail as it padded off on enormous paws.

"The bobcat!" I shouted to the maintenance man after I'd unrooted myself from the spot, run back to headquarters (yes, run—could I have been any more foolish?), and waited for him to arrive so I could tell him about the encounter. "A bobcat!" I burst into my apartment, startling my roommate, who continued to try to get ready for work while I gleefully described the whole affair to her. Then again to my closest friend at the park—a vegetation technician, who didn't mind being subjected to my exuberance first thing in the morning.

"The bobcat!" I exclaimed to my supervisor as soon as he walked into the office. He patiently listened to every detail, right through "tawny coat" and "enormous paws" to "giving a last flick of its long, thick, black-tipped tail as it went." After a long pause, my supervisor looked at me—me still beaming with awe and amazement at my good fortune—cleared his throat, and, trying to suppress a laugh, repeated, "Long, thick . . . tail? A *bobcat*?" Pause. "A small, speckled feline with a short, bobbed tail?" Pause.

Oh. My heart had been so set on a bobcat, my mind hadn't processed what my eyes had seen. All the wildness of the world—the beauty, the unpredictability, the power, the fear—indeed. I had met a mountain lion.

At the beginning of August, I made the drive up to Wyoming yet again—this time for Kemmerer's annual Oyster Ridge Music Festival. The previous year, the bio tech and I had had a happy time together, dancing to bluegrass for days. Again this year, we spent Friday night and all Saturday laughing and dancing, hour after hour, afternoon into evening into night. Perfect weather, friendly crowd, toe-tapping music. Everything was seemingly forgiven or forgotten—my move to Colorado, his return to Fossil Butte, our increasingly strained trips earlier in the summer. We danced and danced, hearts racing in tune to the raucous fiddling.

We paused to rest during the break before the second-to-last band. I remember sitting on a concrete slab—a sidewalk planter? cool and gritty—and squinting at the exceptionally black night sky beyond the streetlights. A bit dizzy from dancing, too much beer. A bit stunned. I don't remember the exact words he used, something along the lines of: the long-distance thing isn't working; we're not working. (Unsaid: he didn't love me. Maybe he never had.) Incongruously major-key chords began to sing in the background.

Of course he was right. I'd sensed it for months—a hollow feeling, a great dark sorrow.

I woke early the next morning, well before daybreak. Intending to slip out of his life as silently as possible, I left while he was still sleeping. (As soon as we'd gotten back to Fossil Butte the night before, I'd wanted to leave for Black Canyon, but he wouldn't let me. I was in no condition to drive.) I didn't make it a mile down the road before I felt like I'd burst. I parked my car at Fossil Butte's Historic Quarry Trailhead and stumbled out into the cool, fresh air. My feet found their way onto the path, first walking, then running, a mad dash. Night was paling toward dawn; the shadow of the butte stood out against the lightening sky. Up and up, through the sagebrush, toward the bright line of sunrise. My lungs burned, from the altitude or running or crying or all three. I had to stop. The last time I'd been on that trail, right before I'd left Wyoming—had it only been four months earlier?—everything had been buried in snowdrifts. Now, wildflowers were blooming, the audacity. Same view, out across the valley—the railroad, the highway, the ridge to the south, beyond that the Uintas, then Colorado, the curve of the earth. But so meaningless, only horizon and sky. No coyote yipping, no meadowlarks trilling. Not even any wind—where was the wind? This was the *plains*, how could it be so still? Why wasn't a blizzard howling or thunder crashing? How could the sun rise so calmly, so cloudlessly? So canyonlessly?

The day was already bright and hot by the time I returned to my car. I drove back to quarters to say goodbye to him after all, then left for real, following the lonely highway south one final time.

CHAPTER 4

Self

Species come and species go. Continents move, oceans open and close. Mountains are born, erode, their sediment reshaped into new ranges and ridges. Though there have been notable catastrophes—during the End-Permian Extinction, also known as the "Great Dying," approximately 251 million years ago, "life was nearly extinguished, ecosystems were devastated, and many long-lived lineages disappeared"[1]—eventually, systems recover and flourish. Biodiversity returned to pre-extinction levels about 10 million years after each of the "Big Five" mass extinctions—a blink of an eye, in earth's 4.54-billion-year history. Life isn't the same, but it goes on. Continents continue to move, canyons continue to erode.

The drive back after the music festival in Kemmerer was the longest yet. *I just need to sit with the canyon*, I kept telling myself—sit and watch mist bellow up from within it, crags come and go; sit and watch sunlight shoot across it and creep down the shadowy walls; sit next to an old gnarled juniper under a sky full of stars, listening to the river's distant thrum—*once I'm with the canyon*, I wanted to believe, *it'll be okay*. Onward.

But then, rolling into Rangely, my car's rotors began letting out a horrible squeal. Sunday in the middle of nowhere northwestern Colorado, failing brakes. (Metaphor?) I again called AAA, then my dad, who said I should be able to make it the rest of the way—160-odd miles and a tortuous mountain pass—before the brakes gave out completely. By the time I rolled gently up to Black Canyon, I was a muddle of misery and gratitude to be alive. I never wanted to drive again. Didn't want to leave. I'd be like the juniper and root my toes into the edge of a cliff, wind myself up toward the sky. I'd be like the mountain lion, prowl softly through the brush. Dinosaur bones, covered by silt and filled with silica. Or the pine cone mold, nothing left but neatly arranged shadow. The river, cutting. The mist, seething. Chinese dragons, all movement and stillness, pegmatite intrusions forever winding through walls of gneiss.

One evening, mid-August, memories of Fossil Butte still raw, not long before my field season was over, I went out for my regular sunset walk and found myself lying at the Oak Flat Loop overlook in the pouring rain, back to coarse, wet boulders, face to the roiling clouds, crying. Crying as though I could fill the canyon with my sorrow, as though the river would carry it away. The river roared and rain fell, from the low clouds splash onto the rocks down past the rim of the earth into the inner canyon—Black Canyon, so spectacularly, obliviously deep.

Silence.

In that silence, lying there at the edge of the canyon, filled with that hollowness and sorrow, I cried until soaked to the skin and completely drained, empty. Only then was I finally ready to feel the solidity of the rock and hear the sound of the space. Space below the horizon and above the earth. Space between two thousand-foot walls of nearly two-billion-year-old bedrock. Space swirling with the wingbeats of swallows, the laughter of ravens. Mist.

In that moment, I finally understood. That's who I'd become: thin shell of the earth broken open, exposed to the infinite sky.

I am part canyon.

PART II

Questions Cloud-Hidden Peaks Pose

DENALI NATIONAL PARK AND PRESERVE, ALASKA

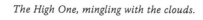

The High One, mingling with the clouds.

CHAPTER 5

Scenery and Wild Life Therein

Cold breeze and intermittent rain notwithstanding, I was more comfortable standing on the platform between the railcars than I would have been inside, sitting in a cushioned compartment, watching scenery roll by like a movie reel. I spent nearly the whole train ride breathing in fresh subarctic air and leaning out to watch the wilderness unfurl: marshy pools reflecting snowcapped peaks; turbid rivers braiding between gravelly banks; mile after mile of spruce-filled forest, occasional stands of birch budding with the fresh green of late May. Every now and then, the train's speakers crackled to life as the conductor shared the name of a landmark or announced, "Moose on the left—we have a moose on the left!" Other than that, there was a soothing rhythm to the ride, a gentle sway to the cars; a reliable clackety-clackety against the rails and a set path—north, no need for me to wonder or worry about where I was going. All I had to do was marvel. "The freshness, the freedom, the farness," like Robert Service, "O God! How I'm stuck on it all."[1]

I was on my way to Denali National Park and Preserve for the summer, to look for fossils again, a year after doing so at Black Canyon. I'd just finished graduate school and sought a bit more adventure before settling into (or, for that matter, looking for) any long-term plans. Freedom—that's what I felt. Excitement, confidence, curiosity, and an exhilarating sense of possibility. Promise. Progress toward *Nuannaarpoq*—Arctic peoples' "extravagant pleasure in being alive."[2]

I felt it as soon as I'd arrived in Anchorage, flying in past snow-capped peaks rising out of a sea of clouds. After taking a shuttle from the airport into town, I'd put on my not-very-waterproof raincoat and goofy rainhat and wandered the city through a cold, persistent drizzle, grinning indiscriminately at cars, fellow pedestrians, and shorebirds swooping along the tidal flats. Scent of salt in the air, clouds hugging the horizon, an edge of wildness atypical for an urban setting, mountain slopes tugging at the periphery. *Is it the place, or my state of mind?* I scribbled in my notebook once I'd retreated to the warmth of a brewpub. *(What's the difference?)*

The next morning, I boarded the blue-and-gold cars of the Alaska Railroad, anticipation building with every mile north. Mountains, forest, muskeg, more mountains. As much as I didn't want the ride to end, it was thrilling to finally hear the conductor announce, "Next Stop: Denali Depot." I gathered my bags, swapped my rainhat out for a wool cap, and stepped off into a fresh, gray-green world of spruce trees, mountains, and mist.

My supervisor met me at the station and took me on a tour of the web of roads, paths, and buildings that would take weeks to learn to navigate properly. (Because there are so many employees at Denali—the usual variety of Park Service personnel, as well as employees and interns for the nonprofit Alaska Geographic and staff for the concessionaire Doyon/Aramark—there are multiple living areas and even a full cafeteria.) After being shown to my room—the top of a little cabin tucked into the taiga, with a view through the trees of a mountain I'd later know as Sugarloaf—I had just enough time to unpack before dinner. From the cafeteria, I found my way to the nearest trail. *To [Mirror?][Oxbow?] Lake, in the late evening light*, reads my first notebook entry, *Magic*.

Horseshoe Lake, I corrected later. By the end of the season, I'd visited that lake several dozen times, nearly every morning. The well-trod trail through the forest and down to the quiet water made for a perfect prebreakfast hike; ideal to start every day with beavers and ducks and fresh, piney air.

What joy, the first days of exploration! Getting a feel for a new landscape, mentally marking areas to return to. Although I knew that I'd have the luxury of time and the ability to return to locations to soak them in more deeply, at first, I felt like every tourist, brimming with curiosity and giddy with newness. The morning after I arrived, I switchbacked up to literally breathtaking views at the Mt. Healy Overlook, then followed Rock Creek Trail to the sled dog kennels in the afternoon. (There, I signed up to walk—or, more accurately, to be dragged behind—a three-year-old, sixty-pound Alaskan husky named Sylvie at least three times a week all summer, helping her keep in shape for mushing come winter, and giving me an excuse to walk even more than I would have on my own.) The next day, I caught a shuttle bus to Savage River and walked the road back to quarters—fifteen miles of leaden skies, spruce tilting drunkenly in the tundra, caribou, bear, porcupine, and a spine of cloud-shrouded peaks I'd learn to call Healy Ridge. (*World cool, fresh, glowing, wild, real, surreal—what adjectives are there? It still doesn't quite seem possible, this place*, that day's summary in my notebook.) Out and back along Triple Lakes Trail on day three, a partly sunny, almost warm Memorial Day. (*Looked up at the big, sharp mountains and wondered, am I really here? What am I living, the blues whites browns greens grays?*)

Although my legs were tired from so much hiking, I was restless, anxious not to miss a minute of anything. I couldn't stay inside, much less sleep, while moose were stomping through the forest and beavers swimming through the lakes, while the sky still glowed with lingering crepuscular light. After dinner that evening, I stepped out of my cabin intending to make a short loop around Rock Creek, but as soon as I started down the trail, I never wanted to stop, never wanted to turn around, felt I could have walked forever, off into the pale northern night.

What is it about places such as Denali—their beauty, their bigness, their wildness—that makes them so inspiring? What is it about northern landscapes that provokes such "Imagination and Desire," as Barry Lopez subtitles his masterpiece, *Arctic Dreams*. Impossible questions: "How do people imagine the landscapes they find themselves in? How does the land shape the imagination of the people that dwell in it? How does desire itself, the desire to comprehend, shape knowledge?"[3] Profound truths: "people's desires and aspirations [are] as much a part of the land as the wind, solitary animals, and the bright fields of stone and tundra."[4] Such raw land, unfamiliar to most visitors, seems open terrain for dreams and desires. "And, too," Lopez adds, "the land itself exist[s] quite apart from these."[5]

Alaska Native peoples, wildlife biologists, petroleum geologists, artists, and Lopez himself view and treat these places differently. We all do, seeing them through the lenses of our own experiences, perceptions, and longings. But the actual land—the features, the processes— supersedes any individual understanding, shaped by forces beyond our knowledge and beliefs. Wild places are so remote and yet so intimate, so ferocious and yet so fragile, so hidden and yet so exposed, that they remain a constant source of mystery, discovery, fear, and delight. What was I seeking there, amid that bigness and wildness? Understanding, yes, and inspiration. Holiness? Wholeness.

"There are no answers to some of the great pressing questions," Lopez gently reminds us, "You continue to live them out, making your life a worthy expression of a leaning into the light."[6]

At 6 million acres, Denali is the fourth-largest NPS unit, smaller than only Noatak National Preserve (6.6 million acres), Gates of the Arctic National Park and Preserve (8.5 million acres), and Wrangell-St. Elias National Park and Preserve (an astounding 13.2 million acres). (Not counting federal land managed by other agencies, including the 17-million-acre Tongass National Forest, the Arctic and Yukon Delta National Wildlife Refuges, totaling 19.3 and 19.2 million acres, respectively, and the 23.4-million-acre National Petroleum Reserve–Alaska, which is bigger than the state of Maine.)

The park takes its name from the highest point in North America— a 20,310-foot-high mountain known to Koyukon Athabaskan people as *Deenaalee*, which means "The High One." A different label for the peak and, at first, the park—McKinley—was assigned by a gold prospector in 1897 to honor a presidential candidate who would never see his namesake. (McKinley's only connection was that he supported the gold standard.) Federal agencies, including the US Board on Geographic Names and the US Geological Survey, identified the mountain on official maps as McKinley until 2015, when the Department of the Interior honored a decades-long request to recognize the Koyukon people's original toponym. The name of the park had been changed from McKinley to Denali thirty-five years earlier, via the Alaska National Interest Lands Conservation Act of 1980 (ANILCA), which also tripled the park's size and made sweeping changes to management and use of tens of millions of acres of other public lands throughout the state.

Although Denali the mountain is now the centerpiece of Denali the park, the original Mount McKinley National Park was intended to be a game refuge, the borders of which didn't even contain the entire massif. "What need [was there] for a park designation in the mountainous Interior?" asked park historian William Brown of early twentieth-century perceptions of endless land and infinite wilderness in the Alaska Territory. "Certainly the high mountains—girt by sub-ranges, vast gorges, and immense glaciers—needed no protection. So it boiled down to the wildlife."[7]

While spending the summer of 1906 and winter of 1907-8 in the shadow of Denali studying Dall sheep (a white subspecies of thinhorn sheep native to dry subalpine areas of Alaska and northwestern Canada), hunter-naturalist Charles Sheldon became convinced of the need to establish a park preserve that could both protect game species and "allow visitors the same enjoyment and inspiration that he had been privileged to experience"; namely, a "heraldic display of wildlife posed against stupendous mountain scenery."[8] Spurred on by the start of construction on the Alaska Railroad in 1914, which he knew would bring more people and greater demand for wild game in the interior, Sheldon mobilized members of the influential Boone and Crockett Club (a hunting club founded in 1887 by George Bird Grinnell and Theodore Roosevelt) to support protection of the habitat of "a wide area of the best sheep, caribou, and moose country."[9] In 1915, Sheldon addressed a letter to Stephen Mather—soon to be the first director of the National Park Service—on behalf of the Game Preservation Committee of the Boone and Crockett Club, insisting that "[the Alaska Range] must be made a national park." Sheldon based his case on the majestic wildlife and "the grandeur of the scenery and the topographical interest," which he claimed rivaled the Grand Canyon.[10] (Always the Grand Canyon.) Mather agreed, as did Congress. In 1917, President Woodrow Wilson signed enabling legislation for a 1.9-million-acre Mount McKinley National Park, "for recreation purposes by the public and for the preservation of animals, birds, and fish and for the preservation of the natural curiosities and scenic beauties thereof."[11] (But, historian Brown notes, no funds were appropriated until 1921, leaving the park "vacant of protectors, unmarked on the ground, and prey to poachers for more than 4 years."[12])

Two decades later, NPS wildlife biologist Adolph Murie had the "good fortune to be given the assignment" to go to then Mount McKinley National Park (along with his wife and their children) to study the relationships between sheep and their main predator, timber wolves.

Murie's description of his field work *The Wolves of Mount McKinley* discusses not just the population dynamics and habits of Dall sheep and wolves, but also the roles that these organisms play in the subalpine web of life, alongside caribou, moose, grizzly bears, red foxes, and golden eagles. The bulletin contains a wealth of meticulously collected and tabulated data on topics such as the stomach contents of sheep carcasses, nest occupancy of golden eagles, and the behavior of grizzlies, whom Murie found to be "unusually well behaved." It also includes an endearing side anecdote, in which Murie details the life history of Wags, a wolf pup that he raised "for the purpose of . . . familiarizing [him]self with wolf character." Like a proud father keeping records in a baby book, Murie notes everything from Wags's first howl to her first bite of ground squirrel, her first wobbly walk to an incident in which she playfully "carr[ied] away a door mat from the Superintendent's residence."[13] (Although an atypical sort of field biology, the depiction of Wags as a curious, loyal furball countered wolves' reputation as cold-blooded killers.)

Murie's central conclusion—"that predators [namely, wolves] played an important role in an intact ecosystem"[14]—contributed to a larger shift in wildlife management, away from controlling predators or increasing game to thinking more holistically about ecological viability. "In a national park the objective is to preserve a piece of primitive nature where natural interrelationships may prevail," writes Murie,[15] overriding the nineteenth-century Yellowstone model of a "public park or pleasuring-ground for the benefit and enjoyment of the people."

Still, it took another two decades for the Advisory Board on Wildlife Management in National Parks to be convened. Chaired by zoologist and conservationist Aldo Starker Leopold (son of Aldo and brother of Luna), the board echoed Murie, recommending that the NPS make a "major policy change . . . [to] recognize the enormous complexity of ecologic communities and the diversity of management procedures required to preserve them" and to actively restore natural ecosystems. "Above all," they concluded, in a document that's come to be known as the *Leopold Report*, "the maintenance of naturalness should prevail."[16]

When another NPS Advisory Board was convened in 2012 to "revisit" the *Leopold Report*, they updated and expanded it to include not just wildlife but "all natural and cultural resources for which the

National Park Service has . . . 'an enduring responsibility.' "[17] Acknowledging that ecological, socioeconomic, and cultural conditions constantly change and that scientific techniques and principles continue to evolve, the board concluded that the NPS should "steward NPS resources for current change that is not yet fully understood, in order to preserve ecological integrity and cultural and historical authenticity." Moreover, they also called on the NPS to "provide visitors with transformative experiences."[18]

On the surface, it sounds like rewording of the "Dual Mandate" of the Organic Act of 1916, which created the National Park Service and charged it with the seemingly antithetical if not impossible duties to both "conserve the scenery and the natural and historic objects and the wild life therein" and to "provide for the enjoyment of the same in such manner and by such means as will leave them unimpaired for the enjoyment of future generations." For a more than a century, park managers have struggled to find an appropriate balance between conservation and use, wildlife and the visitors who come to ogle it. Under Stephen Mather's leadership, the nascent NPS emphasized recreation and access, reasoning that more visitors would translate into greater public support for parks. The 1950s saw a democratization of visitation, thanks to automobiles and more leisure time for middle-class American families. As Leopold and his board were finishing their report, the NPS was completing a decade-long mission to "improve" and expand visitor services—more roads, more trails, more bathrooms, more buildings, more infrastructure in general, allowing for the rise of what writer and monkey-wrencher Edward Abbey scorned as "Industrial Tourism." "Lee's Ferry has now fallen under the protection of the Park Service," Abbey wrote of a spot in one of the new "National Recreation Areas," created for people's enjoyment instead of for conservation of wildlife or other resources. "And who can protect it against the Park Service?"[19]

By the mid-1960s, though, wilderness preservationists were seeing success and the environmental movement was gaining momentum. After publication of the *Leopold Report*, the Dual Mandate pendulum began to swing back toward scientific research and resource protection. The nuanced, twenty-first-century language of "Revisiting Leopold" acknowledges shifting socioecological systems, emphasizes "stewardship" over management, and especially encourages those "transformative

Dall sheep.

experiences" over mere recreation.[20] Visitors are encouraged to come, yes, and to enjoy their time in parks, but they ought to go away changed, having learned something from the land and the wildlife therein.

Adolph Murie was also ahead of his time when it came to minimizing tourism infrastructure. "The more complete the biotic unit and the larger the area the greater is the opportunity to achieve that ideal," he noted, "but unfortunately few national parks are large enough to be uninfluenced by artificial activities taking place both within and outside their boundaries."[21] Citing examples of human activities that have outsized ecological effects—including construction of an "automobile highway" into the heart of Denali, which "gives the wolves a special advantage" over sheep—Murie began to advocate against development projects. For the remainder of his career, he continued to both study wildlife and battle proposals that would have diminished wildness. In particular, his opposition to a road improvement plan "marked a major transition in the park's history, elevating the park's wilderness character as a major value," as the NPS now celebrates his efforts.[22] The Murie Science and Learning Center at Denali—one of eighteen NPS Research

Learning Centers nationwide, dedicated to scientific research, management, and education—is named in his honor.

Thanks largely to Murie's insistence on wilderness values, today's ninety-two-mile "automobile highway" remains similar to what it was when first cut in 1923-38. It's still the only road into the park's six million acres—a long, thin, single line of gravel. To see anything of the wilderness beyond this lone strip of motorized access, visitors have to hike, ski, dogsled, or fly. (Small aircraft operators are available to transport climbers to base camps in the Alaska range and to take flightseers soaring over the mountains and valleys, perhaps making a glacier landing if conditions and permits allow.) Since 1972, visitors have only been allowed to drive personal vehicles down the first fifteen miles of the road, to a campground and trailhead (one of few maintained trails in the park) at Savage River. During the summer season, road travel beyond that point is restricted to transit and tour busses. Three-quarters of visitors experience the park from one of these busses.

Each day from mid-May to September, dozens of busses navigate the narrow, winding two- and then one-lane gravel road, helping alleviate road congestion and air and noise pollution. Tour busses, driven by certified naturalists, offer interpretation along the way, stopping at rest areas, designated overlooks, the Eielson Visitor Center (deep in the park, at Mile 66), and/or the former gold mining town of Kantishna at the end of the road—a twelve-hour ride, round trip. Meanwhile, transit busses are just for transportation. They're like school busses, not tour coaches—no bathrooms, no cushy seats. They don't offer narration but do pause to allow backcountry hikers, road bikers, wildlife watchers, paleontology technicians, and anyone else who so desires to disembark at any point, and, as long as there are open seats, will stop to pick people up from along the roadside and carry them back to the entrance.

(Ed Abbey again commented on how tourists "are being robbed and robbing themselves" by seeing parks from what he calls "back-breaking upholstered mechanized wheelchairs."[23] "In the first place you can't see anything from a car; you've got to get out of the goddamned contraption and walk, better yet crawl, on hands and knees, over the sandstone and through the thornbush and cactus. When traces of blood begin to mark your trail you'll see something, maybe. Probably not."[24] What would he have to say about bus tours?)

Wildlife is as much of an attraction as the scenery. Drivers and riders keep a constant eye out for the "big five": Dall sheep, moose, caribou, grizzly bears, and wolves. According to a park study on wildlife–vehicle interaction, sheep are the most commonly spotted species, their white coats standing out against the cliff faces they frequent. Sheep also exhibit the greatest behavioral change with traffic, lingering far from the road and refraining from crossing at busy times. Caribou and grizzlies are the second and third most common species, apparently undaunted by the busses. Moose are few and far between, in part because they prefer densely treed areas, making them more challenging to spot. Wolves are a rare treat, seen almost exclusively around Sable Pass, near where Murie stayed while completing his fieldwork.[25]

In 2012, park managers completed a Vehicle Management Plan (VMP), which aimed "to ensure that traffic patterns and volume neither reduce the opportunity for exceptional visitor experiences nor adversely impact the ability of wildlife . . . to forage and play and move near or across the park road."[26] "What better symbol of the success of the VMP will there be," they asked, "than the smiles on awestruck visitors who travel the park road by bus to view and photograph a grizzly and her two cubs *right outside the window*?"[27]

The plan seems to be working. It's undeniably safer to spy on grizzlies from the shelter of a giant metal bus than on foot, and visitors certainly are awestruck whenever there's a wildlife spotting. First, a ripple of excitement when somebody spots one of the big five; then, a succession of gasps as others see the animals for themselves. A scramble as all riders flock to one side of the vehicle for better views. Shutters click as everyone takes the same photograph. Slight rumble of the engine if the driver needs to reposition to make room for other busses filled with other visitors who also want a glimpse. After a few minutes, the driver announces that they must start moving so as to keep roughly on schedule and not overcrowd the road. Forward, then, with renewed hope for more animals, more sightings, the same reaction all over again.

It can be like a wildlife bingo: Grizzly? *Check.* Sheep? *Check.* Another sheep? *Enh, waiting on that moose.* Back at the bus depot, it's more like poker, swapping lists. *I'll see your bear and raise you five caribou.* (Wolves are trump.) No skill involved, just luck. And hope. Dozens of watchful eyes.

I saw my first grizzly from a bus—a golden-backed, brown-humped, three-footed he-bear who had, according to the driver, lost one of his front paws in a trap the previous summer yet managed to survive the harsh winter. Had the driver not mentioned the injury, I might not have noticed. "Tripawed," as he was nicknamed, seemed as massive and powerful as any four-footed creature, fording his way across the deep, swift Savage River as easily if moving through air.

I also saw my first sheep from a bus. ("My sheep," "my bear," as if I get to claim possession, having done nothing more than sit on a bus that happened to be in the right place at the right time.) It was nestled into a sunny ledge above the steep, narrow twists of Polychrome Pass, wholly at home, confident that nothing could harm it from either above or below. (While predators are smart enough not to try to traverse near-vertical cliffs, I'd later re-realize the hard way that it's unwise to follow wild sheep trails anywhere, having apparently not learned my lesson in Curecanti.)

On the walk along the road from Savage River my second day in Denali, I crossed paths with caribou and nearly missed a momma moose and her two calves wading through a shrub-lined pool. The next evening, having discovered a stretch of the Taiga Trail where I could pick up a bit of a cell signal, I was talking to my mom, letting her know that I'd made it to the park, safe and happy, when, partway through the conversation, I came around a bend and saw a cow no more than fifty yards away. She stared at me, huge ears raised, huge nostrils flaring on her huge nuzzle. Huge. Moose are enormous, the more so when encountered unexpectedly. The NPS claims that adult females can weigh seven to eleven hundred pounds and stand six and a half feet tall, but this cow surely weighed a ton and stood at least ten feet, maybe twenty. Were there calves nearby? Was I supposed to stare her down? Turn and run? Moose can run up to thirty-five miles per hour. "Um, mom?" I whispered into my phone, slowly backing away, "Call you back. Moose."

Marmots by the Savage River Trail, ptarmigan near Primrose Ridge, coyote trotting past Kantishna—there were animals everywhere, and surely far more out there than let themselves be seen. For every curious little arctic ground squirrel trailing me on a hike or every gray jay cackling outside my cabin window, there must have been a hundred more creatures watching from behind the trees and under the brush. ("If the snow leopard should manifest itself," Peter Matthiessen could have been writing of a lynx in Denali, "then I am ready to see the snow leopard. If not, then somehow . . . I am not ready to perceive it . . . That it is here, that its frosty eyes watch us from the mountain—that is enough."[28])

Denali boasts 39 species of mammals, 169 species of birds, and 14 species of fish. Biologists estimate populations of 2,230 caribou, more than 2,000 each of both moose and sheep, 300-350 grizzly bears, another 200 black bears, and 51 wolves, all making use of the "wild terrain . . . to roam, rest, migrate, spar, sleep, avoid predators, browse, and do all the other things that large animals do in wild, unencumbered landscapes."[29] Not to discount the 442 documented lichens, 499 mosses and liverworts, and 758 vascular plants.[30] The park teems with wildlife. Caribou prance across the tundra, bear pad down streams, sure-footed sheep skip up their vertical walls of rock. Even if an enormous, ungainly mass of a moose is just standing there, doing nothing but munching on willows, its very presence—its utter *mooseness*—adds power and meaning to the landscape. Solid, snowcapped mountains may dominate the horizon and braided rivers may weave through the valleys, but the inanimate scenery can seem like mere backdrop to the animals—the living, breathing souls of wilderness.

Although I encountered wildlife every time I stepped outside, I was in Denali for three and a half weeks before I saw the mountain itself. Three and a half weeks. I'd already hiked all of the trails and begun wandering off into bogs and along braided rivers. I'd taken the bus several stops beyond Savage and driven an NPS truck to the end of the road. I could identify rocks, plants, and birds and could name key landmarks—Toklat and Teklanika Rivers, Double Mountain, the distant teeth of Fang. But where was The High One? The crown of the continent? *The* mountain? Wrapped in clouds, lost in sky.

As I noted later:

> When visiting a national park, we understand that we won't be able to see and do everything. We have to choose what trails to walk and what ranger talks to attend. We have to hope that flowers are in full bloom and animals are loafing within binocular-distance . . . of all of the things we look for, we expect

the land to be there. The rocks, the ridges, the mountains—those stay put. They are there. They are permanent. They are emblems of strength, of fortitude, of quiet, solid dignity, no?

No.

Here, in [Denali], rivers change course and mountains regularly wrap themselves in mist. Clouds sweep through the valleys and snag on the peaks. Skies hang low and tattered, leaking patches of sunlight and curtains of rain that alternately illuminate and shroud distant features. Want to see the Polychrome Glaciers? Primrose Ridge? Cabin Peak? Take your chances. They're always there, but it's not every day that they are visible. The view is constantly shifting, the scenery rearranged. You never know what you will see. You have no say in the "land" part of your scape, especially if you come to see the highest, grandest and most elusive mountain of all.[31]

From late May into June, there was so much to see and do in Denali that I'd begun to forget that the mountain was even there. Then, one weekend, three and a half weeks into the season, I was headed by shuttle to Savage, planning to walk the road from there. It was a perfect morning for walking—air cool and calm, broken stratocumulus sauntering through a brilliant blue sky, tundra erupting in a rainbow of flowers. Nine miles in, the road rose up out of the taiga and rounded a slight bend, giving everyone on the shuttle a spectacular view of a wide, green valley backed by wrinkles of purple-blue mountains. Although the scene was somewhat familiar by then, it was no less breathtaking than it had been when I'd first seen it. Odd, though, beyond the highest peaks, there was this bright mass, strangely angular for a cloud. Pyramidal, almost. Opaque. Wait, no? As I recall, "I gasped. Audibly. Everyone on the bus gasped. The *mountain*! *The* mountain. Shining, sharp, huge and shocking . . . It wasn't a cloud, but rather the summit of Denali."[32]

Even as I watched, floccus began to gather on its flanks. Within an hour, the mountain was completely gone, tucked in its cloud cloak. It wouldn't be visible again for another week.

According to a study on visitor demographics and activities, eighty percent of visitors are at Denali for the first—and likely only—time. They come from every state in the country and many countries around the world, hoping to see spectacular scenery and animals.[33] While some visitors express disappointment at not seeing enough or the desired species, nearly all glimpse at least some wildlife, and most seem to understand that the animals are free to roam. More than a few are surprised and saddened, though, to find that "all that was missing was a view of Denali."[34] Comments range from the wistful "Wish we could have seen Mount McKinley" to the outraged "We came to see Mount McKinley / Denali . . . We returned two weeks later and still couldn't see it. Could 'rain-check' discount tickets be offered on a standby basis for empty seats for passengers who had reservations on overcast days?"[35] (That comment continued: "The state is mostly wilderness so that aspect of the park did not interest us at all." Perhaps those visitors realized, in retrospect, that Alaska is a poor vacation destination for those not interested in wilderness.)

"Is it out?" riders ask before boarding the busses, discussing the mountain as though it makes a conscious choice as to whether and when it will reveal itself. "Not today" is the most common response, or "not for long." It's partly a matter of geography, partly timing, and a whole lot of luck. Weather conditions are unpredictable in the Alaska Range owing to both the orographic effect and the tumultuous mixing of cold, dry arctic air masses with warmer, moister air from farther south. I can't remember a single day when it didn't sprinkle at least a little, and there were multiple several-day stretches of steady drizzle. (On a positive note: near-daily rainbows!) Visitors who come in autumn when the air is drier or who have plenty of time in the park may be able to wait for better weather for mountain spotting; others just have to book tickets and hope.

Few people can linger at Denali until they see the mountain, especially if it hides for a month at a time. For the eighty-five percent of visitors who stay overnight, visits last, on average, less than three days. Those who stay less than a day spend an average of nine hours peering into some corner of the park.[36] This is enough time to walk a couple of the trails near the main visitor center (all of which are lovely hikes, but shielded from sight of the Denali Massif itself) and drive out to Savage River, pausing at Mountain Vista to hope to get a vista of the mountain, imposing from more than seventy miles away. Alternatively, nine hours is enough time to take the shuttle to Eielson Visitor Center, stopping at Stony Dome to snap a version of the photo used on tourism brochures: park road zigzagging along the side of a wide valley, aiming straight at the heart of Denali itself. From Eielson, which perches above a broad floodplain, visitors can see the mossy toe of the Muldrow Glacier, the northern slope of the Alaska Range, and, thirty-three miles to the southwest, the gleaming white mass of *the* mountain, so enormous that it seems just steps away.

More often, though, Eielson looks out into a confederation of clouds and curtains of rain. Buses don't bother to stop at Stony Dome on overcast days, and visitors are lucky if the rugged but comparatively low Double and Cathedral Mountains are visible southwest of Mountain Vista. "With intense cold locking up moisture, summer skies are often cloudy," the NPS tries to warn visitors. "[Bus drivers] say that only one in three days offers glimpses of the mountain."[37] For all its seeming solidity, Denali is more elusive than the wildlife that prowls its flanks.

Type "Denali" into an Internet search engine, and it will return image after image of a snow-white mass towering over a carpet of tundra or perfectly reflected in the calm waters of Wonder Lake. Road in the foreground, weaving toward summits and ridges as if toward the skyline of a great metropolis. Caribou in a corner of the frame, dwarfed by the wall of rock and ice dominating the rest of the image. Denali capped by streamers of cloud. Denali collecting fair-weather cumuli. Denali glowing with delicate shades of pink and purple. People climbing Denali. People dogsledding past Denali. Rangers in Denali. Busses in Denali. People smiling at the base of, on top of, while gazing at Denali. People photographing other people photographing Denali. A truck named Denali. (Confusingly, "Sierra Denali.")

What you will not see in those Internet images? Walls of mist. Rain and snow swallowing whatever was in the background. Taiga and tundra—brilliantly green in the summer or blazing red-orange-yellow in the autumn—fading up into opaque grayness.

Thanks to tourism brochures and websites, general media, and word of mouth from friends and family, even those who've never been to Denali have an idea of what it is, what it looks like, and what it would be like to experience the park. "Destination imagery"—people's ideas of a place to which they would like to travel—is a powerful motivating

View from Stony Dome (sometimes).

force. Positive perceptions of Denali—The scenery! The wildlife! The adventure of it all!—compel travelers to invest significant amounts of time and money on the long trek to interior Alaska.

While airlines, cruise lines, hotels and resorts, restaurants, guides, and other tourism-based businesses select the most enticing imagery to advertise their services (hence photographs of people smiling under sunny skies, rather than people squished onto a bus or drenched in sleet), scholars are interested in the processes by which potential visitors form mental images of places and "operationalize" these expectations.[38] For example, William Wycoff and Lary Dilsaver discuss the Great Northern Railway's use of promotional imagery to encourage tourists to travel to western landscapes in the late nineteenth and early twentieth centuries: "disarmingly realistic . . . photographs were in fact carefully orchestrated reproductions of landscapes designed to communicate key elements of the Great Northern's visual iconography"—soaring mountains, shimmering lakes, and mythic wildlife.[39] (Sound familiar?) As Brian Garrod explains, "tourism destinations . . . must first be constructed as such, and to do so requires that the essential qualities of that place . . . be taken and shaped into imagery that will be attractive."[40] Curated images promise beauty, adventure, history, or comfort—exotic or Edenic experiences. Cruise lines aren't going to fill glossy brochures with images of clouds, mosquitoes, or clouds of mosquitoes.

View from Stony Dome (more often)—you'd never know the mountain is there.

Of course, our perceptions change when we arrive at and experience destinations—when we feel the cool rain, when we sit on the bumpy bus, when we glimpse that grizzly bear, or, for the fortunate minority, when we realize that the immense white cloud towering in the distance is actually Denali.

Or do they? Garrod also finds that destination imagery can become a self-fulfilling prophesy, what he calls a "hermeneutic circle" of "tourism (re)production": appealing images inspire people to visit a place, set up expectations, and frame our choices for things to see and do; in turn, "tourists seek to acquire photographic images of the place they are visiting," so as to structure, remember, and share our experiences, and "prove to others that [we] have been there."[41] How many thousands of versions of the same photograph are taken each year at Polychrome Overlook and other shuttle stops? Cameras click away at the "Big Five"—is that to celebrate the wildness of such animals, or to document encounters? Do snapshots from Stony Dome "count" if the mountain isn't visible in the distance?

Marketing scholars Hector San Martín and Ignacio Rodríguez del Bosque wonder how destination image relates to tourist satisfaction—are people more likely to be impressed or disappointed in a place with a grand reputation? What happens if our experiences don't live up to our expectations? According to their research, tourists seek to avoid "psychological conflict when they perceive discrepancies between performance and prior beliefs," so they "adjust their perceptions to their expectations in order to minimize or remove that tension," if need be.[42] In other words, we will readily lower or amend our demands to ensure an enjoyable experience. (Their research doesn't explore the opposite—how we react when we have low expectations and are pleasantly surprised.)

The more powerful the destination image, the bigger the expectation and, presumably, the better the experience. Asked to rate the overall "quality of facilities, services, and recreational opportunities," ninety-six percent of visitors to Denali felt that they were either "good" or "very good"—higher approval ratings than those of Yellowstone or Black Canyon.[43] The "experience of viewing wildlife along the park road" was comparable, with eighty-four percent of visitors reporting that they felt "satisfied" or "very satisfied." The park met people's expectations—comments read "enjoyed it," "loved it," "beautiful park," "plan to return," and "thank you."[44]

Yet of the more than seven hundred visitor groups sampled, only three mentioned "saw the mountain."[45] *The* mountain. The High One.

If you haven't had the privilege, fortune, and sheer joy of seeing Denali, statistics will have to do. Elevation 20,310 feet, the third highest of the world's seven summits. One of the world's most prominent peaks, with an elevation change of more than 20,000 feet from lowest contour to the top. (The lowest point in the park is just 223 feet above sea level.) And one of the most isolated summits, half a world away from any others even close to its height. Neighboring Mt. Foraker is nearly 3,000 feet lower.[46]

Geologically, Denali anchors the heart of the Alaska Range, which arcs four hundred miles from the Alaska Peninsula to Canada's Yukon Territory. Made up of a mix of Mesozoic igneous and sedimentary rocks, the range is technically a "suture zone" between accreted terranes—former offshore island arcs that smashed into the continent as the Pacific Plate converged and subducted beneath the North American Plate. (The Yukon composite terrane sits to the north, and the Wrangellia composite terrane and Chugach complex were added to the south.) According to geologist Paul Fitzgerald and colleagues, the range began forming about twenty-five million years ago, when the Yakutat microplate (a smaller tectonic plate squished between the North American Plate and the Pacific Plate) got caught up in the mix and began colliding with North America, ramming and twisting the accreted terranes against the Bering block.[47] In the process, the relatively weaker rocks of the Alaska Range Suture Zone crumpled up between the stronger rocks of the terranes and appear to have risen the most at places where the rocks were weakest and subjected to more pressure due to "restraining bends" along fault lines.[48] The same processes that created the mountains continue: the Denali and Hines Creek Faults are quite active (the park sees an average of three thousand earthquakes per year), and Denali itself is still rising, though only two-hundredths of an inch per year.[49]

Even as geologic forces elevate the range, weathering and erosional forces—particularly those related to ice—are breaking it down and carving it out. Freezing and thawing water shatters rocks, and flowing ice—glaciers—is even more powerful (if slower) than flowing rivers. With its high elevation and high latitude, Denali is what the NPS calls a "stronghold of glaciers," a "land sculpted by ice."[50]

More statistics: more than sixteen percent of the park surface is glaciated (though that area shrank by eight percent between 1950 and 2010). The Kahiltna Glacier—the longest on the Alaska Range—flows forty-four miles down from the southwestern side of Denali, while the Ruth Glacier, which starts on the southeast side, measures 3,805 feet thick.[51] Most of the major rivers—the Teklanika and the Toklat; the Savage and the Sanctuary—are either glacially fed or sourced in seasonal snowpack. The NPS warns hikers that glacially fed waterways "roil with sediment loads" and have multiple "braided channels [that] are continually shifting across wide gravel floodplains,"[52] but these statements can't do justice to the sheer power and terror of the rivers' churning milky gray waters. Nor can metrics convey the might of the glaciers. A description of the Kahiltna—"the unsettling creak, crack, rumble, and groan of the huge river of ice that slowly grinds its way down from the high valleys of the Alaska Range, plucking rocks from the sidewalls and valley floor"[53]—begins to reveal their grandeur.

But of all of these numbers and words, any images or films, none can ever describe or explain *the* mountain, much less the awe of being in its presence. Experience or imagination, only, of a colossal, solid rock-and-ice cloud that keeps itself mostly hidden in sky.

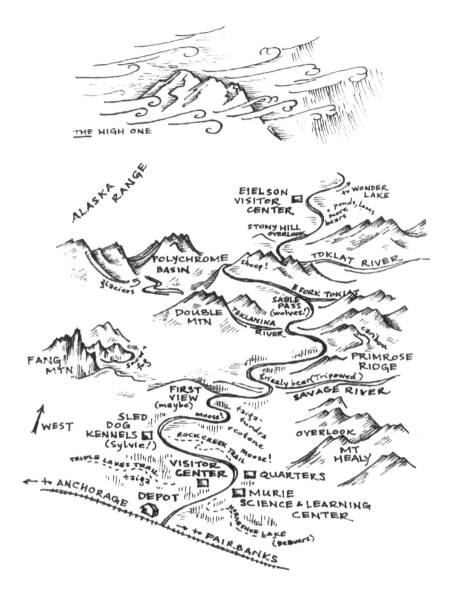

Map of Denali. Fifteen miles to Savage River, fifty-three to Toklat, sixty-six to Eielson, and ninety-two for the entire road. Thirty-three miles between Eielson and the High One. Fifteen miles and a whole lot of hard work from the far side of Fang.

CHAPTER 6

Mountain

I never climbed Denali. Nor did I have any desire to do so. Maybe it's laziness, maybe cowardice, but I've always scoffed at mountain climbing, especially expedition-style treks to "conquer" or "claim" superlatively high or dangerous peaks. That's not to say I discount the effort and skill that goes into the pursuit; mountaineers have remarkable physical and mental stamina. Nor do I scoff at alpinists' aspirations and triumphs; who wouldn't want to be able to say that they were the first to stand on the roof of the continent or pioneered a challenging new route? I welcome hiking invitations and have summited my share of peaks, but I never quite understand the purpose. What does anyone hope to prove by climbing a mountain? What do we hope to learn? What's the good of being *Conquistadors of the Useless*—as alpinist Lionel Terray titles his memoir—an exercise in pure adventure and sheer pointlessness.

During graduate school, I took a field course on mountain geography led by the department chair and my advisor, who specialized in geomorphology and perceptions of mountain landscapes, respectively. Our trip to Rocky Mountain National Park included a visit to the Bradford Washburn American Mountaineering Museum in Golden, Colorado. Looking at the maps and terrain models, the pickaxes and boots of mountaineers filled me with more puzzlement than aspiration. *The "sport," "challenge," "audacity," of navigating/"conquering" peaks—I don't understand,* I puzzled in my notebook. *[Is it a matter of] Pride? Exhilaration? "Spirit of adventure and self-reliance"? . . . [Is it that] men want to feel like gods, look down on mere mortals of the world from afar?* Even when enjoying the expansive views from atop Hallett Peak the next day, I still wondered, *Mountains. What's the allure of mountains?*

(On the way home, I did quite enjoy a stop at "Mount" Sunflower, the high point of Kansas, more a gentle rise near the Colorado border than any sort of true summit. No quest, no triumph, just a view of the sky to forever.)

The eponym of the mountaineering museum, Bradford Washburn, is a legend in Denali mountaineering—a smart and tenacious climber with many first ascent credits (including the West Buttress, the most popular route today), as well as a talented photographer and cartographer whose images and maps of Denali, other summits such as Everest, and landmarks such as the Grand Canyon are still used and celebrated by climbers, scientists, and artists alike. "I've come to hold this great peak and its beautiful but rugged approaches in deep affection—and, at the same time, in profound respect," Washburn writes in the introduction to his illustrated history of Denali mountaineering, *Mount McKinley: The Conquest of Denali*.[1] "We were lucky to climb it when we did," he goes on. "We [he and his wife, Barbara, a self-proclaimed 'accidental adventurer' and the first woman to summit Denali] lived and climbed on the mountain as if it belonged to us."[2]

Mountaineering has changed a lot since his day. More effective and lighter-weight gear, better technology, easier access, and dedicated search and rescue personnel add up to hundreds of people tackling Denali each year. Nearly 1,200 people attempted the climb in 2017; 498 summitted, lower than the average 500–700 summits per year in recent decades.[3] To try to ensure safety and prevent overcrowding, climbers must now register with the park, purchase a permit, and attend an orientation session. Washburn notes, however, "McKinley itself hasn't changed. Just to be in its presence is still as exciting to me as it was the first time I saw it."[4]

There are plenty of achievements and dates—the first ascent (1913), first fatalities (1932), first winter ascent (1967), first solo (1970), first all-female team (1970), oldest climber (aged seventy-eight), youngest climber (aged eleven)—and even more biographies. Heroes such as Walter Harper, Harry Karstens, Hudson Stuck, and Robert Tatum (the first successful summiteers) and villains such as Dr. Frederick Cook (who falsely claimed to reach the top in 1906). Characters such as those who were part of the "Sourdough Expedition," four locals who said they made it up to the shorter North Summit in 1910, fueled only by bags of donuts. (No one believed them until the 1913 team confirmed seeing the spruce pole they'd planted there). Triumphs such as that of Arlene Blum (part of the first all-female team, who went on to lead a famous expedition to Annapurna in the Himalaya) and tragedies such as that of Naomi Uemura (who, fourteen years after making the first solo ascent, made the first winter solo ascent but perished on the descent).[5]

It is inspiring to hear the tales of courage as man pushes himself to extremes. I use the term intentionally, as mountaineering is still predominantly a male pursuit; only twelve percent of climbers in 2018 were female.[6] And it is fascinating to consider how many stories this one crumpled corner of the planet has accumulated, just by virtue of being higher than the rock around it. Like tragic hero George Mallory, I appreciate adventure and "the struggle of life itself upward and forever upward." I understand "that there is something in man which responds to" the natural world with desire and fear and sheer joy. But I don't see the existence of mountains as a "challenge."[7] As someone who doesn't instinctively "desire to conquer the universe"[8] or use peaks as a proving ground for my sense of self, I just don't see why, George Leigh Mallory, *why* climb Everest (or Denali, or any other peak)? What do man's foolish longings mean to a mountain? "The mountains one gazes at, reads about, dreams of and desires are not the mountains one climbs," Robert MacFarlane points out. "These are matters of hard, steep, sharp rock and freezing snow; of extreme cold."

Oh, but also "of unspeakable beauty."[9]

The second time I saw Denali, I was ascending Primrose Ridge—my first solo off-trail trek in the park. On a benign, blue-sky day, mid-June, I caught a shuttle to Savage River, walked the road a mile or two farther, then veered off to the right and began a literal bushwhack up the slopes toward a long, high crest, hoping that I was making enough noise to alert any moose or bears. After an hour of hard work, the stands of willow and spruce began to get patchier. Another half hour and I emerged onto swaths of arctic tundra, soft with mosses, low shrubs, and great shocks of wildflowers. While pausing to catch my breath, I gazed out across the landscape and worried to note clouds building on the western horizon—thick, towering. But oddly sharp—solid? It had fooled me again—the mountain—so tall and prominent as to seem like sky but undeniably stone and gleaming ice.

From the top of the ridge, I had a dazzling view—thread-thin road weaving along the edge of a wide green valley; rim of rocky ledges,

backed by row after row of increasingly sharp, purple peaks; dominating it all, the gleaming white mass of Denali, a good seventy miles
away. Two Dall sheep grazed in a perfect line of sight to complete the
postcard-perfect scene.

"Mass" is the only way to describe the mountain—the exact opposite
of Black Canyon. Not just tall or rugged, not a tooth or fin or swoop—a
mass. Massive. Etymology: *massif*, "solid." In geomorphological terms,
Denali is technically a massif—a cluster of mountains. Very dense, high
mountains. My notebook entry: *"THE mountain! Like a cloud—white,
high—but SOLID."* Impossible, that the planet can support anything that
big. (The crust beneath it is estimated to be up to twenty-eight miles
deep, twelve miles thicker than crust to the north.[10] Tourists sometimes
ask how much the mountain weighs.[11]) Unbelievable, its gravitational
pull. Unforgettable, to have a chance to see it so clearly. Enough, to
know it's there. The whole rest of the season, I was conscious of its
presence, knew it existed, whether I could see it or not, touch it or not.
Even when I'm gone, even if I never see it again, it's there. Robert Mac-
Farlane recognizes this permanence, in both the physical world and
the psyche, writing, "Mountains . . . are simply there, and there they
remain, their physical structures rearranged gradually over time by the
forces of geology and weather, but continuing to exist over and beyond
human perceptions of them."[12] Maybe Mallory was in fact honoring a
deep, ineffable truth: a mountain matters "Because it's there."[13]

From Maurice Herzog's *Annapurna* to Arlene Blum's *Annapurna: A
Woman's Place*, Jon Krakauer's *Into Thin Air: A Personal Account of the
Mount Everest Disaster* to Joe Simpson's *Touching the Void: The True
Story of One Man's Miraculous Survival*, books about climbing expedi-
tions—particularly ones where something goes wrong and team members struggle to survive—repeatedly top lists of travel and adventure
narratives. Walter Bonatti's *The Mountains of My Life*, David Roberts's
The Mountain of My Fear, Hermann Buhl's *Nanga Parbat Pilgrim-
age: The Lonely Challenge*—the best of these books try to explain and
reconcile whatever urge or yearning compelled the author to climb.
They're mystifying, heartbreaking, thrill-filled narratives. Crevasses!
Cruxes! Long months of planning routes, hard days of stocking camps,
split-second decisions that spell life or death. Glorious moments of

blue-white splendor; fearsome, long nights in a cramped, flimsy tent, listening for the rumble and roar of avalanches. Howling wind! Blowing snow! Triumph; defeat! Lonely mortals pitted against eternal elements. Author and mountaineer Jon Krakauer explains, "climbing was a magnificent activity, I firmly believed, not in spite of the inherent perils, but precisely because of them."[14]

In his eloquent and insightful *Mountains of the Mind* (subtitled *A History of Fascination* in some editions), British author and alpinist Robert MacFarlane supplements an overview of mountaineering history with discussions of cultural perceptions, aesthetics, and adrenaline. "Over the course of three centuries," he writes, echoing the thesis of Marjorie Hope Nicholson's classic *Mountain Gloom, Mountain Glory: The Development of the Aesthetics of the Infinite,* "a tremendous revolution of perception occurred in the West concerning mountains. The qualities for which mountains were once reviled—steepness, desolation, perilousness—came to be numbered among their most prized aspects."[15] In seventeenth- to eighteenth-century Europe, scientific advances, evolving socioeconomic structures, and accompanying changes in philosophical and theological beliefs led people to see mountains less as barren wastelands and more as divine gateways to God and spirituality. In the eighteenth and nineteenth centuries, wealthy European men became attracted to the challenge and exhilaration of climbing the Alps. Meanwhile, nineteenth-century American painters such as Thomas Cole and Albert Bierstadt and writers such as Henry David Thoreau and John Muir celebrated and popularized the "sublime"—that mix of beauty and awe so readily accessible in mountain scenery. "Only daring and insolent men, perchance, go there [to the tops of mountains]," Thoreau wrote longingly in *Maine Woods*, before describing his near psychological breakdown while climbing Ktaadn.[16] MacFarlane still describes "those who travel to mountain tops" as "half in love with themselves, and half in love with oblivion."[17]

Mountaineering took on a militaristic, colonial tone in the late nineteenth to mid-twentieth centuries—the golden age of global first ascents. Large expeditions strove to set records and "conquer" peaks (and other geographic prizes, such as the geographic poles) by launching "assaults" and "besieging" ranges: Aconcagua (1897), Kenya (1899), Kilimanjaro (1912), Nanda Devi (1936), Annapurna (1950), Everest and

Nanga Parbat (1953), K2 (1954), Kangchenjunga (almost) (1955), Vinson (1966). Contrast George Mallory's grandiose statement for 1920s reporters who asked why he wished to climb Everest—"If you cannot understand that there is something in man which responds to the challenge of this mountain and goes out to meet it, that the struggle is the struggle of life itself upward and forever upward, then you won't see why we go. What we get from this adventure is just sheer joy. And joy is, after all, the end of life"[18]—with Sir Edmund Hillary's report upon returning to camp after successfully summiting the world's highest peak—"Well, we knocked the bastard off."[19]

With most "first ascent" glory claimed by the mid-twentieth century, some climbers began to seek more challenging and dangerous routes—a tradition that continues to this day. Others lamented this style, instead seeking meaning and grace in the high country. As early as 1970, Arne Naess—mountaineer, philosopher, and founder of the deep ecology movement—questioned "The Conquest of Mountains: A Contradiction?" and interpreted the idea of "conquering" mountains as "infantile profanation," and the "achievement attitude" as "massively destructive."[20] Two decades later, Naess was proud to note that "Mountains are treated with love and respect by a sharply increasing number of climbers"—values that are more in line with other cultures' perceptions of sacredness and his own love for the "great Norwegian mountain" *Hallingskarvet* than most Western tendencies to characterize mountains as grand challenges or outdoor playgrounds.[21] Today, well-known climbers such as Conrad Anker seek both challenge and transcendence. As renowned mountaineer and Anker's former climbing partner, Alex Lowe, wrote of him, "Conrad's motivation for climbing is altruistic and endearingly simple—he reveres the mountains. . . . [Mountains are] where his heart beats, where his soul abides."[22]

Mountaineering is a long tradition, perhaps a human universal. According to scholar Edwin Bernbaum, "whether they realize it or not, many who hike and climb for sport and recreation are seeking an experience of spiritual awakening akin to that sought by people of traditional cultures."[23] Bernbaum's tour of *Sacred Mountains of the World* discusses the cultural and geographic context of specific peaks, region by region, and also synthesizes common themes. From first ascenders who notch a new route to devotional pilgrims who circumambulate peaks, ancient Chinese poets who retreated to wild rugged landscapes to tourists who just want a glimpse of beauty, people worldwide see mountains as "an inscrutable mystery that attracts and repels us with intense feelings of wonder and awe."[24] This mix of attraction and repulsion draws us back to mountain landscapes again and again, "seeking something [we] cannot put into words."[25]

Beyond the activities people perform in mountainous landscapes—climbing, bowing, making art, ogling—mountains themselves are "revered by cultures around the world."[26] From Kailash (divine to Hindu and Buddhist peoples, as the source of several sacred rivers and dwelling place of Shiva and his consort) to Olympus (home of the ancient Greek gods), Sinai (where Moses received the Ten Commandments from the Judeo-Christian God) to Ararat (where Noah's Ark is said to have landed), Uluru (Ayers Rock, sacred to Aboriginal Australians) to Bear Lodge (Devils Tower, sacred to Lakota people in North America), peaks and prominences are "regarded traditionally as places of revelation, centers of the universe, sources of life, pathways to heaven, abodes of the dead, temples of the gods, expressions of ultimate reality in myriad manifestations."[27] Bernbaum attributes this to their prominence: "as the highest and most dramatic features of the natural landscape, mountains have an extraordinary power to evoke the sacred."[28]

In several of these cases, specific peaks aren't seen as mere metaphors for or symbols of sacredness, but as holy in themselves. Bernbaun makes the distinction: "If we say that a mountain is like a temple, we merely point out an interesting resemblance between the two. But if we say that a mountain is a temple, we make a much stronger statement, one that alters our notions of mountains and temples."[29] His discussion of Denali illustrates differences between sacred and secular perceptions. Indigenous peoples of interior Alaska have reverence and respect for "the great height and bulk of the mountain," as reflected in their belief that "it was considered disrespectful to talk about the size or majesty of a mountain while looking at it." Koyukon people, in particular, insist that they "need to be humble before something so large as a mountain."[30] Meanwhile, "white people have treated the mountain with much less reverence," slapping the name McKinley on it, scaling it on a bit of a lark (the Sourdough Expedition), and "conquering" the peak thousands of times.[31]

Part of me wishes I didn't know that anyone has ever climbed Denali—stuck a tree on the North Summit and filled the South Summit with flags. I wish I didn't know that planes shuttle people and gear back and forth to base camp on the Kahiltna Glacier, or that so much effort and expense goes into search and rescue efforts each year. Having seen the mountain, it seems somewhat sacrilegious to think of touching it, much less climbing it. (I even feel a little guilty photographing it, but it doesn't seem to mind.) I wish it were like Machapuchare, never summited ("one of the few places on earth reserved for the gods"[32]), or Amnye Machen, circumambulated. Khumbila, whom Sherpa people "regard as too sacred to be desecrated by climbers."[33] Or Analogue, a "Symbolically Authentic Non-Euclidean" mountain dreamed up by surrealist writer Rene Daumal: *"its summit must be inaccessible, but its base accessible* to human beings . . . It must be *unique* and it must *exist geographically.* The gateway to the invisible must be visible."[34]

My own jaunts up Mt. Healy and Mt. Margaret? Just for the views. Prominences near Double Mountain and Fang? I climbed them for work. Guadalupe Peak, Mt. Sunflower, and other state high points? For fun. Wyoming's Grand Teton, Maine's Katahdin, Washington's Rainier and other notable mountains I've seen and not climbed? Beautiful. Foraker, right next door to Denali? Fine, climb on.

Denali is different. Not because it's highest, though that's an obvious part of it. Nor because it's so prominent, though that too is important. (Hence the popularity of Fuji, Kilimanjaro, and Monadnock.) It's just so magnificently, massively *mountain.* Being in the presence of it gave me a feeling of pure power, of pristine otherness, of what I can only call the divine.

CHAPTER 7

Fang

As much time as I spent gazing at and thinking about mountains, I was in Denali to look for fossils. More accurately, my position as a paleontology / Geographic Information Systems "GeoCorps" intern (through the National Park Service's Geoscientists in the Parks Program, coordinated by the Geological Society of America) involved both field reconnaissance and data management: organizing a decade's worth of somewhat haphazard paleontological information into a usable, searchable, geospatially standardized database. I shared these responsibilities with another intern—a smart, friendly, and unflappable recent college graduate who had both the knowledge and the tenacity to make a perfect field partner. We complemented one another well: while I was more familiar with the NPS procedures for fossil management, she brought a passion for paleoecology, a willingness to ford rivers, and a sensibility to tell when cliffs were too steep to climb.

We were the latest in a series of GeoCorps interns at Denali to document and interpret fossil resources. Like Black Canyon, the park wasn't established with paleontology in mind, and fossils were only recently discovered. As the story goes, in 2005, University of Alaska Fairbanks geologist Paul McCarthy was leading a field trip in the park and stopped in front of an outcrop of the lower Cantwell Formation—a seventy-million-year-old series of sandstone, mudstone, and conglomerate, similar in age and depositional environment to fossiliferous formations elsewhere in the state. While he was explaining "that this type of Cretaceous sedimentary rock commonly preserves dinosaur tracks and that [students] should be alert for them . . . almost as if it was staged, [a student, Susi] Tomsich immediately spied the dinosaur track not far from McCarthy's gesturing hand and asked, 'Like this one?' "[1]

Since then, nearly three hundred fossil localities—more tracks from multiple dinosaur species, a spectacular diversity of bird tracks, a similarly impressive diversity of plant remains, invertebrate traces, possible mammal tracks, a pterosaur hand print, and, most recently, a few bone fragments—have been discovered, filling out a picture of the Late Cretaceous paleoecosystem. Conglomerates, sandstones, siltstones, and shales indicate that rivers wound along floodplains and cut between forested hills, alluvial fans spilled out into valleys, and lakes and ponds filled the lowlands.[2] "Imagine a landscape where redwood-like metasequoias towered over the hills; slim alder-like trees, ginkgos and vines dwelled at the forest margins; and lush ferns, cycads and horsetails packed the swamps," writes a journalist for the National Parks Conservation Association. "Horned dinosaurs . . . grew to 20 feet long and munched the low-lying plants. Duck-billed hadrosaurs roamed in great herds . . . Pterosaurs with 13-foot-wide wingspans swept through the air, and fierce, predatory theropods stalked the herbivores."[3]

Much of the initial paleontological work was completed by Tony Fiorillo, curator of earth sciences at the Perot Museum of Nature and Science in Dallas, a pioneering expert on arctic dinosaurs who has made several significant findings elsewhere in Alaska, and the same researcher responsible for the first discoveries in Curecanti. Within months of the initial discovery, Fiorillo and colleagues documented the track—that of a medium-sized theropod—and located additional fossils, including another theropod track, beautifully preserved bird tracks, and plant impressions.[4] Two years later, Fiorillo and colleagues made one of the park's most spectacular discoveries—a huge slab containing thousands of hadrosaur tracks from both adults and juveniles, indicating that the "herbivores . . . roamed Denali in herds that included family groups."[5] In subsequent years, he helped coordinate a lidar scan of the "Dinosaur Dance Floor," documented the northernmost occurrence of a therizinosaur—a bizarre "four-toed, . . . feather-covered, sickle-clawed, pot-bellied," plant-eating theropod—and discovered and named the tracks of *Gruipeda vegrandiunus*—a small, web-footed shorebird—and *Magnoavipes denaliensis*—a large crane-like species.[6] Based on this work, he has concluded that "the lower Cantwell Formation in Denali has the richest record of fossil bird diversity from a single rock unit in the world."[7]

Meanwhile, paleoecologist David Sunderlin, along with students and park personnel, has used Denali's fossilized leaves, fern fronds, cones, stems, rhizomes, and pollen to better understand ancient ecological dynamics and determine what the paleoclimate would have been like. According to this research, the Cantwell flora are representative of "Polar Broad-leaved Deciduous Forest" and a climate similar to today's Pacific Northwest, with an average annual temperature of about 45°F (compared to Denali's current annual average of 28°F) and growing season precipitation of nine inches in the course of four months (compared to Denali's current average total of ten inches from June through September).[8] The temperatures were part of a global trend, as the earth was just beginning to cool off from the Cretaceous Thermal Maximum, the as yet not fully understood "warmest period in Earth's history in the last ~200 million years," lasting from about ninety to eighty-five million years ago.[9]

According to paleogeographic studies, Denali was at an even higher latitude in the Late Cretaceous than it is now (estimated 65–70°N, compared to today's 63°N).[10] In other words, although winters were relatively warm, they were still long and dark. Paleontologists are particularly eager to investigate how plants and animals adapted to these limitations: did dinosaurs migrate? Hibernate? How many species could such a northerly ecosystem support? And how can this inform understandings of modern arctic ecosystems?

More than a decade after the first discovery of a fossil dinosaur track in the Cantwell Formation, experts agree that Denali is "an exciting, rich, new area for dinosaur studies. . . . Further work will provide the opportunity for a more detailed regional paleoecological and paleoenvironmental understanding of an ancient high latitude terrestrial ecosystem on a greenhouse Earth."[11] This, park geologist Denny Capps reminds us, "helps explain the importance of parks": "When Denali was set aside back in 1917 to protect the current ecosystem, including the sheep that were being hunted down, we didn't recognize that we also had an intact Cretaceous ecosystem . . . Now, any new resources we find are also protected."[12]

"We still don't know what's out there," he points out. My job was to help figure it out.

Given time for orientation and training, the other intern and I didn't have our first field day until mid-June. We made plans to meet with the park's seasonal physical science technician (one of the previous year's GeoCorps interns) at the Toklat River so that she could help orient us to both the terrain and the fossils. As with many subsequent expeditions, it was pouring rain when we boarded a shuttle bus bound for Toklat. On this day, though, as the bus passed Savage, the raindrops became splattier on the windshield, then slushier—snow! Heavy white mush caught on spruce boughs and collected on the tundra, adding extra layers of intrigue to the landscape. (*Satisfying to know that mountains are out there, hidden*, I wrote later, *including THE mountain*.) The conditions weren't conducive to travel, though. We were delayed at one of the stops, waiting for visibility to improve, then again when we disembarked at Toklat, where the technician insisted that we wait. She advised us, "Always be conscientious when it comes to weather. And terrain. And bears. It's easy to get turned around in the fog and hypothermia is a real danger." Of greatest concern: the rivers. Powerful to begin with, they can rise rapidly with distant snowmelt or a rainstorm, going from fordably ankle-deep to impassably waist-deep within a matter of hours.

Midday, the snow turned back into rain and the sky almost began to glow, so we layered up and headed out into the Toklat's wide, braided bed. The river wove through a broad U-shaped valley, with tundra-swathed slopes swooping up into steep, rocky faces and low, dark clouds swallowing everything above a thousand feet or two. Size and distance were impossible to gauge, especially on the first field day. After a couple miles' worth of splashing through channels and clattering along gravel bars, we began to ascend a steepening, narrowing creek. I gave up trying to keep my boots dry and just did my best to keep up with the others and do my part calling out the refrain of "Hey, bear! Heyyyy, bear!" Surely, there were bears and sheep nearby, ptarmigan and wolves. This was their place far more than ours.

And *fossils*! The technician led us up a branch of the creek, then another even smaller drainage, up into the clouds. Rain turned back into snow. Boulders got bigger and slopes more unconsolidated—no longer neatly eroded and reposed. *Petrified wood fragments!*, the other intern was first to spot signs of ancient life. *Invertebrate burrows!*, I

Field day—mountains and rivers and mist and fossils.

then recognized. With that, weather conditions, scenery, and wildlife were forgotten in the excitement of discovery: every next rock might hold fossils. The technician used GPS to get us in the vicinity of the locality's true prize—a huge, three-toed hadrosaur track cast sitting innocently among other boulders. Not the prettiest or most important fossil, but a clear sign that some seventy million years ago, a duck-billed, plant-eating dinosaur measuring up to forty feet long, ten feet tall, and weighing up to five tons (the same size of one of Denali's shuttle buses) was stomping around this place.[13]

This is going to be a good summer, I thought to myself—a sentiment that was only confirmed on the hike back, when the precipitation began to break and clouds began to lift, leaving the world fresh and glistening. The sun even came out. Slopes began to steam and we peeled off mittens, hats, jackets. Even though we barely made it back to the road in time to catch a shuttle, then back to headquarters just in time for dinner, the whole return trip was buoyed by that particular flavor of euphoria that comes with fresh air, a magnificent landscape, a good, long hike, feeling safe and warm after being cold and wet, and, of course, finding fossils.

The day's excitement, clearing weather, and near-solstice nighttime skyglow left me so energized that instead of going to sleep or visiting

Sylvie at the sled dog kennels after dinner, I agreed to go for a hike with one of the park's backcountry rangers—a tall, blue-gray-eyed, red-bearded Thoreau enthusiast with whom I'd previously shared a few rounds of beer. Just a little way out and back along the Triple Lakes Trail, we thought. We both wore sandals. I carried nothing but a camera. A mile or so in, we found the trail was flooded at the Riley Creek crossing, but we weren't ready to turn back so soon. So we plunged right on into the cold, silty, knee-deep water. Another mile or two farther, we reached a section where the trail rises steeply up out of the drainage. A tiring climb, we admitted, but worth it for the views. And we still weren't ready to turn back. To the top, then. From the ridgetop, it made more sense to just finish the whole darn trail—another eight miles to the highway just outside the park, where we could catch a shuttle back to quarters.

Onward! Through the spruce trees, past the breeze-ruffled lakes; horizons filled with unnamed peaks. Completely unencumbered, feeling strong and happy. We didn't get back until well after midnight, sky still glowing and air cool and fresh. Like Annie Dillard, I couldn't help but think, "Is this where we live, . . . in this place at this moment, with the air so light and wild?"[14]

A week later, the backcountry ranger asked if I wanted to go for another hike—this time, up Sugarloaf, a peak that defines the eastern horizon across the Nenana River from the park entrance. *Of course!* I told him, and off we went to climb a mountain. At 11:30 p.m.

It was summer solstice—perpetual twilight, plus not a raincloud in sight. No need for headlamps, nor backpacks; I can't remember if we even brought water. (Though we did wear boots this time.) After scrambling straight up through close, dark woods, the path emerged onto a spine of sharp crags separated by tundra-soft saddles. Upward, upward, we had the whole mountain to ourselves—the rocks, the flowers, the pale pink clouds floating featherlight overhead. Upward, upward, outcrops getting rougher, golden sky duskier—or was it getting brighter again? Time suspended. "A million / Summers, night air still and the rocks / Warm. Sky over endless mountains . . . Even the heavy present seems to fail / This bubble of a heart."[15] A false peak or two before the very top, we made the mistake of pausing to check the time—it was two in the morning. On a mountainside. In Alaska. Torn between wisdom and wildness, practicality and euphoria, common sense won and we decided to turn around, floating down the trail through the dreamlike pastels of predawn.

Later that morning (on very little sleep), the other intern and I hiked up a drainage to see a pterosaur track. Not hard going, but slow, stopping to check out petrified wood, leaf impressions, and invertebrate traces in just about every other outcrop. I'd never seen such a density of fossils; it felt like we were walking through the Cretaceous jungle. Lost in the excitement of discovery, we scrambled up so many cliffs and turned over so many stones that we never even reached the pterosaur manus.

At the end of that week, a miserably mosquito-ridden, brush-blocked, bog-soaked, near-futile fossil goose chase was redeemed by a ridge full of exquisitely preserved angiosperm leaves. The rock layers were so thin and perfectly intact that we turned through them like pages of an ancient manuscript, new fossils to read with every face. More plant impressions the next week, just below a thick conglomerate layer eroded into spires and turrets. I scrambled to the top of one to look out over the broad valley below and crinkled mountains beyond, overjoyed to see just how much wilderness existed and still somewhat amazed at my great fortune to get to see it, to work in such a place.

We measured days in fossils found, miles walked, cliffs scoured, rivers crossed. (Or not crossed, in my case. Instead, embankments traversed, as I went far out of the way to avoid river crossings, which terrified me.) Wildlife encountered. (Sheep, mostly, hoofing around cliffs that might have been full of specimens but were too steep to survey.) Storms caught in. Rainbows seen. I lived in a dream world suspended somewhere between seventy million years ago and emphatically *now*, with the weather and wildlife, mountains and rivers so raw and alive.

The first week of July, the other intern and I got permission to make a multiday expedition to survey exposures of the Cantwell Formation on the flanks of Fang Mountain—true to its name, a grand incisor of a peak—which towers over the headwaters of the equally well-named Savage River. As a safety precaution for us and resource stewardship training opportunity for him, the ranger coordinated his backcountry patrol to accompany us. That made the planning go more smoothly— he knew the terrain, necessary gear (trekking poles, he emphasized,

A host of non-fossiliferous wonders found on a typical field day.

though neither of us had used them before), and necessary protocols (like all visitors, we needed to get a permit and file an itinerary). Having him along didn't, however, make the actual travel any easier, especially since his long-strided pace was much faster than our typical fossil-poking meander.

We began at Mountain Vista on a crisp but sunny morning, divvying up and securing our gear, strapping on boots and gaiters, then setting off southward, only to have to take our boots and gaiters back off again so that we could cross the Savage River. Next, a miserable two- or three-mile stretch through thick brush. While the others skipped ahead, their calls of "Hey, bear!" growing faint with distance, I struggled under the weight of the pack and the unfamiliar appendages of the trekking poles, which kept getting tangled in the shrubbery. At one point, I was so frustrated with them—and with myself for being so slow and uncoordinated—that I tried to fling them away, only to have them bounce off the brush and trip me. Not my proudest backpacking moment.

Finally, we found a game trail that made travel easier, but it still required bog squishing and river cobbling uphill, mile after mile, trees shrinking and shrubs thinning. By midday, the sun was high and almost hot. For the first time that summer, I worried about sunburn and dehydration—I was lugging extra layers and rain gear, not t-shirts or sunblock, and didn't want to keep asking to stop for water breaks. As the hours blurred together, the riverbed got thinner and thinner, then forked. Fifty-fifty chance—we chose to head right. The branch became a trickle, the trickle a dry bed; the valley narrowed to V-shaped slopes of moss and rock. Easier walking but baking sun, blinding rock, heavy pack, doubt that we were heading in the right direction. Late afternoon, just when it seemed as though we'd hit a dead end—what looked like a solid stone wall ahead—the drainage made a sharp left, veering into a deep, hidden valley whose walls gleamed with argillite as if lined with pewter. The near-mythical start of the Savage.

We found a little tundra-carpeted plateau upon which to pitch the tent, fighting to erect it in winds that were funneled down the narrow channel. By the time we'd identified a spot to store the bear canisters, cooked dinner, and tried to eat while debating (well, arguing) the merits versus flaws of Thoreau, sunlight was disappearing from the riverbed, leaving cold shadows in its wake. Deep in that remote, rocky valley, it soon felt more like mid-September than midsummer—brisk wind, dusky light; numb fingers, dripping nose. Although it would have been warmer in the tent, I didn't want to retreat just yet, especially if that meant continuing to argue with the ranger about Thoreau. (How absurd, to fight about nineteenth-century transcendentalist posturings when out in a living, breathing wild place—"rocks, [tundra,] wind on our cheeks! the solid earth! the actual world! the common sense!"[16])

Up I clambered, seeking the weak warmth of what sunshine was left higher on the valley's steep slopes. The platelike argillite shimmered, slid, and clattered underfoot. (Think climbing up a slate roof, except that the tiles aren't affixed to anything.) I should have been worried about the unstable footing, but, unencumbered by my heavy pack and free of those awkward trekking poles, I felt secure—like a Dall sheep, in my element. I didn't go particularly high or far—just enough to feel a solitude I'd been craving all day. I stayed up on the slopes, pondering my preference to be alone, until the sun disappeared and wind stilled, then was ready to slide back down to our tiny, temporary trio of humanity.

The next morning, we woke to a renewed, even icier wind. As much for warmth as out of eagerness, we hurried to scarf down breakfast and get moving. According to the maps, we would need to climb out of our valley and crest a high ridge (and geologic fault) to get over to the Cantwell Formation. After the previous day's exertion, my legs felt like lead. I struggled to get up those loose plates of argillite, sliding backward with every step, again frustrated with my inability to keep up with the others. They called out in excitement as they reached the top of the ridge, as did I when I joined them. The scene on the other side was of an entirely different world—a verdant valley opening eastward into views of hundreds of pointy gray-white peaks and a half dozen caribou, grazing nonchalantly, as if people popped up in their hidden pasture every day.

Fang loomed over us, looking even darker, craggier, and more forbidding up close than it did from afar. While Denali's height and mass are awe inspiring, Fang is terrifying, all jagged pinnacles and precipices, patches of snow accenting deep crevices and debris sliding away from its lower slopes. Eroding spires reveal the carnage left behind as brittle bedrock battles with water and gravity. Although it's not that high—only 6,736 feet—Fang wasn't summitted until the 1960s and perhaps only twice since: "No safe way to do this thing," reported a climber from 1994, citing the unstable, near-vertical cliffs.[17] The mountain looks like it could, at any moment, either pierce the sky or crumble to pieces.

Of course, we weren't there to conquer Fang (though I have to admit that some unexpected, hungry part of me did want to try). We were there to look for fossils. The other intern and I set about poking through piles of mudstones and conglomerates, finding some petrified tree trunks but nothing significant, much less in situ. (The same forces that carve away at Fang's impressive flanks also deposit debris on top of outcrops.) By lunchtime, we'd stopped sorting through unconsolidated float and begun to traverse the mountain's sliding slopes, looking for any intact shelves or ledges. Nothing. Pretty flowers, patches of snow. Fang always scowling—or was it grinning?—toothily down on us. I felt increasingly discouraged and drained. Had the other intern not given me a chocolate bar, I don't know how I would have made it through the afternoon. Up, down, and around we went. Nothing. Cold wind. Sun and shadow. So much rock; plain old rock. We'd had such hope—the geologic and topographic maps held such promise—and had invested so much time and energy. There *had* to be something here.

But nothing was there. As much as we wanted to make a major discovery—or *any* discovery—we couldn't will fossils into existence. Nor could we walk endlessly (unlike the backcountry ranger, who'd gotten bored with our slow study and gone up and down ledges and ravines for the sheer joy of movement). Sometime toward late afternoon, when we came face to face with a group of sheep blocking the only lip of rock accessing Fang's western shoulder, we took it as a sign that we should admit defeat and begin making our way back to camp.

It was much easier—almost fun—to slide back down into the Savage River drainage than it had been to climb up out of it, but the merriment was tempered by pervasive disappointment. Dinner was more somber than it had been the day before, so much so that I almost missed the Thoreau debate. Again, it got cold quickly. The ranger retreated to the tent to read, the other intern stretched, and I sat out sketching wildflowers until my fingers went numb.

Likewise, the return hike the next day was easier but less exciting. We packed up and trudged off through now familiar terrain, no worries about which drainage to choose and a longer stretch staying on the game trail. (No more trekking pole battles.) As we waited to catch a shuttle bus from Mountain Vista to headquarters, I should have been excited for the promise of hot showers, real meals, and a warm room to sleep in. Instead, I felt deflated by the unproductive expedition and rattled by the first rifts in what didn't even yet count as a relationship with the ranger. (How could he revere someone as preachy and pedantic as Thoreau?) I looked back across the landscape we'd trekked. It seemed smaller, less wild. *So much for Fang*, I thought. It may be just a pile of rock, but the mountain seemed to have somehow baited or betrayed me.

Fang Mountain.

What we couldn't have known during that disappointment of a trip (and the series of equally discouraging field days that followed) was that it would prove integral to an opportunity that arose at the end of the month. Tony Fiorillo (*the* Dr. Fiorillo, who has done so much important work in both Denali and Curecanti, and who literally wrote the book on *Alaska Dinosaurs*), Paul McCarthy (the professor who'd helped find the first fossil in Denali and who has continued to do key research), Yoshi Kobayashi (a paleontologist from Hokkaido University), and one of Dr. Kobayashi's graduate students were planning to spend a week searching the far side of Fang. They graciously invited the GeoCorps interns—us!—to join them.

As if research with leading experts in the shadow of Fang Mountain weren't enough, we would get to travel by helicopter. The location was so remote and the team had so much equipment that it would have been impossible to carry it all in and out otherwise. They'd arranged for the permits and made the plans—all the other intern and I had to do was pack our gear. The only complication was that we were scheduled to lead a special tour group to see some of the park's readily accessible fossils midweek. Seeking a way to do both, we discussed the possibility of flying in, spending a couple of days with the research team, then hiking back on our own. Gauging from the maps, the return hike would be challenging but not impossible: a trek of about fourteen miles over two high, sharp arêtes, around unknown cirques, and across unseen slopes back to the north face of Fang; semi-familiar territory from there on out, over the argillite crest into the Savage River drainage, followed by the long slog to the road. Google Earth warned that the higher elevations consisted of rock slides and perpetual snow fields, but nothing looked *that* steep, and we knew half of the route. (And I really wanted to go.)

Thus we found ourselves packing, suiting up, and taking turns boarding a helicopter on a cool morning in late July, with sunlight filtering through a broken sky and forecasts calling for rain. Each trip with a couple of people and gear only took a few minutes in the air—soaring through tundra-green valleys, floating over ridges dotted with white sheep, and touching down in the bottom of a steep-walled cirque—to cover terrain that would have taken days if not weeks on foot. Once we arrived in the cirque, we each hurried to set up tents, then met to hike up onto the western wall, eager to begin scouting. Within ten minutes, we found a mudstone slab full of perfect plant impressions—*Equisetum* stems, fern fronds, leaves with every delicate vein and edge visible. Then another, and another. Fossils everywhere! Scrambling to try to document everything—to take photographs, make measurements, record GPS locations, identify species—the other intern and I eventually gave up with specifics and decided to mark the whole ridge (an ancient alluvial fan, it turned out, with a forest's worth of flooded-down material[18]) as a locality.

For the first hour, I was happily focused with fossil tunnel vision. When I finally looked up from the ground, I was dizzied to find myself amidst mountains upon mountains—endless peaks of the Alaska Range, graying with distance like an ocean full of churning waves frozen under a lowering, darkening sky. How many of them were still unnamed? Was it possible to hike to the distant ridges, the unseen valleys? Who had last been out there, in any of that vastness; when, and why? My mind couldn't quite process it, leaping from seventy million years ago to a viewshed of seventy miles, from unmoving rock to gusty wind. Wilderness. The most wild place I'd ever seen, ever stood in.

(Having merely hopped a helicopter ride to get there, had I earned it? I buried the question as it briefly crossed my mind.)

Research—I was there to help with research, not to marvel at the scenery. (How did people like Adolph Murie manage to mix science and aesthetics? How did John Muir manage to study glacial geomorphology while climbing in the Sierra and waxing on about the sublime? How could Bob Marshall go from diligent descriptions of tree line experiments in one paragraph to rousing anecdotes of adventure in the next?) From the first ridge, we continued west, looking for promising outcrops and ledges. Smooth mudstones, coarse sandstones and conglomerates, thin shales crumbling and sliding away underfoot. Although we didn't find much aside from the first abundance of fossil flora, we did succeed in the main objective—scouting spots to revisit on subsequent days.

If we hadn't identified areas with the best potential and appreciated that spectacular view in the first few hours, we might never have had the chance. Later that afternoon, clouds closed in and it began to drizzle. Once the mountains were lost to the mist, I'd never see them again. We returned to our camping area, put on warm and waterproof layers, then nestled out in the tundra to eat dinner just as it began to rain in earnest. The wind picked up. The clouds got darker, and it poured harder. Yet we all sat and ate and chatted as if we were on a sunny picnic in a city park. If the trade-off for being on that expedition was a bit of sogginess and shivering, I'd take it.

All night, raindrops pattered on the tent. Wind pulled at the stays and made the fabric flap. Clouds thickened to darkness—an odd sensation after so many weeks of light. Come morning, the weather continued to be cold, gray, and wet. Nonetheless, as soon as we finished breakfast (mmm, hot cocoa in the rain), we hiked back up the ridge and split into teams—the other intern with Dr. McCarthy to survey geological cross sections (measuring and identifying different strata, piecing together the paleoecological context), the rest of us to look for fossils. Because clouds had swallowed the mountains, we weren't distracted by the scenery and could focus all of our attention on the work at hand. We crawled up and down cliffs, turning over rocks and looking under ledges, sometimes spreading out to scout and sometimes gathering to discuss discoveries. I lurked close to Dr. Fiorillo, trying to learn how he reads the rocks and homes in on layers with the right depositional

Immersed in the vastness of space and time, south of Fang.

environment. In just one morning, he taught me more about ichnofossils than I'd learned the entire previous summer.

Dr. Kobayashi and his student made the biggest discovery—bird tracks—after lunch. I tried to help document them, but by that point, the sideways-blowing rain had numbed my fingers, so I wasn't of much use. As conditions continued to worsen, we all called it an early day and ducked back down to camp. Dinner was another soggily cheerful affair, only slightly tempered by the awareness that the other intern and I were scheduled to leave the next morning. Soon we'd have to pack up the cozy tent and the rest of our gear, leave the friendly and encouraging group, and hike up a rock-strewn arête into the neighboring cirque. Surely, the weather would break soon?

Rain, wind, and mist, still, at seven the next morning. If anything, the clouds were even lower, heavier, and darker than the previous afternoon. Over breakfast (my fingers almost too numb to prepare my cocoa), we debated waiting to see if the mist would at least lift a little. It seemed foolhardy to hike into terrain that was not only unknown but also invisible. In the rain. Conditions were unlikely to improve, we finally conceded. All we could do was hope that it wouldn't get worse—drizzle turn into a downpour; downpour turn into a snowstorm; all of that moisture loosen a mudslide.

Off we went, wishing the researchers good luck, and them wishing us the same in return. The mist was so thick that we soon lost sight of their bright tents—it was just the other intern and me, negotiating a world of steep rock and cloud. Laden with full packs, we staggered slowly up loose, rain-slicked boulders: step, step, pause; step, step, breathe. Some of those pauses weren't just for breath, but also to take note of plant fossils in the float. *We'll have to expand the first day's first locality into the whole valleyside,* my paleontology brain briefly overrode my burning legs and lungs. Step, step, breathe.

As we trod upward, it got not just steeper but colder. Soon we had to decide between navigating loose scree versus patches of snow. I opted to stay on solid rocks, though they were of questionable repose. *Not too late to turn back,* my rational brain chimed in. After at least an hour of hard work and constant doubt, a horizontal line solidified out of the mist above us—the top of the arête! Energized by this bit of hope, we made the last push—the end of the longest ascent of the day, we thought—and triumphantly peered over the edge.

Oh. A wall of rock to the right—the direction we needed to go. Everywhere else, a snowfield disappearing into nothingness. White snow merging into white cloud.

We deliberated. How high was the cliff? (No perspective.) How deep was the snow? How far did it go, and how steeply did it tilt? (No way to tell.) Should we cut across the top of the snow patch, clinging to the base of the cliff? Should we make a diagonal traverse downward? Could we climb the arête and hope for a way down from it farther on? The map indicated only one more steep saddle (what we'd thought would be the crux), then relatively gentler terrain. But a contour interval of twenty feet wasn't terribly helpful out in this topography. And the clouds were opaque, the snow crusty; how comfortable were we with self-arrest on a steep slope with heavy packs? Should we wait? Turn around? It had taken us so long to make that first mile.

While we were weighing options, the mist swirled and thinned just enough to afford a brief glimpse of a ridge across the snow-swept bowl—confirmation or promise that there really was a world out there. Or, at least, enough of one to lure us on.

Onward! We crunched and slid down the snow to a slightly less steep section with some exposed rock, then made an uneasy traverse, kicking out steps one at a time and trying not to wonder how far it was to the bottom. Also trying to ignore the wind, the cold, and the packs' tendency to tilt. The clouds closed back in. Between the featureless-ness of the snowscape and our intense focus on each step, time itself seemed suspended. Kick, kick, step—was the whole hike going to be an exercise in endurance? How could we ever have thought we knew what we were doing in such a big, hazardous place? Recalling the hours we'd spent ogling maps from the safety of the office, I couldn't help but feel guilty. Had I pressured the other intern into this hike? Was I over-estimating our abilities? Was I prepared for the consequences if either of us slipped? So accustomed to hiking alone—to being accountable only to myself (and to my supervisor, and to my mother) for my not infrequently poor decisions—I felt both extra responsibility and relief. If anything happened, at least there were two of us. We were a team. We were making decisions together. Then again, were we making *worse* decisions, feeling safer together and thus acting more reckless? Kick, kick, step, my mind looped. Were we moving forward? Time flowing? Gravity was the only force with any constant directionality. Even the wind shifted and spun.

Then we were at the base of a cliff. Out of the nothingness, rock—presumably the top of the cirque. For a moment, we were suspended in time and space, surprised to find sandstone blocks containing enor-mous petrified trees. *Locality!* My paleontology brain celebrated. *Do NOT try to revisit*, we included in the site notes as we dutifully docu-mented the find, in continued sideways-falling rain.

Onward, traversing the upper lip of the cirque, below the arête. More snow, more scree, including an old rockslide consisting of unsta-ble boulders that shifted and groaned nerve-wrackingly under our feet. The grade flattened out slightly, enabling us to feel safe enough to begin checking the GPS regularly. ("Hiking IHR"—Instrument Hiking Rules—we decided to call it.) Only then did it feel like we were making progress and not lost in an internal loop—the movement of the little arrow on the screen proved we were moving in the real world. All of the questions in my head began to settle back down, enabling me to concentrate on where we were and what we were doing. Line by line on the GPS, foot by foot in the real world, we slowly and carefully inched along the shoulder of Fang, together.

When we finally reached the ridge that we'd barely caught sight of from across the snow patch—what the map and GPS told us was the saddle—we found it a surprisingly easy climb. Or easy compared to what we'd just crossed. It was solid rock, at least. We scrambled up. Then, for the second time that day, we peered over the top of a ridge, far less triumphantly and more anxiously this time. We had no idea what we'd see on the other side.

Simultaneously, we burst out laughing. Tundra and sunshine! Soft mosses, shallow slopes, and actual patches of blue sky! It was like peeking into an entirely different world—benign, Edenic, entirely unexpected after days of nothing but crag and cloud. Granted, the tundra was at the bottom of the slope, the blue sky was far in the distance, and we still had a long way to go, but it looked so welcoming. After some snow patches, the valley widened and flattened out, curving north toward familiar terrain.

Giving one last glance at the wall of mist hovering behind us—if not magic, the topography must have held it in—we slid down the snow and practically danced along the drainage, giddy with delight. Our packs felt lighter, the air fresher. We ate a luxurious lunch in an alpine valley filled with bobbing wildflowers and whistling marmots—the same soft stretch where we'd seen the caribou on our first trip to Fang. All that was left was to clamber over into the headwaters of the Savage River—over that ridge that had felt so defeating weeks earlier—and trudge back to the road—the same route that had felt so exhausting, now familiar, almost welcoming. Along the way, we occasionally looked back and marveled—we'd been there! We'd crossed that! Even Fang no longer looked malicious. One of the pinnacles resembled a giant Buddha, blessing us with calm, rugged beauty. We'd earned—or perhaps just learned—it.

Maybe *that's* what mountain climbing is about: exploring unfamiliar terrain, learning new things, testing unknown limits, having a meaningful experience, then—the trait unique to upward topography—seeing the tangible reminder of that experience standing tall on the horizon. Unlike the plains, where moments sweep in and out with the skies, and unlike canyons, where the focus is inward and down, mountains expand up and out, prominent and permanent. Mountains are landmarks upon which we hang our memories and dreams.

Fang Mountain again (as seen from Primrose Ridge).

CHAPTER 8

Self

Disasters in the backcountry are usually not a matter of a single catastrophic error or stroke of misfortune but the accumulation of several seemingly minor mistakes or concerns. The Fang expedition could have gone wrong in any number of ways. The terrain was treacherous, the visibility poor. Instead of carrying a compass, we relied on the GPS. Most of our layers were soaked. We'd carried a tent and a little extra food in case we were forced to camp for another night, but that made our packs too heavy. If one of us had sustained an injury, we had a radio and were better off just by virtue of there being two of us, but also we were entirely overconfident because we were aware of that same virtue—there were two of us.

I'd never have attempted that hike on my own. In fact, all of our fieldwork would have been too dangerous alone—the slopes were steep, the rivers strong, the bears big, and the moose ornery. It was much safer to have another person nearby to help or go for help, if need be.

It was also a matter of scientific quality. The other intern and I did better work as a team, with two sets of eyes scouring the outcrops and two sets of feet to traverse different routes; two perspectives on where to go and what to look for. Two of us to identify specimens and discuss their geologic context. Two of us to plan areas to visit, two of us to remember to bring all of the equipment and catch the bus on time, two of us to write our trip summaries.

Moreover, it was a lot more fun to work together. Miles were easier, shuttle waits shorter, and office days more entertaining when there was someone else to talk to. Circumstances that I normally would have found upsetting—getting lost, fighting brush, day after day of rain—seemed [slightly] more tolerable, thanks to the other intern's exemplary patience and good humor. (Mosquitoes weren't any less annoying, but

Cliffs along the East Fork Toklat—too steep to safely climb solo. (Or as a team, for that matter.)

at least we could commiserate.) Better yet, good moments seemed dou-
bly better—together, we exclaimed at the spectacular view from above
Tattler Creek, marveled at the sheep at Polychrome Pass, and laughed
at ourselves as we tried to climb up and slid hopelessly back down the
loose slopes of Double Mountain. She's the only other person with
whom I shared the fear and triumph of the return from Fang.

That said, as enriching as it was to share the adventures, I didn't
pay as much attention to my surroundings when working as part of a
team. Because I knew that she was there, I relaxed slightly, or at least
didn't think as much about where I was putting my feet or whether
a slope would hold. At times, the scenery became mere backdrop for
our conversations, the wildlife spottings pleasant surprises to enliven
our fossil quests. We'd get back from the field and I'd remember the
new localities we'd documented and the topics we'd discussed, but I
wouldn't be able to describe what the landscape had looked like or how

the weather had felt. When it came time to compile trip reports, we filled in details that the other had missed or forgotten—scientifically, making for more complete and more accurate records; personally, indicating that we'd each missed elements, as if we'd divvied up the experience as well as the work.

I'm accustomed to exploring wild places on my own. Skiing alone across great snow-draped bluffs at Fossil Butte. Clambering solo along cliffs at Black Canyon. Before that: deserts, prairies, forests, mostly alone. The months I'd spent climbing, hiking, and traveling with the biology technician in Wyoming and beyond had thrown me for a loop; I hadn't realized that places and experiences could be so much more meaningful when shared with someone. A year later, I both couldn't imagine going back to flying solo—the danger, the work, the loneliness of it—and desperately wanted to be by myself, on my own schedule, immersed in my own senses and thoughts. (A quote from *The Monkey Wrench Gang* haunts me: "And loneliness? *Loneliness*? Is that all [s]he has to fear?"[1])

In their "Solitude: An Exploration of Benefits of Being Alone," Christopher Long and James Averill discuss the importance of solitude in terms of everything from religion to cognition, focusing especially on self-awareness: "the human capacity to reflect upon and interpret one's own experiences."[2] They celebrate freedom, creativity, and spirituality but are careful to distinguish between voluntary solitude, forced isolation, and general loneliness: the first opens to all sorts of positive psychological benefits; the latter two to depression, anxiety, and other illnesses. Also, it matters where an individual ranks on the "Preference for Solitude Scale," first proposed by Jerry Burger.[3] To some people, time alone proves pleasant, serene, and productive; "researchers have found that time alone can allow for valuable self-reflection, creative insights, and a restoration period."[4] To others, it's miserable.

Several studies note that natural settings are considered the "ideal place for seeking solitude."[5] An entire chapter in the massive *Handbook of Solitude* is devoted to the "Restorative Qualities of Being Alone with Nature." In it, authors Kalevi Korpela and Henk Staats summarize that "being away from the civilized world" enables individuals "to relax, refresh, meditate, reflect, and experience a sense of peacefulness within themselves."[6] Picture a Buddhist temple, high on a remote mountainside; a yoga retreat on a distant island; a cabin deep in snowy woods, firewood stacked neatly by the door—all places of refuge, solace, and self-reflection, freed from the formalities and hassles of the curiously labeled "civilized world."

It would appear as though nature is only enjoyable when it's tame and pretty, though. People don't tend to feel relaxed or at peace when they face "difficult and dangerous passages of the terrain, [the possibility of] encountering wild animals, or lack of orientation."[7] Temples and retreats aren't so calming if located in a place prone to avalanches or raging typhoons; cabins not so cozy without a woodstove, running water, or a cell signal in case something goes wrong. Sometimes, Korpela and Staats conclude (in a handbook dedicated to solitude), it's better to be around other people as "a safeguard against getting hurt or lost."[8]

But what if part of the point of being alone in nature is to feel not just relaxation, but exhilaration? Not calm meditation, but heart-beating, legs-shaking, fear-focused attentiveness? To push oneself, to test oneself, to feel alive again, in a big, wild place?

On weekends, I often headed out alone. In Denali, this meant getting a bus ticket, hopping off somewhere, wandering wherever I wanted to go until I was tired or satiated, then flagging down a return shuttle. Almost always, bus riders were curious to know where I was going or where I'd been; what on earth I thought I was doing, hiking solo. *Isn't it dangerous to hike alone?* people frequently asked. Kindly, earnestly; they were concerned for my well-being. *What if you fall? What about the bears?* Twice, variations on *Does your mother know?* (*Sort of,* my reply.)

Although I returned to Primrose Ridge several times and poked around plenty of other peaks and valleys, I only went on one solo backpacking trip at Denali. As I characterized it later, "One trip: two days, sixteen miles, one braided river, one icy glacier, and many, many hours of steady, grey rain . . . A cold, wet, and thoroughly miserable time." And, simultaneously, "more vivid, more real . . . more memorable" than nearly any other experience.[9]

The backcountry ranger helped me choose a destination that fit my criteria: scenic, relatively infrequently visited, no major river crossings—Polychrome Glaciers. He also supplied me with a lightweight tent, waterproof pack cover, bear canister, bear spray, and much unsolicited advice. (I politely declined to bring trekking poles.) While packing the night before, I kept telling him that I was accustomed to hiking alone and was by that point reasonably well acquainted with backcountry travel in Denali. Moreover, unlike field work, I wasn't planning to scale any cliffs or crawl into ravines. If the weather deteriorated, I'd turn back. My only intents were to touch the toe of a glacier and feel spectacularly strong and attuned to the world.

When I stepped off the camper bus near the East Fork of the Toklat River, with a wave and a "good luck!" from the driver, my senses immediately heightened. Sounds were sharper, colors brighter. I was acutely aware of being alone in *Denali*, where the mountains were bigger, the distances greater, the wildlife wilder than any place I'd ever known. Once the busses stopped running for the night, I'd be a dozen miles if not farther away from any other soul; if anything happened to me, how long would it be before anyone could find me? Even with my hiking plans on file, the landscape in real life was so much bigger than the tiny "Unit 8" on the backcountry map.

So much bigger in real life! I strapped on my too-heavy, as always, pack and set off. After carefully picking my way down a scree- and brush-filled incline, the first real challenge entailed crossing a stream gushing with snowmelt. It wasn't particularly wide or deep, but I always fear the rivers—the cold pull of the water, the unstable boulders underfoot. It was both a relief and a minor triumph to make it across with no incident. From there, the trekking was straightforward, following gravel bars and skirting brush, slightly uphill, aiming for the central of several parallel valleys, each of which contains a tongue of ice oozing down from the northern slopes of the Alaska Range. Several hours of relatively relaxed walking out, I paused to rest, looking back toward the park road across a wide expanse—what I later learned is called the Plains of Murie in Adolph's honor. A tiny green bus rolled by, only noticeable because it was moving and the rest of the scenery was still. As with prairie landscapes, I'd lost all sense of scale—was the bus miniscule, or the mountain behind it enormous? Was the valley a mile wide, or ten? If visitors were taking photographs at Polychrome Overlook, would my bright red pack show up and mar the naturalness of the scene? Would it be visible enough if rescuers had to search for me? I felt both conspicuous and insignificant, out among the rocks and moss and rivers.

While I sat sprawled out on the tundra, pondering, a gust of cold wind hit my back. I turned away from the Plains of Murie—which weren't exactly sunlit but were sort of glowing, with diffuse light leaking through thin layers of altostratus—and looked up toward the glacier-filled valleys. Clouds were coalescing, quickly. It soon began to sprinkle. Time to don rain gear and resume hiking.

I'd intended to pitch the tent and stash the bear canister, sleeping pad, and sleeping bag as soon as I was out of sight of the road, then continue to the glacier and back with a lighter pack. When I rounded a corner into the narrow central valley—an unexpectedly lush meadow of ankle-high wildflowers, surrounded by mountains and ice, slopes disappearing in mist—I changed my mind. The cliffs focused a fierce wind. Clouds thickened and churned. A brief last glimpse of sunshine before it began to rain in earnest. What if the tent blew away while I was gone? What if I twisted an ankle or was attacked by an animal—how stupid would it be to get caught out here without food or shelter? *Alone*—I had to remember that I was *alone*, responsible for my own safety, my own decisions, lugging everything I needed on my own back, slow and steady.

Perhaps instead of continuing on, carrying everything, I should stay there and hope the clouds would blow past as quickly as they'd moved in. The most prudent thing to do would be to acknowledge the deteriorating weather and turn around, before the rivers started to rise. (For that matter, I'd have been safest not bothering to come in the first place.) While I was considering the options, a small group of caribou materialized from the clouds and trotted purposefully toward the Plains of Murie, as if to indicate that I was a fool to go any farther. A marmot popped out of the rocks to whistle a warning, in agreement. "No," I shook my head and actually spoke out loud, addressing caribou, marmot, and mountains, "I'm still going." Onward, I'd decided. Of course, my motto—onward—leaning into the wind.

Farther, higher—up a long, continuous incline, through the last of the shrubs, then the mosses, eventually to a landscape of nothing but rock, lichen, and a churning, silt-gray stream. Dragon water, "the awesome force of change."[10] A half mile later, I found myself scrambling up, down, and around hummocks of glacial debris, picking a route as if skirting lunar craters. Rocks shifted; the stream frothed; increasingly large patches of dirty old snow and ice broke and slid underfoot. One misstep and I'd be crushed or swept away, I was sure. *Alone.*

At first, the glacier looked like just another crusty snow patch, coated with rocks and silt, disappearing into mist. But as I neared, I realized that the stream was gushing out from underneath a shelf of ice, striped with layers of accretion and glowing with hints of a haunting blue, as if bits of sky had gotten trapped and compressed along with the snow. Side channels burst out of ice caves and trickled out from under ice bridges. The air reverberated with the sound of icemelt. That was it for me—I wasn't going to risk crawling up the ice and inching along the glacier when I had no idea how thin or unstable the top could be. *Alone.*

I did, though, lean out over the churning stream long enough and far enough to brush off some rocky debris and touch the glacier. Mitten off, hand on ice. Hard, rough, cold. Shadowy, translucent. A different form of dragon, "lazing in the form of . . . glaciers that scour . . . high peaks away."[11] Ancient, endangered.

That done—goal achieved, though I hadn't realized until then that that was what I was seeking—I was eager to get away from the cold, the stream, and the unstable ice. As quickly and cautiously as possible, I turned around and threaded back through the moraine, still laboring under the weight of the pack. I made it out of the narrow valley—that world of ice, rock, and water recolonizing with lichen, then mosses, then flowers—and perhaps a mile out onto the windswept and rain-drenched Plains of Murie before calling it a day. Although the hike itself wasn't that far or steep, pervasive fear, persistent attentiveness, and continued rain combined to leave me feeling exhausted and soaked, wanting nothing but to crawl into the tent and feel warm and secure. First, though, I had to select a campsite. Weighing the reality of the weather against the possibility of grizzlies, the wind and rain won and I chose a hollow behind a slight hill, trying to ignore signs of fresh digging in a patch of bearflower. Then, pitch the tent, hoping I was hammering the stakes in well enough for them to hold against both the wind and rain. Locate a place to eat dinner. Not bothering to cook or even boil water for tea, just swallowing cheese and rain-soggy bread. Locate a place to stash the bear can. Identify landmarks to use to relocate the bear can among the featureless shrubs and mosses. Readjust the tent stakes. Then, finally, retreat to the flimsy nylon shelter for a night of fitful sleep—dreams of bears, punctuated by the occasional need to re-stake flapping corners.

Early the next morning, I woke to a clearing sky and peaks shining with fresh snow. Shivering in the cold air and feeling slightly silly for having been so afraid of ice and bears the night before, I performed the camp rituals in reverse—bear can, raw oatmeal, break down the tent, and shoulder my pack. The tundra trudge, gravel bars, and that technically unchallenging but psychologically unnerving stream cross-ing all proceeded quickly, without incident. I was back at the road by midmorning, barely twenty-four hours after I'd started hiking.

Compared to the rest of the summer—three full months in Denali—twenty-four hours was nothing. Yet those hours burn especially sharp and bright in my memory. Mine alone. As I summarized later:

Long after I have warmed up and my backpack has dried out, I can still feel my fear as I picked my way along the lateral moraine, acutely aware that any slip would send me sliding into a rocky stream. I can still feel my frustration as I huddled into a muddy cutbank, trying to get out of the wind long enough to eat a soggy granola bar. I can still feel my exhaustion as I trudged across interminable stretches of squishy tundra, not even bothering to detour around brush or bearflower. I may not have enjoyed those days, but I really *lived* them.[12]

Of course, I didn't have to trek far off into the backcountry to find solitude, much less adventure. Most weekends, I was content to walk along the park road—to see the scenery at a pedestrian pace, to have a better chance of encountering wildlife, to set my feet free and loosen my mind.

Two weeks after my first walk from Savage back to headquarters—an introduction to the drunken trees tilting out of the tundra, the moose standing in bogs, the low clouds pierced by occasional sunshine, and the snow-dusted Healy Ridge backing the northern horizon—I decided to try another section of road, from Savage more deeply into the park, to the Teklanika Campground at Mile 29. Actually, I meant to stop and catch a bus back from the Sanctuary River Campground at Mile 23, but I was feeling so strong after the first part—up a long stretch with

One of the Polychrome Glaciers—manifestations of "dragon that wanders in the form of continents drifting through their massive slow-motion collisions; dragon thrust up into towering peaks, lazing in the form of mile-deep glaciers . . . dragon breathing through the ceaseless modulations of weather that are slowly wearing this mountain away with mist and rain" (Hinton 2012, 79).

sweeping views of Double Mountain to the southwest and Fang Mountain's sharp pinnacle to the southeast, around a steep, wooded curve, and across the Sanctuary River bridge—that I decided to keep going, past pools of water reflecting broken blue sky, through a dusty section of taiga to a slight rise and more sweeping views of distant Double,

Walking the park road east of Savage.

and finally down a seemingly long final stretch alongside the Teklanika, where I resorted to counting off each signpost. I enjoyed that day so much that I did it all over again the next day, with better weather and better ability to comprehend the landscape the second time around. (Bus drivers and maintenance staff told me later that they were confused to see me at the same spots in the middle of nowhere, two days in a row. They soon got used to me—the smiling road walker—and always waved hello. Bus riders often waved, too, or just gawked and took photos, making me feel a bit like a moose.)

Two weeks later, I went from Igloo Creek Campground (Mile 34) to the Toklat Rest Stop (Mile 53). It was the best stretch yet—rugged valley between Igloo and Cathedral Mountains (which Adolph, his brother Olaus, and Howard Zahniser, the father of the Wilderness Act, climbed in 1961), a mist-filled Sable Pass, the photogenic view at Polychrome Overlook, and a lupine-lined stroll to the braided meanders of the Toklat, complete with a pika, a bear, a fox, and several sheep.

After that, I decided that I might as well walk the whole darn road, section by section. The day I walked from Eielson (Mile 66) back to Toklat, the mountaintops were lost in the clouds for the entire shuttle

Walking the park road up Polychrome Pass.

ride, and a full fog descended once I'd disembarked and began traveling on foot. To me, that part of the park consists of fog-filled valleys,
fog-lost ridges, drainages flowing from fog into fog. My boots crunched
endlessly down the dirt road as if I were on a gravel treadmill. The only
excitement came when one of the maintenance staff passed me, then
braked and drove back to pick me up, giving me a ride past a momma
bear and her two cubs, who were playing and eating berries not more
than twenty yards from the road. I don't like to think what could have
happened if I'd startled them, emerging alone from the mist, nor do
I want to know what else I passed and passed me, unseen. It was a
wonderful day.

I saved the last stretch—Eielson to Wonder Lake (Mile 85)—for my
final weekend in the park, mid-August. As fortune had it, I couldn't
have chosen better weather. When the shuttle left the depot at 6:30
a.m., the sun was already intense, glowing across willow and spruce,
casting crepuscular rays from behind the scattering cumulus. Only a
few minutes into the day and a few miles up the road, the shuttle came
around a bend and there it was, rising up from behind the horizon,
gazing out across countless unnamed peaks, ringing down from the

blue sky, more bright and glorious than I'd ever seen it before—the mountain. *The* mountain.

Thank you, mountain. My mind and notebook filled with gratitude, *Thank you, sky.* I almost believed that they'd conspired this impossibly clear view just for me, a goodbye from the High One.

This rush of appreciation was followed by a surge of sorrow. Looking out across the landscape—Double Mountain in the foreground, then was that Sable? Igloo and Cathedral? Did I know the names and profiles of the lesser peaks?—I realized just how little I'd seen and done that season, how short and limited my experience had been. So many ridges unclimbed, so many wolves unseen. *I haven't seen this place,* my handwriting became more of a scrawl, *don't know it, can't know it. What's beyond Primrose? Behind the other side of Fang? Colors in autumn? Snow in winter? Under the Northern Lights?*

What was worse, the few parts that I thought I'd seen turned out to be untrue, or incomplete. Throughout the shuttle ride, the mountain kept peeking out (peaking out?) in unexpected places. Before and after Polychrome, past Toklat—locations the other intern and I had spent several days surveying, not dreaming that the mountain was with us the whole time. At Stony Hill Overlook, of course, I might expect it there, though hadn't dared hope to see it top to bottom, snow to tundra. Eielson, too—possible, though not probable. But I thought I'd known the other landscapes, mountainless. It was like visiting a familiar city block only to realize that a skyscraper had been there all along, towering above the others but invisible.

The day was an exercise in exclamation points and question marks, awe and sorrow, pure presence and pre-nostalgia. After disembarking at Eielson, I walked and walked, skirting the edge of cliffs above the Muldrow Glacier, out along the open tundra, past loon-filled kettle lakes and fireweed already tinged with the colors of fall. Walked and walked, under the watchful eye of Denali, whose big white mass soon began to snag streamers and puffs. As the hours progressed, more clouds collected and the sky became more shadow than sun. The mountain was gone again, still there but unseeable, unknowable. Sky darker. Ribbons of rain filled the extravagant emptiness to the west, where the McKinley River braided away across the horizon. It was like I was back on the plains again—one vast merging of land and sky. I lost focus and just walked, fearing that this would be my last chance for months to be able to feel so alone and free, in a place so purely wild. (Years, it turned out, until I felt that same sorrowful euphoria again.)

I flagged down the day's final bus just before Wonder Lake, then cried most of the ride back, hating having to leave that raw, magnificent landscape, late afternoon light low and lamentatious.

Countering if not undermining my craving for solitude, I spent the rest of my free time with the backcountry ranger: watching movies, walking Sylvie the sled dog, continuing one long discussion on wildness, adventure, art, meaning and purpose in life, and other similarly light topics. While we shared many perspectives—most notably, an idealistic, purist wilderness ethic—we also recognized and mercilessly probed more and more points of disagreement. Thoreau was just the start.

In late July, we made another after-dinner dash, this time up to the Healy Overlook. It began well, spinning up switchbacks and dashing across straightaways, anticipating the broad view down the Nenana River valley. When we reached the overlook and the end of the official trail, about halfway up Mt. Healy, of course that wasn't enough; we kept going, along an unmaintained trail farther up the ridge. A half mile or so later, I wanted to stop. He was aiming for the very top.

I don't know what was different about that night. Granted, it was overcast, cool, and windy, but not rainy and there was still plenty of light. True, the soles of my feet had begun to crack and bleed after several days in wet boots, but they didn't hurt that much. I had no real excuse; I just didn't want to hike any farther. *Slow down*, I thought. The weeks of frenetic movement and constant newness were wearing me down. I hadn't paused to breathe all summer. Bus rides were the only chances I'd had to sit still, and even then, the world was moving around me, mountains and grizzlies rolling on by. I wanted to allow myself—to allow both of us, together—an hour or two to soak in the scenery, to be comfortable with ourselves in that place, instead of always dashing on ahead, farther, higher, faster.

Simultaneously, I also wanted to not want to slow down. If we went up Healy, from there, I knew, we would decide to keep going. We'd end up fifteen miles west at Savage the next morning. Another grand adventure! Exhilarating, no? I should like that, right? My ideal (and façade) of nonchalant derring-do. No matter how far, how long, how high, how wild I hiked or climbed, it would never be enough for him, or for me. Echoes of Big Bend with the bio tech all over again. I couldn't.

I turned around, leaving him wondering what had happened, where we'd gone wrong.

Soon thereafter, we went to a music festival in Anderson, halfway to Fairbanks. The days were perfect—sunniest stretch of the summer. We brought a growler, pitched a tent at the far edge of town, and waded hip-deep across the wide, silty Nenana River to explore a series of shifting gravel-bar islands. Each evening, though, once the music and actual festivities started, the bluegrass reminded me of the festival in Kemmerer—had it only been a year earlier? I didn't want to dance. Didn't want to go to a music festival ever again. Didn't want to be around singing, happy people. Wanted to stay on one of the river islands forever, to be on Primrose Ridge or out at the Polychrome Glaciers. Wanted to be alone. Needed to be alone. We argued.

We argued an argument that had been brewing all summer—not the one about our all-too-similar need for independence, but our all-too-different notions of a meaningful life. He's a philosopher and traveler, eager to go as far and do as much as possible, to forever see new places and learn new things. I'm a walker and dreamer, happiest burrowing into places—learning the names and shapes of the landforms and water bodies; gauging the moods and rhythms of the weather, the wildlife, the seasons; tracing the history, both human and natural; staying put long enough to let the land open up, reveal, merge. Trying to *feel*, in the sense of the classic Chinese glyph, which scholar-poet David Hinton translates as "heart-mind in the presence of landscape-color" or "the landscape-color of heart-mind."[13] Perhaps Robert MacFarlane's comparison between a pilgrim and a mountaineer best represents the difference between us: I "content . . . [my]self always with looking along and inwards to mystery," while the backcountry ranger "longs to look down and outwards onto total knowledge."[14]

Except that I was far from content. "Nothing holds still in this ongoing process of sincerity," Hinton notes. "What happens never happens enough. It is, instead, possessed always of a restless hunger."[15] Hunger, hunger, never enough, still not quite right. Like Peter Matthiessen before his trek through the Himalaya, I'd spent the whole summer "wandering from one path to another with no real recognition that I was embarked upon a search, and scarcely a clue as to what I might be after. I only knew that at the bottom of each breath there was a hollow place that needed to be filled."[16]

Still, that canyon-shaped hollow, dragons seething.

My second-to-last weekend in Denali, the backcountry ranger and I hiked up Primrose Ridge—my favorite spot in the park, if I had to choose one—for our final full day together.

It was appropriately cool and drizzly, with a low cloud ceiling hovering just above the ridge, so close I could reach up and touch it. We moved through the narrow space between earth and sky—a peculiar, otherworldly layer; a long, lonely expanse of rock, lichen, and cloud. All ours, all we had. (Though of course *the* mountain was out there, too, unseeable to us earthbound mortals, but gleaming somewhere far above the clouds.) Charmed or unsettled by the sense of intimacy, of solitude but not aloneness, we broached the subject of what to do next, after the season was over—was I just going to leave, bye? (That's what I do—onward.)

Then, the miracle of Alaska—only in a place like this, on a day like this, could we be reminded of the selfishness of our questions, the impermanence of our individual concerns, and the unavoidability of our humanness, by the arrival of a caribou. A bull, powerful, with antlers and mane silhouetted against the mist. How long had he been watching us, silently gazing down from a high crag? Then another, behind him: a cow, slender and alert. Stillness, wildness, and dignity. All I could ever hope to be.

Minutes or hours later, they'd seen all they needed to of us, and trotted off, leaving us alone again but freed from all our doubts and anxieties. Free to just experience what time we had left there. The clouds began to lift, alternating between pockets of sunshine and sprinkles of rain. We headed west, through the sun, rain, wind, and more rain to Primrose's northwestern slope. There, we scrambled down a small saddle and up an outcrop for a view of the Sanctuary River, shimmering into the distance. Then, another miracle: sunlight began to illuminate the ridge and the sky behind. A full rainbow arced the length of the saddle, christening the ridge—and us a part of it—with color, with happiness, with hope.

Caribou, Primrose Ridge.

Fleeting.

On the train again, on the way back south to Anchorage, standing on the platform between the railcars, watching the mountains and
rivers and bogs speed by, I breathed fresh, spruce-filled air as deeply
into my lungs as possible, trying to hold it there forever. *I'll be back*,
I kept whispering, as if the land cared. I'll be back for the caribou, the
rainbows, the far side of Fang. I'll be back for autumn, winter, spring.
I'll be back to walk the final miles to Wonder Lake and Kantishna, then
re-walk the whole road, again and again until I know every twist and
turn. I'll backpack alone again. I'll find more fossils. If not Denali, then
somewhere else with mountains and rivers, expanses of tundra with
huge seething skies overhead. Someplace big, wild, alive.

This, I scrawled in my notebook—this hunger, this hope, this presence of landscape-color. *Remember, this is what matters.*

I'd become part mountain.

PART III

Sky, and I Invite Clear Wind for Company

ADIRONDACK FOREST PRESERVE, NEW YORK

Cumulonimbus starting to rise over Algonquin, as seen from Wright, in the heart of the Adirondack High Peaks. Mountains so small, compared with the clouds.

CHAPTER 9

Steward

In the interview, my prospective employers asked why I wanted to be a High Peaks summit steward, responsible for speaking with hikers and protecting arctic-alpine vegetation atop the tallest mountains in New York State. I could have cited John Muir's driving purpose: to "do something for wildness and make the mountains glad."[1] I could have discussed Gary Snyder's bioregionalist ethic: to "find [my] place on the planet. Dig in, and take responsibility from there . . . feet on the ground."[2] I could have paraphrased the Lorax: I "care[d] a whole awful lot."[3]

Instead, Aldo Leopold came to mind. "I want to learn to think like a mountain," I answered, realizing as the words came out of my mouth how absurd that sounded. Mountains don't think. That's one of their merits. No matter how many symbols, intentions, and dreams we ascribe to them, they're simply there, stonehearted. Even if my interviewers got the reference, it wouldn't make any sense—Leopold's essay "Thinking Like a Mountain" is about apex predators and ecosystem dynamics, not about keeping recreational hikers from trampling rare and sensitive plants.[4] Nor is it about learning to appreciate mountain landscapes, much less seeking beauty, sacredness, or the sublime. Certainly not about the merging of self with landscape—a sort of egocentric death or wilderness enlightenment, which is what I think I meant.

At least, I knew not to be totally candid: I still didn't quite understand why people love mountains and figured that a summer spent hiking up to the top of the same few peaks and staying there all day, every day might afford some insight. I'd rarely returned to a summit more than once and had never stayed long enough to really look around. According to geographic theory and basic observation, time and repetition in the mountains would equate to numerous and varied perceptions that in turn would develop into deeper appreciation, right?

Plus, I wanted to know what it was about *these* mountains—the Adirondacks—that people so love. Ever since I'd moved to Upstate New York (straight from Denali), people had been rhapsodizing about the State Forest Preserve and Park, telling me I *had* to go explore the "Daks" or the "North Country." They'd cite mountains and lakes, as if the nouns would be self-evident. Lean-tos and loons. Memory-filled summer vacations and ski trips. The superlatively *most* beautiful sunrises, *most* spectacular sunsets, *most* marvelous wilderness. (Also: black flies, deer flies, mosquitoes. The steepest, most boulder-strewn trails, the most boot-sucking mud and most soul-sucking rain. Adirondackers take perverse pride in their discomforts.)

As soon as they learned that I like to hike, acquaintances in New York asked, "Are you a forty-sixer?" as if it was an affiliation with some not-so-secret society or honorific that I could append to my college degree. Turns out, it's both—forty-sixers are people who've hiked all forty-six of the Adirondack mountains with an elevation above four thousand feet. (Technically, there are only forty-three or forty-four such peaks—three of those originally identified and climbed in the early twentieth century turned out to be below the mark, while one that may measure four thousand feet was not included—but the "46er" hiking group honors the historic legacy rather than the geographic recalibration.)

Not only was I not a forty-sixer and had no desire to be certified one, I'd never hiked *any* of the peaks. Although I grew up in Western New York, I was hardly aware that the Adirondacks existed. I only vaguely recall a trip my dad and I did some time in high school or college—to a lean-to in the woods somewhere, by a lake with a big rock in it. (Every lean-to is in the woods, and every Adirondack lake has a big rock.) When moving to New York after spending most of my adult life out west, I had to look up the name of the state high point—Mt. Marcy, elevation 5,344 feet. Having now hiked it nearly a hundred times, I can't believe there was ever a time when I didn't know every foot of the trail up and every square inch of the summit atop Marcy.

The more that people talked about the Adirondacks, though, the more curious I became. At six million acres—the same size as Denali—Adirondack State Park is the largest protected area in the continental United States. With only half of those acres owned by the state and the rest privately owned, it's also one of the few places in the country where people can live and work within a park's borders—currently it is home to 140,000 residents in several dozen towns and small cities. The three million acres owned by the state are managed as the Adirondack Forest Preserve—one of the country's oldest protected areas, established in 1885. Most unusually, in 1894, New Yorkers approved writing protection for the forest preserve into the state constitution. What is now Article XIV, Section 1, reads: "The lands of the state, now owned or hereafter acquired, constituting the forest preserve as now fixed by law, shall be *forever kept as wild* forest lands."[5]

The "forever wild" clause and the place it protects have inspired several key figures in American conservation and preservation. Before he tried his hand at ranching in the Dakota Territories and long before he adventured in Yellowstone and Yosemite with the likes of John Muir and John Burroughs, Teddy Roosevelt began exploring the wilds of the Adirondacks. (Though, in his era, the "wilds" were a mix of sanitariums, luxurious resorts, active logging, and forests recovering from a generation of timber harvests.) He continued to visit well into his political career. In fact, then Vice President Roosevelt was returning from a conquest of Mt. Marcy when he received word that President McKinley was dying and he would soon be leader of the country, empowered to extend his conservation ethic to the rest of America. Gifford Pinchot, a staunch conservationist appointed by Roosevelt to be the first chief of the US Forest Service, also recreated in the Adirondacks, recording the first winter ascent of Mt. Marcy.

Perhaps the greatest of Adirondack heroes—Bob Marshall—grew up tromping around the woods near his family's summer home in Saranac Lake. It was Bob, his brother George, and their friend and guide Herb Clark who began a crazy quest to try to hike all forty-six four-thousand-foot peaks in 1918—a time when there were few trails and most of the mountains hadn't ever been summitted. They accomplished the feat in 1925, inspiring the forty-sixers who now literally follow in their footsteps. After his time in the Adirondacks, Marshall went on to explore ever bigger, more challenging wildernesses in Montana, Alaska, and Washington, DC, completing epic hikes, working for the Forest Service, and, in 1935, cofounding the Wilderness Society. In turn, Howard Zahniser, early executive secretary and executive director of the Wilderness Society, retreated to the Adirondacks while writing draft after draft of the Wilderness Act, taking inspiration from the mountains and streams as well as the "forever wild" spirit that protected them. If New York could set aside big wild areas and fight to keep them untrammeled and pristine for generations, he believed, then surely the whole country could protect the "enduring resource" of wilderness.

Zahniser was introduced to the Adirondacks by Paul Schaefer, one of many local heroes who worked to ensure that the forest preserve really was kept wild. Throughout the mid-twentieth century, Schaefer led several grassroots campaigns to uphold Article XIV, including one to prevent construction of a dam that would have inundated "forests unlimited, dotted with lakes, sparkling in the sunshine. Rivers threading like quicksilver through the plains and into the evergreen woods."[6] Contemporaneously, Grace Hudowalski, cofounder of the Adirondack 46ers, the ninth forty-sixer, first female forty-sixer, and correspondent for aspiring forty-sixers, spent her life encouraging people to get out and enjoy the mountains. "I never talked about anything but mountains," she reminisces. "I talked about them, I wrote about them. I gave speeches about them."[7] Asked how she became interested in mountain climbing, her George Mallory-esque response was: "Well, the mountains just happened to be all around me, so I climbed them."[8]

In addition to the individuals who have taken inspiration from and worked to help protect the Adirondacks, numerous nonprofit organizations have coalesced around various causes, from the Adirondack 46ers to Schaefer's Friends of the Forest Preserve, Protect the Adirondacks, and new Adirondack Wilderness Advocates to the Adirondack Land Trust and a local chapter of The Nature Conservancy. One of the largest organizations, the Adirondack Mountain Club (abbreviated ADK so as to not get confused with the Appalachian Mountain Club's AMC), was founded in 1922 to help conserve, preserve, and promote "responsible recreational use" of the forest preserve. These mountains must surely be special if all of these people and all of these groups had found and continue to find such meaning in them.

The ADK was one of the first resources I discovered when I began looking into the Adirondacks. While the state Department of Environmental Conservation (DEC) provides some basic information about forest preserve history, regulations, and trail conditions, its focus is more on resource protection and visitor safety than on interpretation. The DEC relies on other entities—such as the State University of New York's College of Environmental Science and Forestry, Paul Smith's College (both of which operate interpretive centers in the park), and the ADK—to help with public outreach. In addition to running the High Peaks Information Center (HPIC) at the trailhead for several of the most popular hikes, including the main trails up Mt. Marcy and Algonquin Peak, the second-highest peak and only other mountain above five thousand feet, the ADK publishes maps and guidebooks, leads skills classes and guided hikes, offers educational and interpretive programming, and operates both a frontcountry and a backcountry lodge.

In clicking through their website, I saw that the ADK hires summer employees, including summit stewards, who are "responsible for educating the hiking public about the rare and fragile alpine communities of the Adirondack High Peaks Region . . . [and] conducting biological inventories and monitoring." Sounded intriguing. Better yet: "Stewards spend five days at a time camping in remote backcountry sites and complete strenuous hikes each day to a nearby summit." I have "a strong desire to be challenged physically and mentally," I thought, and enjoy "working in the remote backcountry in extreme conditions."[9] I sent in an application.

Thus I found myself in a phone interview, saying that I wanted to learn to think like a mountain. Admittedly, I didn't know anything about alpine ecology or Adirondack landscapes, but I'd done work in environmental interpretation and field research. Plus, at Black Canyon, Denali, and beyond, I'd had to cross rugged terrain in sometimes inclement weather. "Sure, I can complete strenuous hikes," I told the interviewers, "and can tolerate being out in the wind and rain all day."

I had no idea what I was getting myself into. Later, I found myself thinking back to one particular scenario posed to me during the interview: "Say you've been out in the woods for four days and it's been raining the whole time. Everything's soaked. You're supposed to hike to the summit again today but know that there won't be that many people on a weekday with bad weather. Is it still worth it to go up?" My reply: "Of course, I'll put on rain gear and go up anyway! If it's my job to protect the plants, I'll be there!" Easy to *say*; harder to *do*, when I actually found myself pulling on wet socks, scraping slugs off my thermos, and getting ready to hike up a mountain and stand in the rain for a fifth straight day.

My interview must have satisfied the summit steward coordinator; she offered me one of the spots. As soon as I knew I'd be spending my summer on the mountaintops, I began researching the Adirondacks in earnest. I tried to learn the geology and hydrology, the ecology and the human history. I looked up photographs and articles, studied maps, checked books out from the library. I even taught an environmental history class with an emphasis on centuries of "Contested Terrain" in the Adirondacks, as historian Philip Terrie describes it.[10] But it was hard to identify plants from books, and harder still to gauge the shapes of peaks from maps and photos. Hardest of all was to understand just what people meant by "rugged" trails. Adirondack trails are a whole different breed, unimaginable to anyone accustomed to tidy switchbacks. I'd done hikes with plenty of elevation gain and loss before; I'd followed game paths along cliffs, forded rivers, fought through brush, but I was entirely unprepared for "trails" that were blazed long before anyone understood or cared about erosion. Adirondack routes follow the shortest paths, straight up streambeds and directly across ridgelines. Through bogs. Over cliffs. Despite best efforts at maintenance—the ADK has a professional trails crew; the DEC has rangers and backcountry caretakers; countless volunteers dig trenches, clear brush, repair bridges, and encourage hikers to stay in the trail corridor—the puddles just get deeper, the boulders more exposed, the slabs more slippery, year after year. No amount of reading could have prepared me for an "Adirondack mile," as strenuous as five in any other terrain.

The trails are part of the "charm" that I wasn't expecting. Then again, I hadn't really known what to expect. That was one of the reasons for going—to explore a new place, to enjoy and help protect wilderness, and, of course, to learn to think like a mountain.

It was raining as I drove north into Adirondack Park, ready to report for my first day of work. Mile upon mile of green forest faded into gray fog. If there were mountains out there, I wasn't going to see them. Rustic towns sat on the shores of eponymous lakes—Indian Lake, Long Lake, Tupper Lake. Rain-rippled water reflected low clouds; mist swirled between tall pines—the epitome of North Country scenery. After hours of peaceful driving, the bustle and panache of Lake Placid were a bit of a shock. I knew that the city had capitalized on its legacy as a two-time host of the winter Olympics, but I wasn't prepared for the crowded Main Street lined with carefully designed storefronts à la a posh Colorado ski town. I never got used to Lake Placid, which seemed to host a major event every weekend—an admirable model for a year-round recreation-based economy, but obnoxious to try to run errands in.

From Lake Placid, it's only a few minutes to the ADK's Adirondack Loj, where I'd be based for the summer. (Spelling courtesy of Melvil Dewey, a proponent of phoneticism and early co-owner of the property.) When I turned onto Loj Road, it was raining harder than ever. I had no idea that I wasn't able to see one of the park's most beloved panoramas: profiles of several of the highest mountains—including Mt. Marcy and Algonquin—corrugating the horizon. For many people—including me, now—this scene triggers happy memories of time spent at the Loj and hiking the High Peaks, but it was just more green and gray on that first encounter. When I reached the end of the pothole-laced and forest-lined road, I parked at the HPIC and went looking for my supervisor.

The ADK property has the feel of a summer camp—paths winding into the woods; campsites featuring picnic tables and fire pits; a big lake, a big lodge (Loj, to Dewey), and an aura of cozy adventure. The Loj itself is an elegantly rustic wooden structure, boasting guest rooms, a dining area, and a soaring great room complete with moose head affixed to a stone fireplace. Nonpublic spaces—the kitchen area, staff dining room, and offices—are tucked in the back and on the second floor. The structure sits near Heart Lake, a twentyish-acre body of fresh, cool water nestled amid the mountains, ringed with white pines and enchanted with loons. I'd eventually come to know and love the reflections and moods of Heart Lake better than my own backyard, but when I walked out onto the dock for a look around on that first day, I couldn't see across to the other side. Rising mist. Pattering rain. Pine-scented air.

After meeting my supervisor, I claimed a bunk in the yurt shared by summit stewards, then tried to find my way back through the woods to the Loj. The rest of the day was full of introductions—meeting the rest of the team, beginning training in plant identification, following a trail around Heart Lake, and waiting for dinner alongside dozens of other seasonal ADK employees. (Meals were always delicious but chaotic, continuing the summer camp vibe. Seasonal employees—mostly college students, working in the Loj or the HPIC as maintenance staff or as education interns—piled into the staff kitchen to wait for Loj guests to finish being served, then jostled to get the remaining food once the chef gave the okay.) Back at the yurt, before chatting with the other stewards until we fell asleep, I managed to scribble down my first impression: "Mountains out there somewhere. Wait and see."

"Conservation"—using natural resources and places wisely, sparingly— and "preservation"—showing restraint and respect; keeping meddlesome human hands off wild corners of the world—are traditional practices and ethics in public land management. While conservation versus preservation debates have been raging since the days of Gifford Pinchot and John Muir, the underlying hope if not belief is that people will find places such as national and state parks meaningful and be inspired to help protect them. As wilderness management expert Chad Dawson writes of the Adirondacks, "The future of the Forest Preserve and the Adirondack Park itself rests on the support of the people of New York State. It is imperative that a wide diversity of New York State citizens learn to know and love the Adirondack Park and its Forest Preserve lands since we often protect only what we know and love."[11] Importantly, he also notes that people can learn about and care for a place vicariously: "Not all the citizens of New York State need set foot on Forest Preserve lands to know and love and, thus, protect them."[12]

"Protection" takes on the connotation of financial or political support—providing funding and enacting legislation to ensure the maintenance of natural and historical conditions.

"Stewardship"—from root words meaning "house" or "pen" (as in animal sty) and "guardian"—is an increasing practice within public land management. Instead of merely encouraging visitors to come to parks, have a good time, then go home and maybe send money to friends groups or write their governmental representatives, the aim is for people to take an active role in taking care of resources and places by maintaining trails, removing invasive species, picking up litter, and contributing to education and interpretation programs, usually during organized events such as National Trails Day or via longer-term commitments such as the Adopt a Lean-To Program. As Guy and Laura Waterman—writers, ethicists, and longtime caretakers of alpine areas in the White Mountains—write in *Backwoods Ethics*, "The goal should be to have everyone be a steward of this lovely landscape. To the maximum extent possible, we want to see every hiker who walks above treeline conscious of the special kind of environment he or she has entered, and . . . heedful of where to step so as to preserve the resource for future years of hikers."[13] (In a subsequent paragraph, they also acknowledge "the right of the mountain to exist on its own terms, a certain respect we owe to the land independent of our selfish enjoyment of it."[14])

Conservation and preservation efforts may be based on science and legitimized by public policy, but they are still inspired and fueled by aesthetics and ethics. Even more so, stewardship is driven by place attachment—love for particular locations and willingness to put time and effort into caring for them. Explaining what had motivated him to dedicate his life to protecting arctic-alpine vegetation in the High Peaks, botanist Edwin Ketchledge once told group of forty-sixers, "For 29 years I've climbed in this country . . . In a pantheistic sense, all of this . . . is part of me."[15] In return, stewards get satisfaction out of seeing tangible results: building a cairn or saving a swath of plants leaves a real, meaningful legacy on the landscape. Positive feedback loop: both the experience of stewarding and the results can deepen an individual's or group's sense of attachment, and thus enhance commitment to further stewardship.

As training got underway, I was enamored with the *idea* of stewardship—giving back to wilderness. Any wilderness. The Adirondacks? In terms of sense of place, I was starting from scratch.

Rain turned to snow overnight. Wetter and colder, still no mountains. While a couple of returnee stewards trudged up the trails (it was Memorial Day weekend, busy no matter the weather), newcomers began wilderness first aid training alongside the Trails Crew—a friendly but intense lot that take the mantra "work hard, play hard" to extremes. The first aid scenarios didn't so much make me feel confident and prepared in the case of a backcountry emergency as they made me aware of the variety of terrifying and painful accidents or illnesses that could happen, bee stings to broken bones, hypothermia to heart attacks. I wondered how I'd survived so many years wandering around wild places. And I should have recognized this as a sign that this place and job would be more different than I'd realized. I wasn't going to be alone watching plants grow, much less looking for fossils; I was going to be hiking heavily trafficked trails up to popular summits, in part responsible for helping any hikers in distress.

After training, there was just enough time to scramble up Mt. Jo—a short and supposedly "easy" hike up a bump overlooking Heart Lake. The trail is only a mile long but requires a heart-thumping, leg-burning seven hundred feet of elevation gain. As my first Adirondack "summit," Jo was an introduction to straight-up-the-mountain-style hiking. Boulders, rocks, and roots seemed dangerous enough; ankle-deep snow and still-falling slush made it even more preposterous. And those seven hundred feet up and down? For the rest of the season, I measured all other hikes in "Mt. Jo" units, as in: *It's only two Mt. Jos from here to the summit of Algonquin? Surely, I can do that!* And, *I still have another Mt. Jo to go up Haystack? I'll never make it.*

People actually enjoy this? I wrote that evening. *Still no mountains.* Even little old Jo was in the clouds.

In need of fresh air and broader perspectives after more first aid training the next day, I went up Jo again. This time, I paused on top. It had stopped raining, and patches of blue were beginning to appear overhead; I could finally see the rest of the world. What a world it was: Heart Lake shimmering below, a sky mirror sitting in a surprisingly vast sea of forest; forest-green hills rolling off to the horizon and rising up into the clouds; white-dusted peaks beginning to emerge, one by one. Algonquin, Colden, Marcy, I'd later learn their names. Everything around me was named, known, mapped, measured. Logged, mined, dammed, regrown. Laced with trails and studded with lean-tos. Written about, talked about, argued over, dreamed. But my first glimpse across the tree-carpeted, snow-shining landscape, bumps and hollows illuminated by swiftly rolling patches of sunlight, was of a spectacularly, unexpectedly wild place. *This* was New York? Ah, this was the *Adirondacks*.

First glimpse of the classic view from Mt. Jo: overlooking Heart Lake, with Wright in the center background, Algonquin in clouds behind it, and Colden (with snow-filled slides) to the back left, Marcy next to it, also in clouds.

Having asked for hiking recommendations and not yet learned that to an Adirondacker "relatively flat and easy" equates to a thousand-foot elevation gain requiring ladders, logs, and both hands and feet to navigate, I went to Avalanche Lake the next day, having been promised that the landscape there was especially scenic.

The first two miles from the trailhead at the HPIC to Marcy Dam are relatively flat, though more muddy than easy. Now that I've walked that stretch of trail hundreds of times and can recite just about every twist, tree, and rock along the way, I wish I'd written down my first impressions—did it feel long? Now: a breeze. Rough? Rather compacted. Remote? Wide highway.

I didn't linger at Marcy Dam, which is now a popular picnic spot and camping area. What had been one of the High Peaks' most scenic and beloved views—Mt. Colden's landslide-lined slopes reflected in the water of a small reservoir—no longer existed, as Hurricane Irene had washed away part of the dam in 2011, draining the pond. Because the dam, built by the Civilian Conservation Corps in the 1930s, served no practical purpose and would have been too expensive to rebuild after the storm, the DEC decided to begin dismantling it in 2015, provoking an outcry from people who remembered and cherished the view. One downfall of so many people loving the Adirondacks is that many want it to stay exactly the same—no new regulations, no trail reroutes, no erosion or succession. Meanwhile, newcomers like me have no concept of or connection to a structure and scene we never witnessed. By the time I first saw it, the pond was mostly gone, leaving behind decidedly unscenic mudflats, which will eventually regrow into lush wetlands.

Several trails converge at or continue from Marcy Dam: one that's accessed from the Loj trailhead or another from a trailhead at South Meadows Road, following an old truck road; one that heads off to Mt. Marcy; and another off to Mt. Colden (eleventh highest peak in the state) or to Avalanche Lake, tucked in the narrow gorge between Colden and Avalanche Mountain (a trailless minor peak, overshadowed by the MacIntyre Range towering over it). The trail to Avalanche Lake follows Marcy Brook for a mile or two, then splits to ascend a narrowing pass. Although the route was rugged, markers few and far between, and signs' mileage contradictory (another joy of Adirondack hiking—signs frequently list different distances), it wasn't until I reached the pass and had to fight downed brush and balance on broken logs that I began to feel like I wasn't simply following a trail, but actually earning my way into a place where natural processes still reigned. When I emerged out of the woods onto the sunlit, snow-lined shore of Avalanche Lake—an inland fjord, with rock walls plunging straight into dark water, cascades ribboning down from high ledges, birdcalls echoing from every direction—I finally sensed an edge of wildness.

I sat on a rock to peel off my mud- and snowmelt-soaked boots and socks, enjoying the mix of warm sun and icy water. Suddenly, I heard a loud *crack!* from high to the left, followed by a scraping, whooshing sound. A wall of snow slid down Colden's steep, bare slope, soared off of a ledge, and crashed into the lake, sending a cacophony of waves splashing in every direction. "*Avalanche* Lake!" I thought, disbelieving my fortune to be there at exactly the right moment to experience such a celebration of snow and gravity.

But as I sat and watched the waters calm, hoping to see another chunk of snow come flying down, I heard voices interjecting from the pass. I hurried to put my boots back on, embarrassed to be caught barefoot, basking in the sun. By the time the people arrived—only two of them, though they'd sounded like a dozen, intruding on the silence—I was on the trail again, clambering over massive boulders and sketchy ladders along the lake's eastern shore.

The views were indeed impressive—most notably the Trap Dike, a gash in the side of Colden formed by differential weathering of an igneous intrusion—but I let myself get annoyed by the couple's conversation, which, trapped and amplified between the rock walls, didn't fade or muffle with distance. Soon, there were more voices, and more. Just like that: from no one else to five or six groups in this bottleneck of a hiking corridor. Everyone was friendly—eager to say hello, tell me about their hikes, and ask where I was going / what I was doing / was I a forty-sixer. "We're making the full loop up Algonquin—peaks 36 through 38 if we can hit Iroquois and Wright, too." / "We're scouting out the Trap Dike, thinking of climbing it tomorrow." / "You're hiking alone?" But I wasn't ready for, much less accustomed to, the camaraderie and communal spirit of hiking in the Adirondacks. I sought serenity and solitude, wild forces at work, not a social gathering.

People, people everywhere, the scenery and the snow were overshadowed in my notebook entry for the day. *Who am I to begrudge them their company?* I questioned myself. *Why does it take away from my experience?*

Why do so many people love this place?

One more day off before training resumed. I spent it hiking Mt. Van Hoevenberg—a twin to Mt. Jo with equally sweeping views, though less popular, perhaps because the trail is longer and involves a submerged section through a beaver pond. Afterward, I took the South Meadows truck road around to Marcy Dam from a different direction—also a less popular route, likely because it's longer than the approach from the Loj. In reverse, this became my regular weekend walk—a long, flat, relatively peaceful loop.

Before dinner, I poked along the shores of Heart Lake. About a quarter of the way around, I discovered a bench, nearly hidden from the trail and tucked far enough into the woods so as to be less visible from the water but with a perfectly framed view of mountains. (Marcy, Colden, Wright, and Algonquin, I'd learn.) I immediately chose or recognized it as "my" spot—the place I'd come to when I wanted a touch of seclusion. The place I'd come to when I needed to get away from the yurt or the Trails Crew or the busy staff kitchen. The place I'd come to to write, to draw, to think. The place I'd come to to sit and study the lake and mountains and sky and ponder myself in relation to them.

While classical Chinese poets would celebrate the view from Heart Lake for its symbolic mirror-calm clarity—"It's this lake's mind, that gaze holding the mountain utterly"[16]—landscape scholars would point out that the scene fits all of the requirements for landscape aesthetics, by any theory: biological survival (water, food, and fuel all nearby); prospect refuge (I could see out but was safely hidden in the trees); cognitive engagement (coherent skyline, yet mysterious ridges and valleys); and principles of design (varying lines, textures, and color). But I think I enjoyed the view from the bench—and, better yet, from a kayak or by swimming out to the middle of Heart Lake and simply floating on my back—because it was relatively open. Although the landscape wasn't as expansive as any seen from a summit or out across the plains, compared with the close, dark green of the woods, the broad, flat stretch of water gave me space to breathe. I could see the wind ripple and sometimes roil its surface, listen to raindrops plunk and hear echoes of owls around its shore. Even on the calmest mornings, when it perfectly reflected the world around it, seeming to open even more space in the forest, mountains, and sky above, it held hidden dragons, beginning to waken from their winter slumber, now exhaling mist, "ris[ing] and ascend[ing] . . . into thunderclouds . . . [and] life-bringing rains."[17]

Sitting by Heart Lake, I wrote that evening, *Wavelets. Cool breeze but not cold. Cirrus sweeping past, stratocumulus rolling in. Those mountains—those old, solid mountains, am I really supposed to climb those? Every day? Wonder what the world looks like from up there.*

Guess I'll know soon.

Cascade was my first Adirondack four-thousand-footer, as is the case for many new hikers and aspiring forty-sixers. As the shortest trail at the time (only 2.4 miles)—with ready access from the highway, comparably less elevation gain (1,940 feet), and spectacular views—it's often touted as the "easiest" high peak or "best bang for your buck." When visitors ask, "What mountain should we start with?" or "What's a good, not too hard hike?" at hotels or in online forums, they're almost always told Cascade.

Mirror-calm waters of Heart Lake, exhaling mist and opening to mountains beyond.

"Eas*iest*" does not mean "easy," however. "Short" translates to "steep." A "1,940-foot elevation gain" still requires going up 1,940 feet. Unlike many other Adirondack hikes, which start with long, gradual approaches then get steeper closer to the summits, and which have some flat or downhill sections that afford breaks from a relentless ascent, the climb to Cascade is consistently, unforgivingly up, straight from the highway. People who expect a pleasant jaunt—and thus come wearing flip-flops, toting small children, or without any water or other supplies—are often unpleasantly surprised. That said, many of those who make it to the top are enormously proud of their accomplishment. I can't attest to how they feel back at the trailhead after more than two knee-pounding, ankle-straining miles straight *down*.

On a cool, beautifully sunny day, with the snow mostly gone, trillium starting to bloom, and huge white cumulus lollygagging overhead, our group of stewards in training went to Cascade to learn trail maintenance techniques. Hiking techniques, too. Earlier, while doling out gear for the season, my supervisor had suggested taking a pair of trekking poles. I could use them for balance, she'd said, and they'd save my knees on the descents. I'd conceded to try them, privately assuming I'd find them as useless and frustrating as I had in Denali. But within the first few hundred yards of the Cascade Trail, as I used and needed the poles to half-pull, half-push myself up the mountainside, I recognized my arrogance for what it was. Trekking poles are indispensable in the Adirondacks—crucial for testing puddle depth, self-arresting during slides, balancing over log bridges, pulling/pushing with on the way up, and especially bracing against on the way down.

Although we stopped often during the climb up Cascade—to clean leaves out from a water bar here, to dismantle a rock stack there, to learn the names of plants just about everywhere—my legs still burned and my forehead dripped with sweat. The first half of the hike is like an uneven, awkwardly tall staircase. The next third involves sections of scrambling, including one particularly steep slab with views opening out across the landscape. (Although not nearly as bad as *The* Slab on the trail to Algonquin, not to mention cliffs on Saddleback or slides on Macomb, this rockface is enough to deter hikers who are afraid of heights.) That leaves an all-too-brief stretch above tree line, finally feeling exposed and free.

Unlike true alpine summits, which have always been too high and too harsh to support anything but specially adapted arctic-alpine vegetation, Cascade was forested until 1903, when a massive wildfire left the summit bald (and also burned through several towns and incinerated the original lodge at Heart Lake). In the century since, subalpine species recolonized the summit, but those plants are at risk owing to an ever increasing number of hikers, many of them unaware of their potential impacts. The whole trail is a widening, muddy mess, with herd paths and shortcuts braiding in and out, but the summit is in the worst shape, with only a few forlorn patches of soil left.

We were there to protect that soil and the grasses and sedges holding it down. This was the first year that, thanks to the Adirondack 46ers organization, the High Peaks Foundation, and other donors, there was funding to support a steward on Cascade on weekends. (Several years later, the 46ers also started the Trailhead Steward Program, with volunteers talking to hikers about safety and environmental protection before they even hit the trail.) Because the peak is so popular, it's a good place to introduce people to or remind them of hiking etiquette. Each weekend, stewards give hundreds of hikers the "Rock Walk Talk"—an explanation of the importance of stepping and sitting only on rocks, not plants or soil. Or, when it gets especially busy and groups wander all over, we abbreviate the conversation by repeatedly calling out "Please don't step on the plants!"

On training day, we focused on trail maintenance. At lower elevations, we "brushed in" particularly bad sections—filling social paths with big, ugly branches so that they no longer look like possible routes or, at least, making then look unwelcoming, keeping hikers in the main corridor. We also cleared dead leaves and other detritus to allow the trail to drain more efficiently. Fewer puddles means fewer people trying to walk around puddles to avoid wet feet. (Impossible, to avoid wet feet in the Adirondacks.) Above tree line, we edged the vegetated patches with rocks as visual cues to stay on the trail, in case people didn't notice the large signs reading "Revegetation Area: Please Stay on Marked Trail" in both English and French. Initially, I disliked how unnatural these rock lines looked, not to mention the signs and shin-high string fences used to keep people out of sensitive areas. *They're such blatant intrusions on the wilderness character!* I remember thinking. *Trammels!* I bristled. It only took a few days' worth of watching people walk through the rock lines, step over the string, and read then defy the obvious signs to convince me of the necessity for barriers. Some days, especially on Cascade, I would have been perfectly okay with erecting ten-foot-high chain-link fences if I thought they'd be at all effective at keeping people off the plants.

We spent the afternoon learning the principles of cairn building. Although cairns may just look like piles of stones, they have to be carefully placed and constructed so as to guide people along trails in foggy, rainy, and snowy conditions, and so as to be stable even in high winds or when tampered with by hikers. It can take a full day or two to build a good cairn, not including the time it takes to find rocks that are just right—large, heavy, flattish. Our group only got as far as dismantling one of the existing cairns in need of repair and getting a good, sturdy base in place before reassembling temporary top layers and hiking down for the day. Working on it piecemeal, whenever we had the chance, it took us most of the rest of the summer to build that poor cairn properly.

Before starting the rock lining and cairn building, though, we learned what proved to be the most important lessons of the day. First:

when we emerged out of the trees and saw the great dome of rock before us, we all made a beeline for the top. No matter how tired I was or what the conditions were like, at that point, the summit seemed so close and so achievable that I wouldn't have stopped for anything. I wouldn't have wanted to talk to a steward. I wouldn't have listened to weather warnings. If I'd fallen and broken a leg, I probably would have crawled until I made it to the benchmark. I feel the same motivation on every other mountain, and presume that many other hikers feel it, too: once I reach the alpine zone, I'm going all the way. This matters less on Cascade, where there's only about a quarter mile of exposure, maybe half an hour to the summit and back into the relative protection of the forest. But on Algonquin or Marcy, where there's more than a half mile of steep and exposed terrain above tree line—at least an hour to the summit and back—this top-or-bust mentality is foolhardy. Subsequently, whenever hikers chose to continue up in the middle of thunderstorms, I simultaneously shook my head at and sympathized with them.

Next: as soon as we got to the summit, we sat. I don't think I even looked at the landscape. As I remember it, we sprawled on the rock and began pulling water and food out of our packs. I'd have found a more sheltered spot if the weather had been bad, and I'd like to think that I wouldn't have stayed at the very top if there were other people who wanted to tag the benchmark, but I probably wouldn't have moved for any other reason or spoken with a steward right away. Upon reaching a summit, some people whoop and holler, some people high-five. Some immediately start taking photos or making phone calls, some turn right around and begin hiking down. Some—most—just want to sit and eat. All reactions are valid in their own ways (except maybe the phone calls), so long as they don't interfere with others' experiences or affect the vegetation. People need their moments with the mountain.

Last: with her trademark mix of astuteness and patience, our supervisor let us have time to eat and soak in the scenery. Only once she sensed that we were ready to listen did she start to talk, identifying notable features: Lake Placid due west; Highway 73 shooting toward us; the rocky outcrops of Pitchoff directly across the road, backed by the Sentinel Range; Whiteface the lonely point to the north. (Because it stands on its own, separated from the rest of the High Peaks massif, sharp and sometimes snowcapped, Whiteface looks taller than its

4,865 feet. People often mistake it for Marcy.) Hurricane, with its eye-catching fire tower to the north-northwest. A sliver of Lake Champlain backed by Vermont's Green Mountains. Then, peak after peak, west and south: Giant, the behemoth looming over Keene Valley; the Dix range, a collection of several separate summits; Porter, the tree-covered ridge next door; Big Slide's swooping wave; behind it, the "Great Range" in all its glory—Lower Wolf Jaw with a long, bright slide, Upper Wolf Jaw, Armstrong, Gothics' bare rock gleaming like a medieval cathedral, the saddle of Saddleback, toothy Basin, Haystack, and the high dome of Marcy . . .

I can't possibly ever learn all of these, I silently panicked partway through her recitation. Did *everything* out there have a name and trail?

. . . Colden like a volcano cone, low between Marcy and Algonquin. Wright blending in with Algonquin. Santanonis in the distance. Street and Nye . . .

None of them meant anything to me. While other stewards nodded with understanding—*Ah, I just hiked Lower Wolf Jaw!* and *What a view*

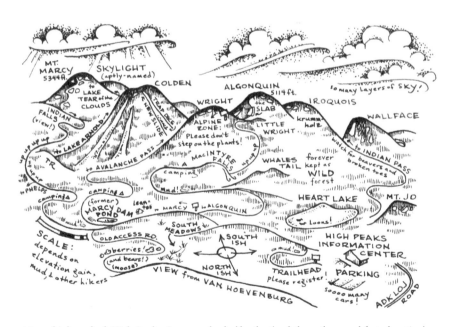

Map of Adirondack High Peaks. Seven and a half miles (and three thousand feet elevation) from the Loj/High Peaks Information Center trailhead to Marcy, two to Marcy Dam Pond, three and a half to Algonquin, and worlds apart to Skylight.

of Big Slide!—to me, the peaks were just crinkles in the vast forest, their names abstract, their stories untold. My supervisor's knowledge was overwhelming, the others' responses intimidating. It was like moving to a foreign country, not speaking the language and not knowing the customs.

But then, a familiar name:

. . . Mt. Jo, the bump at the toe of Wright . . .

And another:

. . . Van Hoevenberg, another bump, with the white tubes of the bobsled run cut into its side . . .

I'd been to both of those! I'd walked the twists of the trails and seen the views from the top. I'd planted memories like mental flags on them. When the others looked out across this landscape, they weren't seeing mountains; they were seeing mementos. That whole view was a range of possibilities, landmarks for future experiences.

We hiked Algonquin the next day for botany training, alongside DEC rangers, an ecologist from The Nature Conservancy, and a former summit steward turned bryophyte expert. Considering how challenging Cascade had been, at only two and a half Mt. Jo units, I was worried that I wouldn't make it up Algonquin's four Mt. Jos. Even more unthinkable: I'd soon have to hike it multiple days in a row.

Thankfully, our group went slowly, stopping to learn about the plants and the birds. The first mile along the trail toward Marcy Dam weaves through a mixed hardwood forest full of maples and beech, ferns and trillium, more clubmosses than I ever knew existed. After splitting off to the right, it begins to ascend alongside MacIntyre Brook. (The whole range—Algonquin flanked by Wright to the north, Iroquois and Marshall to the south—is known as the MacIntyres, after Archibald McIntyre, an early nineteenth-century prospector / investor / iron mine owner.) For a monotonous mile, there's little change to either the terrain or forest, excepting a turn through an enchanting stand of white-barked birch with groves of lady's slippers pinking up between moss-covered boulders. Then the trail begins to steepen, featuring rock staircases and the first cliff scramble before crossing the base of MacIntyre Falls.

I'd later hear and feel this waterfall roaring with storm runoff and wonder if I'd be able to get across the torrent. Oppositely, during dry spells, I worried about people running out of water, as barely a trickle dripped into near-stagnant pools. I don't remember what it was like this first time. Mostly, I was grateful for a chance to stop and eat snacks. Halfway, we celebrated, though it was only halfway in terms of distance; the greatest elevation gain and steepest sections were yet to come.

Up and up, hardwoods giving way to spruce and fir, breaks in the forest affording glimpses of blue sky filling with cumulus cotton balls. After another scramble across from Little Wright (a thirtyish-foot-high chunk that split off from the main mountainside—one of several such "little" peaks, created courtesy of the northeast-southwest trending fault system), we were rewarded with a view toward Whiteface. Then back into the trees, which were getting smaller and scragglier; the soils thinner, the trail eroded down to grainy bedrock. When we reached the sign at the junction with the trail to Wright Peak, I rejoiced to see that it was "only" nine-tenths of a mile to the summit of Algonquin.

Nine extremely challenging tenths of a mile. Harder than the notoriously steep grades on Gothics and Haystack; harder than the last push up Mt. Marcy, which is only awful to those who don't realize how many false summits there are. Maybe not as hard as the trail leading from the south side down to Lake Colden, which seems near-vertical, but, after seventy-odd trips up and down it, I rank the stretch from the Wright junction to tree line on Algonquin as my least favorite in the park. For a quarter mile, rock faces get steeper and steeper, culminating in The Slab—a long stretch of exposed, seemingly near-vertical bedrock. Many hikers are intimidated by the grade and exposure so try to skirt the edges, clinging to roots and branches, killing the trees and widening the bare patch, making the rock ever more exposed. "Dash up in one go," our supervisor recommended. "Then rest for a second at the bottom, then scurry up without stopping." Once we made it up, she cheered, "Almost to tree line!" not mentioning that the next quarter mile of rocks and trees seems more like ten.

Finally, we arrived at a sign announcing that we were about to enter the alpine zone. There's still another Mt. Jo to go from this point, but at least there are views—a north-facing semicircle, looking back at Cascade, Big Slide, and the rocky fin of Wright. At this elevation, the few black spruce and balsam fir that can survive the high winds and rime ice are stunted and flagged, with branches growing in one direction, away from the wind—*krummholz*, this phenomenon is called, from the German for "crooked wood." Higher up, arctic-alpine plants are even more diminutive and hardy, forming a mat of mosses, grasses, sedges, and dwarf shrubs hardly higher than my ankles. But we were on the final push—no stopping to marvel at the vegetation or views. *Mountain top!!!* my note from the day, with more exclamation points than explanation of how it felt to achieve the summit.

Same as with Cascade: the first things the group opted to do were to take off our boots and eat lunch. Once sated, we began our lessons. Geology first (or maybe my rock-minded brain just picked up on it best): the High Peaks Massif is composed of anorthosite—an intrusive igneous rock similar to granite but relatively rare and of origins that aren't fully understood. It crystallized as part of the Canadian Shield roughly 1.15 billion years ago, was buried deep underground, resulting in faulting and intrusions such as the Trap Dike, and only domed back up to the surface about five million years ago, likely due to a hot spot in earth's mantle. This is one of the reasons why the Adirondacks are a circular mountain range, unlike the Greens, the Whites, and other elongated ranges in the Northeast. Geologically, the Adirondacks are separate from the Appalachians.

During the Pleistocene Ice Ages, advancing and retreating ice sheets up to a mile thick scraped across the massif, scouring out valleys such as Avalanche and Wallface Passes along existing fault lines, plucking off the sides of slopes (Big Slide is a lovely example of a roche moutonnée, smoothed on one side and a cliff on the other, where rock was peeled off), and dropping piles of debris (moraines as well as lonely boulders called erratics). Wind, water, and gravity continue to shape the landscape. Particularly after large storms, rain-soaked soils slide off steep slopes, leaving behind bright scars of exposed bedrock. In 2011, for example, Irene alone exposed more than forty significant slides.[18] No fossils in the High Peaks, but it's a great region to study geomorphology.

When the ice sheet retreated at the end of the most recent glacial episode, it also left remnants of plants it had carried down from arctic tundra farther north—small, hardy species whose scientific names hint at their places of origin or ideal habitat. *Minuartia groenlandica*: sandwort, as thrives in Greenland. *Diapensia lapponica* and *Rhododendron lapponicum*: diapensia and Lapland rosebay, both echoing Lapland in northern Scandinavia. *Rhododendron groenlandicum*: Labrador tea, which is suited to both Labrador and Greenland. All of New York State was once coated in tundra, but in recent millennia, boreal forests crept northward and upward, followed by the mixed hardwoods that now fill the Adirondack lowlands and much of the rest of the state. On the tops of the highest and most exposed summits, though, conditions are far too harsh for anything but arctic-alpine plants, which are adapted to thrive in short, cool, and cloudy growing seasons, to tolerate acidic soils, and to survive rime ice in the winter and high winds year round. For example, diapensia—a trademark arctic species—grows in a cushion shape to retain warmth, has small, waxy leaves to prevent desiccation, and contains anthocyanin, a reddish pigment that both enables it to photosynthesize on cloudy days and protects it from ultraviolet damage on rare sunny days. Most species adapt by staying small and close to the ground. For example, Lapland rosebay is morphologically the same as a regular rhododendron, except that its brilliant fuchsia flowers barely grow bigger than the size of a fingernail. Similarly, the gnarled trunk of bearberry willow (*Salix uva-ursi*) may take a century to grow to the thickness of a person's thumb.

As perfectly adapted as these species are to the harsh conditions, they're not at all accustomed to being stepped on by anything bigger than a snowshoe hare. A misplaced human footfall can damage the grasses, sedges, forbs, or mosses beyond self-repair. Worse yet, if plants are trampled to death, the exposed soils and moss mats are more susceptible to erosion. Once the soil is gone, it takes centuries to redevelop, thanks to slow rates of decomposition and such little organic matter in the alpine zone.

In all of Adirondack Park's six million acres—and all of New York State, for that matter—there are only about eighty-five acres of arctic-alpine vegetation left, interspersed between about twenty isolated locations. Several of those locations—the summits of Marcy, Algonquin, and other High Peaks—are also prime hiking destinations. Unfortunately, early twentieth-century hikers in the Adirondacks (and worldwide) were unaware of just how rare and fragile mountaintop vegetation is. Historic photographs show smiling groups picnicking and pitching tents in the seemingly lush alpine meadows, oblivious to the plants crushed underfoot. As climbing became more popular and

*Arctic-alpine flora: diapensia (*Diapensia lapponica*).*

the Adirondacks more accessible in the mid-twentieth century (thanks to demographic and socioeconomic changes such as an increasing population, more affordable personal automobiles, and more frequent vacation time, as well as construction of the "Northway"—Interstate 87, connecting New York City and Montreal), the summits started to look worse for the wear. Photographs from the 1960s show networks of herd paths, exposed soil, and, worst of all, huge patches of bald bedrock, with both plants and soil gone.

Then Edwin Ketchledge came along. Botanist, professor at the State University of New York College of Environmental Science and Forestry, ADK member, and 46er number 507, Dr. Ketchledge was the hero of alpine ecosystems in the Adirondacks. While completing his round of the forty-six, he began to take note of hiker-caused damage and decided to find ways to repair and prevent further destruction. In the late 1960s, he attempted to transplant native alpine species to affected areas, essentially facilitating natural processes of dispersal and recolonization. But alpine plants are extremely sensitive to microclimates (minute, place-specific differences in terms of wind, temperature,

*Arctic-alpine flora: bearberry willow (*Salix uva-ursi*).*

and sunlight, as well as soil chemistry), so they don't transplant easily. When transplantation didn't work, Ketchledge began experimenting with the introduction of nonnative grasses, enlisting hundreds of students and volunteers to help lug seeds, fertilizer, and lime (to increase soil pH) up to the summits year after year. Although he took a risk by deliberately introducing nonnative species, he correctly hypothesized that Kentucky bluegrass—a common lawn grass—would only be able to survive the extreme conditions long enough to hold down the soils and allow native alpine species to successfully start growing again.

Noting that it would be pointless to patch up the damage if people continued to wander willy-nilly around the mountaintops, Ketchledge also saw the importance of keeping people on the trail and off the plants. Again, he enlisted students and volunteers to help, this time to build scree walls, place stepping stones, and brush in side paths to reroute trails over bedrock or to provide a single, clearly delineated path. They erected large wooden signs to educate, warn, and plead with hikers just below the summits: "You are entering an Arctic-Alpine Plant zone. The plants are rare, fragile, and very much endangered. Walking and sitting on them will kill them! Please walk only on the trail and on solid rock surfaces." With faith in human goodness, Ketchledge believed, "in general, the public is amenable to restrictions when it understands the reasons behind them."[19]

Lastly, recognizing that not all hikers pay attention to the trails, stop to read signs, or understand why or how to prevent impacts, Ketchledge insisted that "continuing educational efforts [are] necessary."[20] Taking a cue from the Green Mountains, where "ranger-naturalists" had been stationed atop Mt. Mansfield and Camel's Hump since the early 1970s and had proven successful at "controlling visitor impacts and halting loss of tundra" simply by speaking with hikers, he enlisted the ADK, The Nature Conservancy, the 46ers, and the DEC to sponsor the Adirondack Summit Stewardship Program beginning in 1990.[21]

In the decades since, the program has expanded from two stewards to a team of five, plus more than twenty indispensable, dedicated volunteers. Coverage has broadened from Marcy and Algonquin to include Wright and Cascade Peaks, with trail maintenance on other alpine summits. Meanwhile, duties have developed beyond hiker education (though that's still the cornerstone) and trail work to include ecological monitoring: stewards collect data on everything from the presence/absence of particular species to plant phenology (the timing of growth and reproductive activities, such as leafing out, budding, blooming, and fruiting), and often assist visiting scientists with their research (for example, helping resurvey transects established by Ketchledge in 1984).

Since 1999, stewards have been monitoring changes using repeat photography—taking photographs of the exact same spots from the exact same vantage year after year to track the growth or decline of vegetation, exposed soil, and bedrock. This research shows a statistically significant increase in vegetation on stewarded peaks when compared with non-stewarded peaks, proving that the vegetation is resilient and that the program has been a success. "The presence of a summit steward as an educator in these alpine areas may serve as a significant deterrent to further trampling in these areas," the ADK program coordinator attests.[22] So long as people stay on the trails, the arctic-alpine ecosystem has the potential to resume its post-Pleistocene, pre-twentieth-century glory.

As someone accustomed to working with rocks—objects that stay put, don't change that quickly, and hold millions of years' worth of earth's history—I felt a bit overwhelmed by the ecological aspects of the job. Ecosystems—even the specific, relatively small, supposedly limited components and dynamics of the alpine zone—seemed to have too many moving parts to keep track of.

Plants. I was supposed to start with the plants—to learn to identify the two dozen or so most common species. Or three dozen, four dozen. The grasses, the sedges? The mosses, the lichens? What about not just names, but niches? Where is each species most likely to grow—behind a rock, in a bog? And their leaves, their flowers, their stalks—they were always *changing*, one day a shoot and the next in full flower. Botanist Nancy Slack's place-specific *Adirondack Alpine Summits: An Ecological Field Guide*[23] became my most treasured book; I memorized every page and often used it to help hikers who asked me to identify something they'd seen on the trail. But each entry only had one or two photos. How was I supposed to tell what anything was when it wasn't in bloom, or if the leaves were a slightly different shape, or if the hikers hadn't looked all that carefully? ("White petals, or pinkish. Four, maybe five.") All season long, I brought sketches and photographs to my knowledge-able and patient supervisor, trying to figure out what I'd found growing in some odd crevice.

If I thought the plants were bad, though, the *birds*. At least the plants are rooted and relatively still. The birds flit and flutter in and out of the krummholz, swoop low past the summits, sing out glee-fully while staying infuriatingly hidden from sight. Little brown this, little brown that, trills and tweets and raucous garbles. I learned and promptly forgot species in the low-elevation mixed hardwood forest around the Loj—Which is the black-throated green warbler, and which is the black-throated blue? *Zee-zee-zee-zoo-zee* versus *Zoo-zoo-zee*? I spent several days sitting at the trail junction just below the summit of Mt. Marcy with only a Bicknell's thrush for company and still didn't learn its fat profile and ray-gun-like song. Fortunately, I had only a few, distinct species to deal with at the actual mountaintops: white-throated sparrows, with their white throat feathers, yellow eye patches, and optimistic, unmistakable *Old Sam Peabody-Peabody-Peabody* ringing out all day long; white-breasted, slate-gray-backed dark-eyed juncos who show up every day at noon, almost like clockwork, to pick up after people's picnic crumbs; and, unignorable, ravens, who appear on sunny days at two in the afternoon to show off for admiring crowds by soaring on thermals. On rain-drenched days, ravens came to croak at me alone, mocking the silly wet human huddled behind a rock.

Insects? Those have a phenology, just like the flowers. One week, the summits were overrun with twice-stabbed ladybeetles (which look adorable until they nip at exposed skin, scraping off salty sweat); the next, sawflies. (Sawflies, which look a lot like bees or wasps, love two particular erratics atop Algonquin; they swarm anyone who tries to sit there, scaring hikers into thinking they've sat on a hornets' nest.) Ants, on sunny days. (During my third season stewarding, we tried to conduct a survey of ant species, having heard about research on them in other northeastern alpine areas. Turns out that ants are fast, elusive little creatures—we amateurs were fairly inept at collecting them.) White admirals, occasionally; rarely, a luna moth. More types of beetles than I could count. Once a year, a lonely sugar maple borer, with its distinct yellow-and-black Rorschach design. Deer flies at lower elevations, and deer ticks. Black flies always, everywhere, rain or shine, cold or hot, flying in eyes and crawling in ears, leaving rows of angry little welts around the edges of socks and sleeves and along the nape of the neck, seemingly immune to bug spray and more clever than bug nets. "They help pollinate the plants," I told hikers at first, trying to make the best of a bad situation, but soon I gave up. I don't know that black flies serve any useful purpose, except to test people's patience. Anyone who writes of the summertime joys of hiking or boating or pic-nicking in the Adirondacks is deliberately omitting or trying to forget the misery of the black flies.

Beyond the living components, what about the ecological chem-istry, the morphology, the way that water pools in some spots and flows away from others? What conspiracy of wind, sun, snowbank, and soil encourages gentians to thrive in one grove and Labrador tea in another? Why do the soft, white heads of cottongrass bob in one par-ticular bog while another fills with the small pink petals of cranberries, crowberries, and bilberries? I could have crawled over every inch of the summits of Marcy and Algonquin (to some degree, I did) and strived to learn every single plant (as others have, quadrat by quadrat), and still not understood the complex, mysterious web of life in each small area. John K. Wright's observation remains just as true today as it was when he was speaking to fellow geographers in 1947: "Even if an area were to be minutely mapped and studied by an army of microgeographers, much about its geography would always remain unknown, and, hence, if there is no *terra incognita* today in an absolute sense, so also no *terra* is absolutely *cognita*."[24]

On our first training hike up Algonquin, while we were memorizing the names of plants and locating plots for MountainWatch (a long-term phenological research project run by the Appalachian Mountain Club), I remember feeling torn between wanting to learn everything—everything about not just alpine ecology but also the geology, geomorphology, hydrology, ecology, topography, history, sociology, psychology, and phenomenology of the whole mountain range; and the whole park; the whole world—and wanting to just go back to rocks, to focus solely on something I understand, old and solid.

"Do this:" Byrd Baylor urges in *The Other Way to Listen*, "go get to know / one thing / as well / as you can."[25] Focus. Work. Stay put, become part of a community, both human and non-. Find my place and dig in. Do something for wildness. Think like a mountain.

No, Baylor advises, "It should be / something / small / . . . Don't start / with a mountain."[26]

I was going about it all wrong.

On my next day off, I had no desire to labor up another peak. I wanted a long flat walk (that is, only several hundred feet of elevation gain and loss; still bogs, boulders, ladders)—Indian Pass, in the valley west of Algonquin.

Indian Pass was featured in Charles Ingham's famous *The Great Adirondack Pass, Painted on the Spot*—a painting that shaped perceptions of the American ideal of wilderness. Ingham first saw the pass while participating in a geological survey to the then little-known High Peaks region in 1837. Expedition leader Ebenezer Emmons—a geologist and eponym of High Peak Mt. Emmons—invited Ingham along to help record, illustrate, and thus verify their discoveries, just as painter Thomas Moran would join Ferdinand Hayden's geological survey to Yellowstone in 1871. Emmons was eager to explore territory he'd spotted the previous summer while conducting a survey commissioned by state governor William Learned Marcy. From atop Whiteface Mountain, he'd noted "a high peak to the south which appeared to him to be the highest in the state which, as far as was known, had never been climbed."[27] To join him in the 1837 survey/summit quest, Emmons recruited Ingham alongside a team of scientists—including meteorologist William Redfield, eponym of Mt. Redfield—and men relatively familiar with the area terrain, including Archibald McIntyre, Iron Works co-proprietor David Henderson, local guides, and "three unknown woodsmen."[28] As Emmons recorded, the team of about fifteen men "ascended the east branch of the Hudson to its source, which we found to be in a small mountain meadow, 10 or 12 miles northeast from the iron works at McIntyre, at the base of the summit of what finally proved to be the highest point in the group of mountains."[29] On August 5, they climbed that highest summit and named it in honor of the governor who'd sponsored the expedition but who would never so much as glimpse his namesake.

The view from Mt. Marcy must have been spectacular—a sea of trees bluing to the horizon, wholly intact in that era, with logging still much farther southeast and MacIntyre's ironworks the only possible sign of human presence. Instead of recording the grand wilderness or man's triumphant conquest of the state high point, though, Ingham chose to paint *The Great Adirondack Pass* two valleys over from Marcy—a towering cliff below a broken sky, with two tiny, almost unnoticeable human figures insignificant before the vast landscape and literally overshadowed by giant boulders. There's so much drama in the scenery that the people are an afterthought, their shapes and colors catching the eye as out of place. That's the point. The painting exemplifies the Hudson River School aesthetic—storm-filled, staggeringly beautiful images of American wilderness as envisioned and popularized by artists such as Thomas Cole, Asher Durand, and Frederic Edwin Church in the 1830s through the 1880s. In addition to romanticizing the pastoral scenery of the Hudson Valley, the artists celebrated aspects of the sublime—that mix of beauty and terror, awe at forces greater than mankind—they saw in the Catskills, Adirondacks, and, later, the American West, making the case that "the most distinctive, and perhaps the most impressive, characteristic of American scenery is its wildness."[30]

I wanted to experience some of that wildness in the Adirondacks, to get a glimpse of the sublime. Sort of. So I tossed food and water into a pack (no map, compass, or other safety gear—this was just a day hike), strapped on my sandals (yes, sandals; I still hadn't learned that "relatively flat" means something different in the Adirondacks versus everywhere else I was accustomed to hiking), and headed southwest from the Loj up Indian Pass Brook, eager to stand in the same spot as Ingham and be as amazed by the place as he was.

After a couple of hours of plodding through undistinctive woods, hopping across puddles, and slipping on dew-soaked boulders, I was decidedly unenthusiastic. It was humid out. Buggy. Distances kept getting longer: one sign said 2.8 miles to a place called Scotts Clearing, then, a half hour later, another sign told me I'd come 1.4 miles but still had 2.0 miles to the clearing. At least the opening at Scott's Dam—a remnant of late nineteenth-century logging—afforded a bit of a view up the valley and a respite from the close monotony of the trees.

By the time I got to a section of trail that was, thanks to a beaver dam, completely underwater, I was ambivalent about everything Adirondack. On one hand, I was glad that beavers had returned to a habitat from which they'd been nearly extirpated; on the other, what sort of developed "trail" sends me crawling over steep boulders, past snow-filled crevices, and through shin-deep muddy water? Granted, I appreciated having a trail to follow so that I didn't have to bushwhack, navigate, or really care where I was except to wonder how far it truly was to the pass, but mindlessly following a trail is *not* a wilderness experience. Then again, if I wanted a wilderness experience, I was free to wander off into the woods. But I *hate* being in the woods, where I can't see anything of the sky.

Lost in thought and not watching where I was going (not that I could tell where I was going, mid-beaver meadow), I jammed my right little toe on a rock or root and felt a sickening crunch. Shooting pain. Was the place trying to make me pay attention? Or trying to get back at me for not liking it? What did the place know or care about what I thought?

Stupid for wearing sandals, stupid for coming to the Adirondacks, I hate trees and bugs and mountains, my summary of the hike, after I'd limped on to see the semi-impressive views from the Pass's Summit Rock—the steep wall/face of Wallface to the west, radiant hills and valleys rolling out to the south—then hobbled through the beaver meadow, down the boulders, and however many miles back to the Loj.

Typical trails: mossy, muddy, sun-drenched path up Marcy.

That evening, frustrated with the hike (and my swollen, throbbing toe) and eager to get away from the boisterous Trails Crew, I sought my spot of solitude at Heart Lake. Barely acknowledging the soothing landscape, I plunked down on the bench and continued scribbling into my notebook: *What am I doing here? Not just the Adirondacks, the whole darn state? Is there any wildness in the East? Will I be able to get back to Wyoming or Colorado or Alaska—places I belong?*

Mid-rant, a sound echoed across the water and stopped my pen. Three notes—lingering, longing—low, high, low.

A loon.

Self-pity forgotten, I looked up and across the calm water, listened into the silence. Again, the wail.

I stood and limped to the water's edge, then plunged on in, knee deep, the cold numbing my toe. The loon was at the side of the lake opposite the Loj. It dove under, barely sending out ripples—simply disappeared, like it had never been there. Then, after a surprisingly long absence, it popped back up again, fifty yards from where it had been. Loon, no loon, loon.

Not a waterfall; the official trail—"The Slab" on Algonquin.

Again, the wail. How did a single creature make such a sound? It filled the whole lake—the whole valley, even, from the cliffs of Mt. Jo clear across to the slopes of the MacIntyres—with melancholy resonance. I could practically see sonic waves reverberating between the rocks and trees, water and sky; could certainly feel them articulate and echo away some of my anxiety.

Loon, no loon, loon. This time, it popped up in the middle of the reflection of Algonquin Peak, as if it were floating in air, halfway up a mountain. *Algonquin*, I thought, having not just a name for it now, but also a memory of the trail, the view from the summit back down toward Heart Lake. *I've been there*. And would be there again and again. *Wright Peak*, rocky top almost blending into Algonquin; *I'll eventually take the trail up to Wright*, I thought, not knowing that I'd come to enjoy its weather-beaten, wind-scoured perch best of all the stewarded peaks. *Avalanche Pass*, I couldn't see it, but felt the valley there, behind Wright, before Colden. And Marcy, the high, distant dome—I'd be there soon, too. Names, memories, dreams. Maybe, like Black Canyon, it took a little time for this place to work its magic?

Or maybe the first step to thinking like a mountain is to think like a lake. Scholar-poet David Hinton notes that ancient Chinese philosophers "recognized their most essential nature in [dark and mirrored] pools, for they saw empty mind in still water, that dark mirror replacing the arbitrary contingencies of self with an identity expansive as the mountain distances and bottomless skies it mirrors."[31]

For days after that, my notebook entries were filled with loons. *Kayaking in calm water, sharing the lake with loons.* (Also that day: *Caught in a thunderstorm on the way to Marcy Dam, hate not being able to see the sky through the trees.*) Before training: *Woke early, walked around misty lake, in time to hear loons!* That night: *After-dinner kayak. Sunset-shadowed mountains, one puff of pink cloud in a bright blue sky. Some frogs, some birds, two loons!* During training the following day, on the shores of Heart Lake: *Loons taking off, flapping, flapping, around and around, trying to gain enough altitude to get above trees. So graceful in water; so ungainly in flight.* (Ungainly on land, too. The name "loon" comes from *lomr*, an old Scandinavian word for "clumsy."[32]) That night: *To Lake Placid with Trails Crew. Good beer, fun people, but I missed being with the loons.*

Sitting at my bench, the evening before my first hike up Mt. Marcy: *Waiting. For what? To be cold, to be warm. To be tired. To feel alive. To be someplace wild. Ah, there it is. Thank you, loon.*

Although my notes read like all I did was lurk by the shores of Heart Lake listening for waterfowl, that week was dedicated to Leave No Trace (LNT) training. In my years of rambling around and working in wild places, I'd pieced together my own hiking strategies but had never learned the formal set of principles developed and taught by the Center for Outdoor Ethics: Plan Ahead and Prepare; Travel and Camp on Durable Surfaces; Dispose of Waste Properly; Leave What You Find; Minimize Campfire Impacts; Respect Wildlife; and Be Considerate of Other Visitors.[33]

Principles like leaving what you find and respecting wildlife seem self-evident, though I've seen my share of park visitors picking flowers and feeding chipmunks. Admittedly, I'm always tempted to take rocks from USFS and BLM land. *Not* from national parks or wilderness areas and *not* vertebrate fossils, but I have a weakness for smooth, flat river stones that feel just right in my hand.

The notion of staying on durable surfaces—bedrock or the designated trails or campsites—also seems straightforward, but hikers don't always pay attention to where they put their feet. Thus the need for summit stewards, to remind people to please stay off the vegetation.

Planning ahead and preparing are easier said than done. For all of the times that I've given directions to hikers who'd followed the wrong trail or who'd come without a map, for all of the water and medical supplies I've shared with those lacking basic gear, and for all of the people I've seen shivering in t-shirts or racing to get back before dark, I can recall an equal number of occasions where I myself didn't do research beforehand, got lost, or didn't bring proper equipment (say, wore sandals). The DEC can only do so much to inform visitors of area regulations, and ADK staff can only do so much to warn hikers of trail conditions and inclement weather. As I quickly realized and never quite learned, it's easy to underestimate the Adirondacks.

Because I'm more accustomed to traveling through deserts, prairies, and tundra—areas where there's no need for a fire and oftentimes no access to wood—I hadn't thought about backcountry campfires before. They're apparently a traditional part of the Adirondack experience—fires for warmth, for cooking s'mores, to smoke out the bugs. Unfortunately, the quest for a roaring fire can also cause significant damage and pose risk for wildfires. Especially in popular camping spots, where dead and downed material quickly gets burned through, campers sometimes cut wood from live trees. Recognizing the need for more strict environmental protection, the DEC banned campfires outright in the Eastern High Peaks Wilderness in 1999, causing an uproar among longtime visitors who felt their memories of and expectations for backcountry trips were challenged. As with Marcy Dam, I'd never known so never missed them.

I thought I understood how to dispose of waste, but I was surprised to learn the science behind decomposition of different materials. Orange peels can take up to two years to break down; nylon thirty to forty![34] More so, I was appalled to realize what a problem waste—particularly human waste—has become in the Adirondacks and elsewhere. Judging from historic accounts, there's less litter than there used to be;

pistachio shells, apple cores, banana peels, and the corners of granola bar wrappers are now the main annoyances, though a handful of times each summer, someone leaves a soaked sleeping bag or broken tent on the trail, apparently unwilling to carry out what they'd packed in. Levels of human waste are increasing, however. Like all stewards, I found toilet paper "tulips" alongside—and sometimes *in*—the trail every single day, and soon became adept at burying them with a trekking pole. Even more disgustingly, it's not uncommon to find actual feces in the trail corridor. Yes, the hikes are long, there are few facilities along the way (aside from box privies in a few select locations, installed after the DEC granted approval in 2016), and new hikers may not be aware of the guideline to be at least 150 feet from water or campsites,[35] but you'd think people would at least leave the trail for a bit of privacy. And dig a cathole and pack out toilet paper.

After discussing all of the LNT principles, the summit stewards and interns-in-training played an ethics game in which we were given a few scenarios and asked to rank which we felt was most severe: toilet paper versus dog off-leash versus too-large group; vandalized sign versus apple core versus cell phone conversation. Within a few rounds, I realized I was fanatical about "Be[ing] Considerate of Other Visitors." Playing music, blocking the trails, hogging the summit, taking dozens of photos, sending or receiving phone calls or texts, and chatting via FaceTime may leave no biogeophysical impacts, but to me they were the most egregious examples of abuse, ruining others' wilderness experience and, I wanted to argue, preventing the person(s) engaged in them from experiencing the place as well. *Why do people even bother coming to the wilderness if they're not there to absorb its wildness?* I felt myself getting more judgmental as the activity (and the season) (and the subsequent three seasons) progressed. *Not just other visitors—be considerate of the mountains, the forest, the lakes*; wild-deor-ness, *the place of wild beasts.*

Thirty years ago, Edwin Bernbaum already worried, "Without an intimation of its harmonies reverberating around their heights, mountains become heaps of dust and rock—or glorified pieces of gymnastic equipment."[36] Authors and dedicated Franconia Ridge caretakers Laura and Guy Waterman agreed, discussing case after case of people who "treat the mountain world as a personal playground" and who "exhibit a kind of elitist arrogance: . . . [thinking] I'm licensed to act as I please in the wilderness, introduce what intrusions suit my personal agenda."[37] But Guy trusted that "if we all came to the mountains in the spirit of having the peace and health of the wild mountains foremost in our minds, we would do the right things naturally."[38]

I hope he was right. I *really*, truly, deeply hope he was right.

But first, the precondition, a big "if" to ask for: I hope we—*I*—can go to the mountains with the peace and health of the wilderness foremost in our minds.

The final day of training took us to the fog-engulfed summit of White-face—the only High Peak with a road. "Nowhere else is the beauty and vastness of the Adirondack Park so apparent and so easily accessible," brags the company that operates Whiteface's ski area and road; at the summit you'll find "gorgeous views spanning hundreds of miles of wild land" as well as a restaurant and gift shop, stone "castle," and, why not, "an elevator carved deep inside the mountain top itself."[39] Construction of the road, which began in 1929, required the approval of not just then Governor Franklin D. Roosevelt, but that of all New York citizens. To enable people to drive to the top of the fifth-highest mountain in the state, Article XIV of the state constitution had to be amended, allow-ing an exception to that noble if apparently unpracticable "forever kept as wild" clause. When then President Roosevelt returned to dedicate Whiteface Veterans' Memorial Highway in 1935—celebrating how "we have provided one mountain that [people] can go to on four wheels,"[40] as if the state built not just the road, but the entire landform—it was the fiftieth anniversary of the creation of the Adirondack Forest Preserve. To be fair, historians note that, by that point, "most of the land had already been cleared by loggers,"[41] so a formal highway seemed more like a step up from a logging road than a new incision into the forest.

Simultaneously, Roosevelt's "Tree Army"—the Civilian Conserva-tion Corps—was building campgrounds, dams, and twelve-foot-wide "fire roads" on "forever wild" land throughout the Adirondacks.[42] Original 46er and cofounder of the Wilderness Society Bob Marshall lamented the construction, seeing "roads as the biggest threat to wilderness."[43] (What would he think now, when seventy percent of the park is within one mile of a public road or snowmobile trail—not count-ing private snowmobile or ATV routes—and a staggering *ninety-seven*

percent of the park is within three miles of a motor vehicle corridor or
two miles from a motorized water body?[44]) "Think of being able to see
the Adirondacks, all of them, for a dollar!" Roosevelt marveled atop
Whiteface in 1935.

On training day, it was undeniably more comfortable to sit in a
warm, dry vehicle than to have to hike up a cold, wet Whiteface. The
summit was so socked in, I wouldn't have known I was on a mountaintop had I not heard the whine of the van engine on the way up
and smelled the burning brakes on the descent. In fact, the parking lot,
stone gatehouse, and turret of the "castle" made Whiteface feel more
like a resort than part of a forest preserve. The vegetation didn't seem to
mind, though. The plants that weren't paved over were well protected
behind stone walls and guard rails, flourishing thanks to the calcium-
rich cement used to build the structures.

Whiteface hosts an Atmospheric Sciences Research Center (ASRC)
field station, which has been collecting data on atmospheric conditions and pollution since 1961. It's a perfect place for an observatory,
not only because of the road. As a monadnock ("mountain that stands
alone") or inselberg ("island-mountain"), isolated from the rest of the
High Peaks, Whiteface creates its own weather, channeling winds and
catching clouds. "The fact that the summit is very often enveloped
in cloud has made the observatory an attractive place for scientific
research," writes a team of ASRC researchers,[45] one of whom was kind
enough to show us the instruments and describe his research. ASRC's
main focus is on cloud chemistry and acid deposition: tracking trends
in acid rain concentrations over time, identifying relationships with
sulfur dioxide emissions upwind in the industrial Midwest, monitoring
ecological impacts, and gauging effectiveness of air pollution regulations—all significant concerns in the acid-sensitive Adirondacks, where
the anorthosite bedrock can't buffer low-pH precipitation and where
the forests and freshwater ecosystems have been suffering for decades
as a consequence.

While the weather atop Whiteface isn't quite as extreme as that of
New Hampshire's Mt. Washington, site of the self-proclaimed "Worst
Weather in the World," it's similarly severe, thanks to the combination of elevation and exposure. During our tour, I nervously noted that
the previous week's data included a day with wind gusts measuring a

Cirrus sweeping over a sea of forested mountains and ridges, as seen from Algonquin Peak. Cairn the only tether to earth.

hundred miles per hour. We'd been warned that there are hurricane-force winds above tree line every month of the year, but I'm not sure that I'd believed or understood that statistic, just as I'd discounted the trails, the black flies, and the cold. Like Whiteface, the tops of Marcy and Algonquin are frequently in the clouds and are much colder than lower elevations. (On average, temperatures decrease about 3.5°F for every thousand feet of elevation gain—what's referred to as the environmental lapse rate. When air is saturated—precipitating or in a cloud—the moist lapse rate is lower, but the dry rate is 5.4°F for every thousand feet. In other words, when it's a comfortable, sunny sixty degrees at the trailhead, it's in the mid-forties on the summits, not counting the windchill. When it's forty-five degrees and raining at the trailhead, it's quite possibly snowing up top, even in the middle of the summer.)

I ought to have learned my lesson on that wet day on Whiteface, but it took months to know how many extra layers to pack. Even fifty degrees is bone chilling when you're standing still for hours, and there's no such thing as truly waterproof gear after hours of drenching rain.

By August, I carried a wool jacket and snow pants every day. I quickly realized that much of the season would be spent in a cloud. "From an experimental scientific perspective, mountain sites are quite often the ideal locations for many types of cloud related research," ASRC researchers explain,[46] referring to meteorological, ecological, chemical, and other types of biogeophysical research. In becoming a summit steward, I embarked on an unexpected psychological and philosophical study—the phenomenology of clouds. The sensation of mist pooling on exposed skin and seeping through several supposedly waterproof layers. Recognition of cloud particles of different moisture content and composition—fine fog, heavy droplets, full drops, half slush, ice. The feeling of warmth and accompanying hope when sunlight begins to glow through a dense fog, then crushing defeat when the fog again thickens. Hope again, when one's shadow is almost visible, then despair. Hours or days later, pure euphoria at a first glimpse of blue sky. Pure awe at an inversion—gazing out across a blanket of clouds from *above*, as if looking out from an airplane window or bird's eye. The quiet peace of feathered cirrus, the boredom of flat altostratus, the intrigue of roiling asperitas; a years-long yearning to see Kelvin–Helmholtz waves. The endless joy of ever changing layers. To stand on a mountain is to stand in the sky.

CHAPTER 10

Skylight

For my first day of official stewarding, mid-June, I was stationed on Mt. Marcy. I woke early to rain pattering on the yurt; forecasts called for storms all week. After finishing packing—Enough food? Enough layers? Sketchbook, camera, map, plant book?—I headed to the Loj to eat a quick breakfast and meet my supervisor, who was helping to guide me up and settle in. A little before seven, we donned rain gear, shouldered packs, staggered over to the trailhead, and radioed to let the DEC dispatcher know that we were on duty. I used the well-worn and already familiar first two miles to Marcy Dam to warm up and get accustomed to the weight of my very full pack. (Why had I brought fresh apples? Extra weight.) New territory after we turned toward Phelps Brook, a gradual rise over smoothed boulders and across tippy wooden planks, then relentlessly up for a full Mt. Jo unit. (Oh, those trekking poles; I was always particularly grateful for them through this stretch.) My supervisor paused to let me appreciate the view from Indian Falls—ripples of dense, dark forest rising up the slopes of the MacIntyre Range, summits lost in mist—before resuming the ascent. Five and a half miles in, we reached the "corkscrew"—a section of particularly steep, twisting trail. Having not yet learned the choreography—exactly which boulders to step on and where; how to position the trekking poles; where to rest for a second—I found the going agonizingly slow and demanding, requiring both willpower (to continue hiking up) and concentration (to not twist an ankle in the process). "Does it ever get any easier?" I gasped, legs and lungs burning. "Not really," my supervisor's reply, "but it gets more familiar."

Past the corkscrew, we were rewarded with a flattish half mile through boreal forest—spindly gray-green spruce draped with old man's beard lichen. Through a slight opening in the tree canopy past

the junction with the Hopkins Trail, which connects to another popular trailhead in Johns Brook Valley, I would have had my first glimpse
of Marcy's summit, according to my supervisor. I had to take her word
for it, though: all cloud. A wet section and a few steep boulders later,
we reached Marcy Plateau—the site of a former lean-to, removed in the
1990s owing to the sensitivity of the high-elevation ecosystem, and a
flat patch that supposedly afforded a full view of the mountain. Still all
mist. More puddles and scrambles to the junction with the Phelps Trail,
which heads toward Mt. Haystack—the state's third-highest peak—or
down into Johns Brook. We turned right and, finally: tree line!

We paused to calibrate the weather. If it's too cold or windy, and
especially if there's a threat of thunderstorms, it's safer to stay at that
final trail junction, somewhat sheltered by trees. It's also tremendously
boring. I spent many a "junction day" with nothing to do but pace in
small circles, watch rain drip off my poncho, sing every song I know, or
ration M&Ms, hours punctuated only by the arrival of hikers and the
trills of thrushes. I once spent an entire afternoon at the Wright-Algon-
quin junction watching a slug ooze across a rock. Preferable, on Marcy,
to go up to the first section of bare rock, rising just far enough out of
the krummholz to afford a view, should the rain stop and clouds thin.
Even more preferable, to make it to the bump after that—slightly more
exposed, but tucked next to a lovely subalpine bog. Of course, once
you're that far, might as well head up the next slab, do some trail work,
and study the plants in the first big patch of arctic-alpine vegetation.
Above that, there's a nice sheltered chimney, or, better yet, it's not far
to the very top—past a lush meadow (roped off, with numerous signs
asking people to please not walk through the sensitive vegetation), to
the north-facing side of the summit rock (which boasts a large bronze
plaque, affixed in 1937 to commemorate the hundred-year anniversary
of the first ascent), and the summit itself.

That's where my supervisor and I found ourselves. We tapped the
top (no benchmark on Marcy—someone went to the tremendous and
illegal trouble to chip it off), then tucked behind an erratic that afforded
the most shelter. First things first: we put on extra layers. By that point,
the rain had begun to slow and the cloud ceiling seemed to be lifting.
Yes, there was Colden, the next ridge over to the west, growing more
solid. And the MacIntyres behind it: the top of Algonquin still chopped

off, but Iroquois emerging to its left and Wright to the right, striped with slides. They looked so different from this vantage—I had to relearn and rethink their profiles, triangulate them with what I'd seen from Jo and Cascade. Summit by summit, more consciously than I ever had before, I was weaving a sense of place, adding new strands with each new view. Was *this* what forty-sixers sought or found—a web of connections, trails and summits, across the High Peaks?

More new views, new names to learn. We turned east, windward—Panther Gorge two thousand feet straight down, the sound of Panther Brook audible all the way up from the bottom; on the other side of it, Haystack, looking remarkably like a rough pile of rocky hay tangled in mist. The distant silvery gleam to the south? Boreas Ponds. And that unassuming bulge next door? Skylight, the fourth-highest peak, boasting a small, isolated patch of alpine vegetation.

Skylight—I remember reciting after my supervisor, sensing that there was something different about it. Sleeping in the heart of the High Peaks Wilderness, Skylight is overlooked in comparison with its superlatively tall neighbor, and for that reason it is much less visited, more wild. Even the name is magical—Skylight, a portal to the heavens.

I could have spent all afternoon learning the names of peaks and especially observing how patiently and persistently my supervisor welcomed hikers to the summit and informed them of the need to stay on durable rock surfaces. But the radio crackled to life: thunderstorm warning, wind gusting to fifty miles per hour, possible hail. What we'd taken to be improving conditions was just the lull before the storm. Even as we watched, a wall of black clouds swallowed Iroquois, then Algonquin. With the faintest of sky rumbles, it was time to leave the summit. And to convince arriving hikers that they probably didn't want to be the tallest things in the state when there was lightning in the vicinity.

My supervisor had hiked all the way up specifically to help orient me. Once she felt that I was comfortable and capable on my own, she left for the Loj, leaving me at the junction to eat a soggy lunch and talk to a few more hikers, advising them of the storm and then asking them to please not to step on the vegetation when they opted to continue hiking anyway. After an hour, the thunder stopped and a bit of sunlight began to break through, so I headed back up, hoping that I might be able to spend the afternoon on the summit after all. I made it to the second exposed outcrop before I saw dark curtains of precipitation—what turned out to be hail—dousing the MacIntyres. Back to the junction. Twice more, I bobbed up and down, alternately aiming for sun-shining ledges and racing storms back to shelter, regularly getting blown off balance en route. I ought to have been exhausted by the hiking and discouraged by the weather, but it was absolutely exhilarating—the wind, the rain, the rock. Channeling *uitwaaien*, a Dutch word meaning "to walk in the wind not for self-improvement but for the sheer fun of it."[1]

By midafternoon, I had the mountain to myself. The first bout of thunder must have deterred any hikers who'd set off midmorning. (That proved to be atypical. I'd learn to expect people to show up no matter the conditions or circumstances. Especially on Marcy—if visitors made plans to climb the state high point, well then, they were going to climb the state high point.) Although I was grateful for the solitude, the notion of staying put was odd. Every other time in my life that I'd climbed a peak or prominence, I hadn't lingered for more than an hour at the top—what is there to do other than eat snacks and look at the view? What if there is no view? Was this really going to be my job all summer—to hike up a mountain each morning, then stay there *all day*, busy or not, cold or less cold, sun or rain or fog, almost always wind? Even more so, would I get paid just to stand at a trail junction, alone in the woods, seven miles from civilization, with trees swaying and hail falling and clouds racing overhead? Weren't there cairns to build or plants to measure or fossils to find? (No fossils.) Forced meditation.

One last window of sunshine, late afternoon. I dashed up to the summit and stood alone atop the state, looking out over a landscape whose rises, ridges, and hollows were full of secrets. Light glowed across the treetops, glinted off lakes, and set the summit rock steaming. In its wake, long purple-blue shadows stretched away from every bump and pooled in every valley. From that vantage, I was sure I could see not only all six million acres of Adirondack Park, but also the curvature of the earth. The Green Mountains to the east. Montreal to the north, New York City to the south. (Rain falling on the south side of Marcy flows into Lake Tear of the Clouds, then Opalescent and Feldspar

Clouds flowing and breaking around the High Peaks, as seen from the summit of Marcy.
Colden and, behind it, Algonquin, trying to surface. "All I can see is the dragon-form way
earth tips up and churns into heaven here in these mountains, and how heaven seethes
down to mingle all windblown mist and sky breathing through earth" (Hinton 2012, 144).

Brooks; from there, the Hudson River. It reaches NYC in about two weeks.) And to the west? Beyond the Western High Peaks, Cranberry Lake, Five Ponds; Lake Ontario, Toronto, Chicago, the northern Great Plains. Wyoming was out there, and Colorado. The emptiness of Black Canyon, the mass of Denali.

In that moment, on that mountain, I wasn't wishing myself elsewhere. I could see the sky again. I was *in* the sky. *MARCY*, the summit plaque reads, *also known by the Indian name TAHAWUS, meaning CLOUD-SPLITTER.*

White-throated sparrow, singing its heart out.

Not only was Marcy never called "Cloud-splitter" by native Haudenosaunee or Algonquin peoples, but "TAH-A-WUS" itself was, according to Adirondack historian Alfred Donaldson, "probably invented or first applied [in 1837] by Charles Fenno Haufmann, the versatile Indian scholar, who devised and compounded many another Indian name to meet the whims of his poetic fancies."[2] Late nineteenth- and early twentieth-century Romanticism (and guilt for mistreatment of Native Americans) made "Tahawus" stick. "Names in exchange for land, wild game and a way of life," scholar Sandra Weber chides the poets and plaque makers who promoted its use. "And who cares if they are authentic names so long as they are pretty names?"[3] Cloud-splitter. Cloud-snooper. Cloud-seeker. Mount Sky.

Skylight Peak, the next day. It rained again overnight—torrents that I feared would wash away my tent. (When stationed on Marcy, stewards camp to cut down on the hiking. Full fifteen-mile-long, three-thousand-foot-high treks five days in a row would be impossibly grueling.) Upon waking to overcast skies, I resigned myself to more cold drizzle and began trudging up the trail, even more slowly than the day before, euphoria wearing off. Brook, falls, corkscrew. Good god, was I going to have to go back up this again the next day? Hopkins, Plateau, Phelps. Finally out of the trees, but locked in thick fog again.

Not much wind, nor rain; just mist, drifting quietly through the krummholz. I paused at the first outcrop—no views, but sounds were oddly magnified. I could hear water trickling, sparrows singing (did they ever stop?). My own breathing, my own heartbeat. On to the second exposed area, navigating carefully up lichen-slippery slabs, still learning where to place my feet and poles. Then, unexpectedly, with what I swear was an audible "poof," I popped out of the clouds onto a sky island, sandwiched between a low sea of stratocumulus and a thick, slightly higher blanket of altostratus. The final few hundred feet of Marcy rose above me, looking fierce and craggy, as if fully intending to rip the sky to shreds. To the west, Algonquin was the only other piece of earth visible, plowing through the stratocumulus like a giant anorthosite ocean liner. That was it—two mountaintops, two layers of cloud, and me. All the components of classical Chinese wilderness paintings, poetry, and philosophy: "The pregnant emptiness of Absence in the form of mist and sky . . . the mountains-and-rivers landscape of Presence emerging out of this emptiness and hovering there, on the verge of vanishing back into it; and, finally, within that cosmological process, the human."[4]

I was scheduled to go to Skylight that morning to become acquainted with the trails and to see how the vegetation had fared through the winter, but I didn't want to leave Marcy's summit. Doing so would require descending back into that mundane, mortal world of trees and mist; I wanted to stay above the clouds forever. "No one knows this / mountain I inhabit," I was beginning to see the appeal of mountain sitting, as expressed by poet Han Shan (whose name translates to Cold Mountain), "deep in white clouds, / forever empty, silent."[5]

Work, though. I was there for a job, not enlightenment. After soaking in the panorama, I carefully picked my way down Marcy's steeper, more exposed south face, navigating cairn by oddly shaped cairn once I was back in the mist. The trail led into the forest, then to a junction—Four Corners—with a battered yellow-lettering-on-brown-paint DEC sign pointing left to Panther Gorge, right to Lake Tear of the Clouds, back to Marcy, or straight to Skylight.

Straight! A short climb later, I was above tree line again, mist beginning to thin. Immediately, I recognized that the alpine zone on Skylight was different than any others I had experienced or would come to know. Algonquin boasts a great meadow, Marcy a wide dome. Wright is a wind-whipped fin, Cascade a bald patch, Haystack an exposed ridge, Iroquois the edge of the world. Colden, Gothics, Giant, Whiteface—each have their own character. *Skylight*, though. It's not just the name or the summit itself: the alpine zone is relatively small, and the view isn't any more aesthetically pleasing than other peaks', especially since I couldn't see most of it at first. Sure, an original bronze survey marker from the 1870s is still present and readable, a century and a half after intrepid Adirondack surveyor and champion of preservation Verplanck Colvin hammered it in. And yes, there was, at that time, a giant pile of rocks on the summit, growing courtesy of hikers who believed a superstition that they'd have good weather if they added to it. But those features shouldn't make Skylight any more unique than, say, Wright with its wreckage of an airplane, or Gothics with its cables for hikers to hold on to. Skylight's just special, if not surreal.

Perhaps I feel that way because my first impression was of pure solitude, pure silence: mist dissipating, altostratus breaking, a strip of blue blazing on the horizon. Unlike every other alpine peak in the Adirondacks (discounting wooded summits, from which nothing is visible anyway), there's not a hint of civilization from atop Skylight—no cities, no roads, no titanium mine tailings, no ski jumps. Just mountains and valleys, valleys and more mountains; lakes shimmering in the dark forest. The mass of Marcy looms to the north, all barren and weather-beaten rock, looking every part the high point. Haystack's crags sit lower to the right, the serrated fins of Basin behind. Colden and the MacIntyres stretch to the left, blending into western ranges. A full sky arcs over it all, wider and wilder than the sky over any other summit. Such serenity, such surety; a hint of the numinous.

I felt the same charm when I returned to Skylight the next year. Perhaps the magic continued because I went for sunrise on summer solstice, arriving by headlamp in time to watch pastel peaks emerge from the darkness. Again during my third season, also for solstice sunrise, I had the fresh, bright world all to myself. The spell soured by my fourth season, however, on a windy visit, midafternoon in mid-July, when two other hikers showed up and broke the illusion of solitude. The final time I hiked Skylight—a quick dash up at the end of my final week stewarding on Marcy, still my fourth season in the Adirondacks, a brilliantly sunny Sunday, trails packed everywhere else, but no one on Skylight—I could still sense its magic, despite the monster rock pile spilling out onto the tundra and the plants looking decidedly worse for the wear. Though increasingly weak and fragile, with more and more peak baggers tagging its top and adding a rock to the pile, a heart of wildness still beat in that peak.

Back to my first season, though: once the sun began to break through—crepuscular rays corroborating Skylight's name—it was there for good. As light flooded the forest, I marveled that such a place existed in New York. If I'd thought more deeply about it, I'd have felt gratitude for Colvin and Marshall and Schaefer and all those who'd fought to keep it forever wild. But I was thinking only of myself. *Maybe, just maybe, Adirondacks*, I whispered, not quite articulating. *Maybe I'm starting to like you.*

Giddy with possibility, I danced down to Four Corners, then made a quick dash to Lake Tear of the Clouds, which also seemed particu-larly magnificent, the top of Marcy reflected in its rush-lined water. "A minute, unpretending tear of the clouds," Colvin had aptly character-ized and christened it in 1872,[6] making a case that the state needed to protect it and the surrounding forest, as the headwaters to the Hudson River. After the lung-busting, muscle-burning, wholly exhilarating

Solstice on Skylight.

climb back up Marcy's south face—bare anorthosite, resembling the High Sierra more than the High Peaks—I was greeted at the top by a co-steward and about a dozen visitors. From then on, Marcy was bustling—a nonstop stream of hikers asking directions, eating lunch, getting their photographs taken. Friendly people, all excited to have achieved the state high point, all glad that the weather had cleared, all amazed and appreciative to be greeted by summit stewards. As would prove typical, most thought we were there to answer questions and offer assistance to people, not to protect plants.

Had I been plunged straight into the noise and bustle of Marcy on a typical day, when upward of two hundred visitors show up, making the summit feel more like a roadside overlook than the middle of a wilderness area, my impression of the Adirondacks would have been one of overuse and exhaustion. Trampled, trammeled peak-bagger trophies jutting out of second-growth forest. Every little lake, brook, and bump known, named, conquered, Instagrammed. I wouldn't ever have believed that any wildness was left in the High Peaks.

But I'd had that morning's mist and the previous day's rain—an invaluable first few hours alone with the mountains and clouds. Skylight. A possibility for place attachment if not place identity.

It should have been the perfect job. I was paid to hike every day and sit on a mountain! To build cairns, to measure plants, to talk to ravens. To watch clouds rise, sweep, and break on by. Of course there were highs and lows, psychological and topographic. For every spectacular inversion or sudden storm, there were days of mud, wind, rain, biting bugs, uncooperative hikers, and those trails with their mix of torture and monotony—the same rocks, the same trees; little of interest until I reached tree line. "Dripping with sweat," I wrote of a mid-June hike up Wright, the shortest of our assigned peaks, "and crawling with black flies. This is awful." A string of journal entries from late June—what I was told was an especially cold, wet month—detail some of the low points. "Huddled behind rocks, cairns, and ledges all day, trying to stay out of the wind and rain and feeling sorry for myself." "Wind kept blowing, rain kept falling. Up to the summit. Where else to go?" "Sun and mist and drizzle, alternately getting soaked and drying off. Beautiful, but what does it matter?" By July, just "So tired, etc." August: "Not my place. My whole soul is dragging. Need to get back to the plains . . . Dusty, desperate edge of something." The more I wondered why so many people love the Adirondacks and tried to force myself to like them, too, the more I couldn't help but focus on the discomforts and disappointments, like being told not to think of an elephant and subsequently finding it impossible not to envision herds of them thundering through my savanna of a mind.

Grueling hikes and unforgiving weather notwithstanding, the hardest part was trying to stay patient with people. The vast majority of hikers were kind, especially on blue-sky days or once they'd made it successfully to summit. They shared snacks and stories, were curious about my job, and happy to share their stories with me in return. They listened politely and sometimes even with interest to my overview of the rareness and fragility of the arctic-alpine ecosystem, and for the most part agreed to abide by DEC regulations—dogs on leash; no camping above thirty-five hundred feet; day groups fewer than fifteen people. Except for one French-Canadian couple who flat-out refused to leave a patch of alpine vegetation on the leeward side of Algonquin on a chilly, windy August afternoon—their reasoning, word for word: "We're cold . . . people are more important than plants"—no one seemed to knowingly want to damage the trails or mountaintops.

While there were several first-time hikers, especially on Cascade and Marcy, many people had been coming to the Adirondacks for years—families, forty-sixers, those for whom "forever wild" is an essential part of their identity. I witnessed dozens of marriage proposals and one actual wedding—priest, bridal party, and all. Every now and then, someone would ask if they could scatter the ashes of a parent, sibling, spouse, or friend, explaining, "this was his/her favorite place in the world." There were people who'd been planning their trip for years, people who'd come on a whim, and hikers who'd gotten turned around and showed up on the wrong mountain. Hikers running, wearing kilts, walking barefoot, carrying cats. Big dogs, little dogs; dogs running circles around their owners, dogs that had to be carried all the way down. Kids bouncing with excitement and kids who decidedly did *not* want to hike a foot farther. Parents carrying babies and grandchildren leading grandparents. Boyfriends/girlfriends eager to introduce their significant other to the world of hiking and boyfriends/girlfriends upset that their significant other had dragged them up the steep, muddy side of a mountain. Camp groups, church groups, Facebook groups. There were singers, flutists, trumpeters, mandolinists, bagpipers, and one tubaist who lugged his instrument all the way up Marcy. (As if bagpipes weren't impressive enough!)

Upon arriving on the summit, people whooped, high-fived, sang choruses, flew kites, did handstands, blew bubbles, lit cigars, took selfie after selfie after selfie. Guzzled water, Gatorade, coffee, hot cocoa, beer, whiskey, champagne. Devoured candy bars, gorp, sandwiches, pretzels, crackers and cheese, noodle soup, subs, leftover pizza, an entire watermelon. Yes, sometimes tromped across or tried picnicking in the vegetation. Tucked out of the wind. Leaned into the wind. Yelled "Halloo!" into the mist. Stared at their smartphones.

An odd and interesting slice of society—thousands of people who share the desire, or at least the willingness, to clamber up a High Peak, though they may have little else in common. Young and old, clueless and overprepared, showing off brand-new Arc'teryx and sporting patched-up old flannels, physically fit and far less so. "Despite the hardship and fear encountered on the heights, people return again and again," mountain scholar Edwin Bernbaum writes. "Religious pilgrims are drawn to a power or presence they sense in a peak; tourists come to gaze on splendid views; trekkers return to wander in a realm set apart from the everyday world."[7]

Asked why they visit the Adirondacks, visitors are remarkably consistent: to "experience natural environment and scenic beauty," to "experience an environment free of litter and human waste and impacts," to "enjoy physical activity, challenge, and exercise," and to "feel a connection with wilderness and wild forests as important places" are common responses.[8] Based on decades of research on sense of place in the Adirondacks, Chad Dawson—an expert who literally wrote the book on *Wilderness Management*—identified "eight dimensions of wilderness experiences," ranked in order of importance to visitors: Natural Environment, Personal and Social Experiences, Physical Activity, Exploration and Remoteness, Solitude, Connections with Nature, Remote Travel Skills, and Connection with Other Wilderness Users and Inspiration.[9]

The Adirondacks are apparently living up to expectations. In a 2008-11 study of visitors to forest preserve lands, ninety-four percent of survey respondents felt satisfied or very satisfied with their experience, and the same percentage said they're likely to return for another trip, though earlier surveys indicated that visitors were less pleased with the amount of litter, lack of information, and number of other users in wilderness areas.[10] Moreover, people return again and again: in a 2002 study, nearly sixty percent of those who had previously visited the High Peaks Wilderness reported returning to that specific unit several times a year.[11] Depending on the survey, only one to seven percent are first-time visitors to the park as a whole, versus seventy percent in Black Canyon and eighty percent in Denali.[12]

Participants in a study on sense of place identified the characteristics that most influence their attachment to special locations in the High Peaks: "exceptional beauty" and "wilderness."[13] While nearly half of those surveyed believed that the "place is part of my personal identity," more than a quarter said that it was not important whether or not a "place has spiritual meaning." Instead, their emotional ties were based on feeling "refreshed/restored," "relaxed," and experiencing "serenity/ peace" or "wonderment."[14]

Interestingly, "of the . . . respondents who experienced place attachment to a particular locale [in the High Peaks]," one researcher found that "nearly three quarters . . . felt there was a suitable substitute for their special place."[15] An important distinction: place *dependence* is a "functional attachment to a particular setting"[16]—a "form of attachment associated with the potential of a particular place to satisfy the needs and goals of an individual."[17] This means that some people feel a sense of accomplishment when they complete steep, rocky trails, or paddle out to remote, forested isles, or sit by the shores of a calm lake to sip coffee and watch mist swirl. They love the Adirondacks because it's a place where they can pursue these goals. Take them to the White Mountains or the Boundary Waters Canoe Area, and they might feel similarly fulfilled. That deeper place *identity*, meanwhile, is "the symbolic meaning a particular place has to an individual"[18]—"a means of creating and maintaining one's self" or "source of self-definition" centered on a specific location.[19] Mt. Marcy, Skylight, Heart Lake, no substitutes.

The concepts aren't mutually exclusive. Hikers seeking to climb all forty-six peaks may both pursue a personal goal and find their sense of self wrapped up in the mountains they climb. Mountaineers might long for "the physical and emotional satisfaction of accomplishment" as well as the feelings of "immers[ion] and intima[cy] with the natural world, [being] a part of nature itself rather than a passive passenger over its surface."[20] "Affective relationships with parks and wilderness areas are a potent source of self-definition on personal, biological, and national levels," researchers proclaim.[21] All the people out on those mountaintops have their reasons for being there: the father who dragged his kid up Cascade through sideways-falling rain pellets one awful day; the child who was crying and clinging to his father while rain pummeled down on us. The woman who fell and broke her wrist on the way up to Marcy, then continued to the top anyway; the group of friends who were so intent on hiking Marcy that they wouldn't turn around when one of them broke her wrist. The Meet-Up group from New York City bent on running the Great Range. The man who brought his friend's ashes to Algonquin, thirty years to the day after they'd climbed it together. Dozens of volunteer summit stewards who instead of hiking for fun dedicate full days to standing on a single mountaintop, talking to hundreds of hikers about the vegetation and the general joys of the Adirondacks. Retired DEC Ranger Pete Fish—famous for having summited Marcy 777 times—who showed up on Cascade one busy afternoon wearing a kilt and a huge smile. They all have their reasons for coming to this place. "Something [in the Adirondacks] grabbed a hold of him more than 50 years ago and never let go," a reporter wrote in an article on Fish. "He likes open summits, the islands of rock in the High Peaks that, as he put it, 'make you feel like you're on a mountain.' "[22] (Perhaps Fish put it best. Asked " 'What brought you to the Adirondacks?' ", he answered with a twinkle: " 'A car.' "[23])

And me? Midway through my quest to think like a mountain, what was I seeking, what did I find? Sure, I wanted to see some "natural environment and scenic beauty," to engage in physical activity and develop remote travel skills.[24] I *wanted* the place to have "spiritual meaning"[25] and, better yet, to become "part of my personal identity."[26] I wanted what Ketchledge promised—"when you finally reach the summit, you have arrived at a totally different world from that in which you started . . . You [will be] in a 'new place,' having conquered the mountain."[27] Yes, Bernbaum, I was "seeking an experience of spiritual awakening"; I longed "to glimpse a vision of transcendent power and mystery," "to experience the world anew," to "transcend . . . the earth and touch . . . the sky."[28]

But there was a mundaneness to it all. The bugs. The rain. The mud-splashed and boulder-strewn trails. The crowds, endless crowds. One hundred people. Two hundred people. Three. Midday on Mt. Marcy and all day on Cascade, fifty people would arrive on the summit simultaneously and sprawl out, sending me racing from corner to corner, frenetically trying to speak to everyone and protect the poor fragile plants. "Oh, *these* plants?" people would ask when I pointed at the signs asking them to please stay off the very vegetation they were sitting on or standing in. Even the clouds—my favorite part of the job, watching the clouds gather and drift, roil and dissipate—left me feeling unsettled and dissatisfied. Couldn't anything in this place just sit still for a second, quiet down, let me hold time like a rock in my hand?

Mid-July: Rain and rain and rain. I woke on my final day of another week on Marcy very much not wanting to hike up a mountain. The scenario from the original interview taunted me—"Say you've been out in the woods for four days and it's been raining the whole time." It was no longer a hypothetical. Sigh. I pulled on my wet socks, scraped slugs off my thermos, and set out. As forewarned, the hike wasn't any easier, but it was more familiar. By this point, I knew how to trekking-pole-vault the puddles and scramble up the slick spots. And, as expected, the already soggy raingear quickly soaked through.

Aside from the wind shaking drops off branches, though, conditions weren't all that bad in the forest; the trees buffered the weather. I really shouldn't have gone above tree line. I *knew* I shouldn't go above tree line. Needed to learn to meditate through junction days. But when I reached the trail sign pointing out the final turn to the summit, I continued up into the krummholz. No longer blocked by the trees, the wind scoured raindrops across stones and sent me reeling. First outcrop, second; cairn, cairn, cairn. If I hadn't had the trail memorized, I would have had trouble navigating through the wind and fog, and still struggled and lurched with the gusts. How easy it would have been to get disoriented. How simple, to slip off a ledge.

When I made it to the summit (I *knew* I shouldn't go all the way to the summit), I snuggled in below the plaque. I just wanted to get out of the wind for a bit. Then, I'd change out of my wet clothes and put on extra layers. Maybe do some trail work. As soon as I stopped moving, though, I lost all motivation. It was cold—low fifties, maybe? Forties? I *knew* I should change, eat something, drink some hot tea, but that all seemed so arduous. It was easier to curl into a ball and shiver. For a while, I felt sorry for myself, then angry at myself, then angry at the mountains, then ashamed of myself. I was getting dizzy, nauseous. I tried to focus my attention on the bedrock—the only thing I could see, the only thing I knew—and recited *plagioclase*, *labradorite*, until my mind lost the words for the minerals and I stopped shivering.

At some point, two figures loomed out of the mist—botany stewards who were spending the summer gathering data to continue Ketchledge's research. The only other people who were dedicated and crazy enough to be up there on a day like that. They too had taken wilderness first aid training and recognized symptoms of hypothermia more objectively than I did. Somehow, they managed to talk me into leaving the summit, then patiently waited as I slowly uncurled and accompanied me as I began stumbling down the mountain, numb feet barely connecting to my slushy brain.

Once again, I'd discounted the wildness and underestimated the power of natural processes in these peaks. Would I ever learn humility here? Respect? Was I stubbornly closed to whatever it is these mountains could teach me?

End of July, also on Marcy: I woke to rare, precious sunshine. Same old oatmeal and awful instant coffee for breakfast, but they tasted so much better in the bright, gentle warmth. The hike up was enchanting: moss steaming, lichen dripping, shafts of sunlight cutting in. Above tree line, mist breathed up from the endless green forest to join fleece-white cumulus bobbing by. No black flies?! For such beautiful weather, the summit was remarkably quiet, with a slow but steady stream of visitors, including a group of friends on an annual Adirondack hike who'd only intended to climb Phelps but missed the turn, so decided to just keep hiking—an extra seven miles and thousand feet of elevation. Right on schedule, juncos at noon, begging for lunch scraps, and ravens at two, soaring on thermals, the show-offs. Then hikers and birds all left, and I had the top of the state all to myself.

Buoyed by the lovely day, I decided to try a different, longer route back to the Loj, swinging around to see Lake Arnold—a pool nestled between Marcy and Colden where, rumor had it, there were bright little carnivorous plants called sundews. Feeling strong and eager, I headed down the south side of Marcy—decidedly my favorite stretch in the park, with its exposed bedrock and view out across millions of forested acres, speckled with shadow under a mackerel sky and shimmering blue in the afternoon light. Past Lake Tear of the Clouds—that minute, unpretending gem, my heart glowed with fondness. The descent down Feldspar Brook was steeper than I'd expected. Although trying to move carefully, I also had to hurry to make it back in time to radio in to the DEC. I sped through an obstacle course of bog "bridges" at the Feldspar lean-to—actually just floating logs, precariously unmoored from their bases—faster than I would have liked, then dashed up muddy pitches toward Colden, heart pounding, faster, faster, barely acknowledging the loveliness of the lichen-draped forest as I raced through. More bog bridges. Another descent down a creek bed. Just as I was beginning to marvel at just how far this lake must be from the rest of the world, I encountered a junction sign—Lake Arnold, half a mile back. In my haste, I'd completely missed it, blown by what I was looking for. Even after so much mountain sitting and mountain watching, I'd not learned anything about patience from the old, imperturbable peaks.

Mid-August: For my final weekend, I aimed to climb the Trap Dike on Mt. Colden—Class IV scrambling up a narrow intrusion of gabbro weathered into a steep cleft between even steeper walls of anorthosite above Avalanche Lake, then up an exposed landslide scar to the summit. Although this now seems to have become the most popular route up Colden (to the great consternation of DEC rangers, who keep getting called out to rescue stranded or injured parties), at that time, the slide was fairly fresh—created courtesy of Hurricane Irene—and the newly scoured dike relatively unclimbed. Guidebooks hadn't yet been updated, and only a couple of websites hosted trip reports that told readers to bring a rope, wear a helmet, bear left to get onto the slide, and not go unless the weather's perfect. (The crux of the climb is at a high chute two-thirds of the way up the dike, whose vertical face is slippery under best conditions and much riskier when gushing with a waterfall.) Also, don't go alone. But what else was I supposed to do? The slide and Trap Dike had been taunting me all summer—a long, bright stripe falling down into a deep, steep gash; a last opportunity to find adventure in the Adirondacks.

Early on the sunny midweek morning, I followed the by then familiar trail up to and around Avalanche Lake, chatting politely with a dozen other hikers en route. "You're climbing *that*?" A father and son duo asked me, looking warily across the lake to the near-vertical dike, still dark in morning shadow. "Alone? Do you have a rope and climbing shoes?" I was wearing my usual L.L. Bean duck boots. "That doesn't seem very safe," they tried to talk me out of it. Even after I turned off the marked trail and began skirting the lakeshore around to the base of the dike, I could still hear others' voices echoing through the valley. Before I started the climb—admittedly, with a healthy dose of fear, though without changing out of my Bean boots—I looked back across the lake, only to see the father and son sitting on a rock, watching and presumably waiting to call the rangers to rescue me or retrieve my body when I fell. Annoyed and insistent on proving them wrong, I flew up the dike. Even the waterfall, which ought to have given me pause, was just another chance to prove to those hikers (and to myself) that I could do anything that the Adirondacks threw at me. Thankfully, I was out of sight of the lakeshore at the spot where I had to figure out how to transition from the dike onto the slide—I went too far, then chose a route without any foresight, so spent a few long minutes clinging to tiny foot and handholds, unsure how to go up, down, sideways, or anywhere in between.

The slide itself was the closest I came to exhilaration—a long, steep walk up bright, gritty rock, pausing every now and then to look back at the expansive views. Still a touch of trepidation (oddly, I kept thinking to myself, *don't drop your water bottle*, worried that I might send it careening thousands of feet down into Avalanche Lake) and a lot of leg-burning, heart-pounding effort, but that enhanced the feeling of flow. *Just me, free to climb*, my record of the day's conquest, undermined by the realization that that's all it had become—something to check off a list. *Back* [to the Loj] *in time for lunch*.

That afternoon, unable to sit still, I strolled out to Marcy Dam, crossing paths with several returning day hikers who saw me heading out into the woods at four in the afternoon, wearing sandals and carrying no gear, and thus commented on the late hour and my inappropriate footwear. I stood at the edge of the former dam and stared at Mt. Colden—the bright streak of the slide that I'd climbed just a few hours earlier. A few clouds floated through the pastel sky, their shadows undulating across the forest below, emphasizing the relief between Colden and the shoulder of Wright. Although the water in the former Marcy Pond was low, there was enough there to reflect the scene, slight ripples blurring the lines between mountains and clouds.

I didn't understand. The scene had color, texture, movement—all the basics of aesthetics—why couldn't I see the beauty? And the place offered challenge, adventure, joy, even solitude, if one planned and worked for it hard enough—why couldn't I find the meaning? *So many* people love the Adirondacks—why, even after three months rich with plant stewarding and mountain sitting, couldn't I?

View east from Algonquin: Lake Colden in the lower right, with Mt. Colden rising up to the left, full of landslide scars, the brightest stripe falling into the Trap Dike. Unseen behind the dark, forested rise (Avalanche Mountain): steep-walled Avalanche Pass. Marcy the high dome in the background, low ridge of Gray and lump of Skylight immediately to the right. Redfield and Cliff behind Lake Colden, blending in with the sunlight and shadows.

Mid-August: My last day on Algonquin, for what I thought was forever. Of course, the summit was obscured by clouds, and it began raining as I scaled The Slab. No point in bothering to put on waterproof gear at that point; I waited to put on dry layers until I reached the top and could tuck under the only erratic that affords any shelter. Perfect timing: the mist parted momentarily, revealing views of mountains wrapped in sky—delicate sleeves of fog below the summit and thick waves of steel above. One tantalizing glimpse, then the clouds closed in and it began to rain again. For an hour, I wandered around the summit, trying to get out of the wind. Then another hour, same thing. Everything completely gray. Juncos my only company. The first hikers didn't arrive until after noon—a father and son who wanted to continue to Iroquois. Then a guy aiming for Lake Colden down a trail that would be more waterfall than rock. Hours alone, eternal while ticking by, but one gray blur in memory. Even the ravens didn't make an appearance.

Lifetimes or a blink later, I was pulling on my gaiters, getting ready to hike down for the day, when I glimpsed a bit of color and substance emerging from the mist below. Forest! Colden! Then the Flowed Lands, the Trap Dike, Iroquois . . . everything! All around me—Wright, Street and Nye, the Santanonis, Whiteface's sharp point piercing up through distant layers, all dark and rain-drenched beautiful. There was a *world* out there! The sky was still dark to the west but breaking open to the north—*blue* shone through! I ran all around the summit, laughing at a place that would do this to and for me—keep me socked in and miserable for hours, only to emerge bright and brilliant. *I don't understand what you're trying to tell me, world,* I said to the mountains, shaking my head and grinning, *but thank you.* In response, a full rainbow arced across Avalanche Pass.

(I know, I know, Rene Daumal: "You'll often surprise yourself talking to the mountain . . . And you'll imagine that the mountain answers . . . Just keep in mind . . . that your dialogue with nature was only the outward image of a dialogue with yourself."[29])

CHAPTER 11

"Wild"

I never meant to return. I never wanted to go back. Yet there I was, making the familiar turn onto Loj Road on a foggy May morning with a mix of optimism, curiosity, and resignation. The first season had left me feeling unfulfilled; there was still more work to do. I knew that it was going to be cold sometimes. My knees were going to hurt. People were going to chatter and disrespect me and the vegetation and the spirit of wilderness. But for now, I was glad to reacquaint myself with the scent of the air, the swirl of the mist, the view from my favorite old weather-beaten bench on the shores of Heart Lake. Rain on the roof of the yurt, pitter patter.

It was reassuring to return to the ADK family—that group of welcoming, dedicated, and enthusiastic individuals who love the mountains and, to some odd degree, the bugs and mud. And it was comforting to reacquaint myself with the trails and summits and skies. My first weekend on Marcy featured an appropriate assortment of mist, rain, hail, and sunshine. Wright laughed in waterfalls. Avalanche Pass glowed gray-white mist, hints of distant cliffs. A return to Indian Pass registered as "Trees. Mosquitoes. Nothing much. No broken toes." Skylight: Skylight!

I learned new things during training—more bird species, more Leave No Trace facts—and found that familiar topics had more resonance. When the steward team gathered to watch *The Mountains Will Wait for You*—a biopic on Grace Hudowalski—I felt proud to be carrying on her legacy. I didn't really believe I'd earned the title of summit steward during the first season. Yes, I'd carried out the duties, but the place itself was irrelevant to me; I just wanted to protect any and every scrap of wilderness, no matter where. Only after leaving and returning did I start thinking of my role as tending to specific arctic-alpine plants on specific summits—diapensia, deer's hair sedge, sandwort; on Marcy's high dome, Algonquin's lush meadows, Wright's exposed fin (and, begrudgingly, poor Cascade's bald patches). Maybe I was taking Gary Snyder to heart, finally "[f]ind[ing] my place on the planet. Dig[ging] in"? Or was I still scratching at the surface?

The first few weeks went well. I knew what to expect in terms of weather, trail conditions, and hikers, and what to look forward to in terms of sky-scapes, new routes, and sparrows. As a returnee, I helped new stewards with orientation and training, though I was still unprepared for a day on Whiteface that was even colder and soggier than it had been the year before. The food at the Loj was just as delicious, the Trails Crew just as crazy fun. The water in Heart Lake was warm enough for swimming. The loons were back! Not so much a sense of belonging, but certainly one of longing, still; yearning to understand.

By late June, the euphoria had worn off.

In the middle of a five-day stretch on Marcy, I caught a cold—hack-ing cough, runny nose, squeaky rasp of a voice. I didn't want to abandon the mountain, though, so I dragged myself up the long, arduous trail. The plan was that, rather than chatting with everyone as usual, I'd speak to hikers only if they were damaging the vegetation. I should have known better. It was a Saturday. Cool, drizzly weather notwithstanding, any weekend—especially the first one of the summer—would be busy. Not just busy—*overrun* with hikers, more than two hundred of them, an unending chain, all arriving and seeking shelter from the wind and rain. All asking questions, making requests: *How's the trail to Haystack? When's this weather going to break? Here, take my photo.* More than a few flattening the poor patch of grasses that made the ecologically sound but anthropocentrically poor choice to try to grow on the leeward side of the summit.

I answered questions, snapped photos, and chased people out of the vegetation. Again and again. Although I could barely breathe for cough-ing and it felt like swallowing a porcupine to talk, it was my job to be there to protect the plants. It was *not* my job to take photos, though that came with the territory. As the hours wore on, a knot of fury and sor-row tightened somewhere between my stomach, heart, and sore throat: *What are all of these people doing on this peak? Why are they here, what do they want, what's the point of it all? Why can't they read the signs or respect the plants? Oh, this poor mountain.*

(The mountain couldn't care less what such small, fleetingly present people think of or do on it. Yes, Rene Daumal, "The mountain is only rock or ice, with no ears or heart."[1])

(Then again, maybe it does care that we're leaving long-term impacts, eroding the trails. Making the trails in the first place. Maybe it needs a few people be there to protect it?)

(Mountains are mountains. They don't need protection. Mountains don't care. Mountains don't think.)

(*Think like a mountain* . . .)

From that day on, I was exhausted. Irritated. Infuriated. Mind as dark and churning as the skies. It seemed impossible to have any semblance of solitude in the High Peaks—morning or evening, weekend or weekday, blue skies or downpour, the place was always crawling with people. Parking lots were full by nine in the morning; chains of cars stretched down the road. There were traffic jams on trails and no places to sit on summits. Toilet paper accumulated at every junction. The radio crackled with constant traffic: separated parties, lost dogs, twisted ankles. So many people. So many unprepared people. Those recurring questions: Why were they there? Was this the "wilderness experience" they sought? Was there any wildness left in these mountains?

As I blogged (well, fumed) to a generic hiker, midseason:

Why ever you go, whatever you find, is it worth the impact you have on the place? Do you leave a tattered trail of granola bar wrappers, stacked-rock "sculptures," footprints ripped into the soft mud or moss? Even if you practice proper LNT principles (kudos!), do you absorb any . . . wildness, or do you return more self-impressed than -aware?

If you want exercise, that's great, but please don't treat the mountains as an outdoor gym. If you want to spend time with friends, that's great, too, but please don't equate the forest with your local bar . . . If you want to witness beauty, that's meaningful, but please don't view the plains as pretty scenery . . . Please don't dismiss any big, wild place as merely the backdrop for your small personal exploits and desires.

Sharing Cascade with a few hundred friends, any sunny afternoon (only partway up the trail, not even the summit).

I don't mean to judge, I really don't. Everyone has their own reasons for hiking, backpacking, paddling, climbing, skiing, etc., and of course they're all valid when they add meaning and joy to life. When individuals let their interests and ambitions supersede the integrity of the wilderness, though—when people damage ecological stability and pilfer natural beauty in the process of ill-informed or poorly-practiced "recreation"—that's when I judge. Harshly.[2]

To be fair, I issued the caveat: "It's been raining for a week, and I'm angry. Not at the rain, which is quite enchanting—mist swirling up from the valleys, droplets pattering on my poncho, sparrows singing merrily away, the whole forest reeking with life—but at the people."[3]

Wilderness purist—I know, I'm attached to the idea of huge, rugged, primeval areas, where man or woman is a visitor and does not remain. Who does not travel in a large, mindless camp group or Scout troop. Who does not trample vegetation or harass wildlife. Who doth not carry a smartphone.

Laura Waterman, at least, seems to agree, writing in the appreciation for her husband, Guy, in the newest edition of their seminal book *Wilderness Ethics*:

> Wildness is imperceptibly eroded away. It is chipped at over time by those who want to . . . locate a trail up a hitherto pathless ridge, . . . or are overly hasty in their use of helicopters, . . . or in traveling in large groups, or in whipping out their cell phones . . . These can be good things (except for possibly the cell phones!) or not. Each much be carefully weighed; measured against what is gained and what is lost in terms of mountain solitude and wildness.[4]

"A wilderness," as defined by the Wilderness Act of 1964, is

> an area where the earth and its community of life are untrammeled by man, where man himself is a visitor who does not remain. . . . [A]n area of undeveloped Federal land retaining its primeval character and influence . . . and which (1) generally appears to have been affected primarily by the forces of nature, with the imprint of man's work substantially unnoticeable; (2) has outstanding opportunities for solitude or a primitive and unconfined type of recreation; (3) . . . is of sufficient size as to make practicable its preservation and use in an unimpaired condition; and (4) may also contain ecological, geological, or other features of scientific, educational, scenic, or historical value.

The field of wilderness management emerged alongside passage of the act. Managers of parks, forests, and protected areas containing this ineffable thing called "wilderness" needed principles and guidelines to explain what conditions they were supposed to be managing for and to determine how to achieve them. They mined and parceled the act to identify distinguishing characteristics of wilderness, which they put into rubrics to evaluate: untrammeledness; undevelopedness; naturalness; ability to "offer . . . outstanding opportunities for solitude or primitive and unconfined recreation"; presence of "other features of scientific, educational, scenic, or historical value." Wilderness management, then, as explained in the fourth edition of the same-titled textbook/manual, "applies concepts, criteria, guidelines, standards, and procedures derived from the physical, biological, social, and management sciences to preserve naturalness, and outstanding opportunities for solitude or primitive, unconfined recreation, in the stewardship and protection of resources and values in designated wilderness areas."[5] Note: "stewardship" of both resources *and* values.

But how to measure "untrammeledness" and compare it with, say, "naturalness," or "solitude"? Howard Zahniser—author of the Wilderness Act—chose to use the odd and archaic word "untrammeled" specifically to signify that "wilderness . . . is unhindered and free from modern human control or manipulation."[6] He wanted wilderness managers to be "guardians not gardeners."[7] But if natural forces are allowed to dominate, invasive species could creep in, or wildfires rage; without deliberate intervention, nonnatural conditions may arise. Meanwhile, where's the cutoff for "solitude"—two people? Ten? A parade of noisy summer campers? To some purists like me, solitude is broken by the presence of just one other hiker, whereas "to people from the cities who [a]re used to elbowing their way through crowds on streets and subways," students researching visitor demographics and preferences in the Adirondacks explain, "a summit with a scant 30 people milling about might indeed fit their definition of wilderness."[8]

Moreover, if policies are put in place to limit the number of people and their actions when in wilderness, does that undermine "untrammeledness"? "From one perspective," observes environmental law professor John Copeland Nagle, "wilderness management is an oxymoron. To manage wilderness . . . is to defeat the very wildness that defines it. But from another perspective, wilderness management is essential to preserve the qualities that comprise the wilderness. An unmanaged wilderness . . . could cease to be a wilderness at all."[9] Fifty years after passage of the Wilderness Act that he helped campaign for in the 1950s and 60s, former director of the Wilderness Society Stewart Brandborg doesn't hold his tongue: "It makes me mad as hell to see that some in the agencies . . . have reduced wildness to just one of four or five qualities of wilderness. It has diminished the central importance of wildness."[10]

In the Adirondacks, the federal definition of "wilderness"—and, with it, wilderness character—was adopted with the first Adirondack Park State Land Master Plan (APSLMP) in 1972, with an interesting twist: instead of keeping the expectation that a designated area will be "protected and managed so as to preserve its natural conditions," the Adirondack Park Agency added that an area could be "protected and managed so as to preserve, *enhance and restore, where necessary,* its natural conditions,"[11] favoring the natural over the untrammeled, allowing more gardening than guardianship. The current APSLMP insists that "the protection and preservation of the natural resources of the state lands within the Park must be paramount. Human use and enjoyment of those lands should be permitted and encouraged, so long as the resources in their physical and biological context *as well as their social or psychological aspects* are not degraded."[12]

The DEC has made a noble effort to preserve physical and biological naturalness in the Eastern High Peaks—rerouting trails, removing lean-tos at sensitive sites, banning campfires, requiring use of bear-proof canisters, and partnering with organizations such as the ADK to enhance public outreach. The whole goal of the summit steward program is to ensure that the biological resources aren't degraded. We use cairns, scree walls, string fences, signs, and ourselves to keep people who are using and enjoying their public lands from destroying the arctic-alpine vegetation. By all accounts, we've been doing a good job—the plants are growing back, even as hikers arrive in record numbers. When the summit steward program began in 1990, stewards talked to an average of sixty-four people per day. In my first year of stewarding, that number was up to eighty, and well over a hundred in my final season, with weekends and holidays seeing three to four times that. After holding at between ten and twenty thousand hikers per year for the first two decades of the program, the number of contacts has skyrocketed up to nearly forty thousand. In 2018, a steward spoke with the half-millionth hiker. As Laura and Guy Waterman put it (forty years ago!): "The woods are overrun with solitude seekers."[13]

Adirondack residents, nonprofit organizations, and land managers are debating how to deal with the influx of visitors. Or even whether there *is* an issue with overuse or just "massive usage spikes which overwhelm existing infrastructure and resources" when lovely weather and holiday weekends align.[14] Enforce parking regulations? Invest in infrastructure and more rangers? Issue hiking permits? Require orientations or licenses? The first option is used, though hundreds of cars can still be found parked along busy highways within miles of popular trailheads.

The second option is expensive but also being tested, with busy trails such as the one up Cascade being rerouted and revamped, and some indication that the DEC will hire more staff. The final two options can be effective elsewhere, but they conflict with the founding legislation and intent for Adirondack Park. As local writer and activist Pete Nelson notes, there's a "long-held tradition and value in the Adirondacks, that the Forest Preserve is open for all to enter and enjoy as they please, with no gates, booths or fees. That's a remarkable, unique value and I think we compromise it at our peril."[15]

For now, the DEC is holding community meetings and convening a High Peaks Strategic Planning Advisory Group, tasked with "ensuring public safety . . . ; protecting natural resources and recreation infrastructure . . . ; providing a quality recreation experience; supporting local economic vitality; and . . . making decisions based on science."[16] A near-impossible balancing act, to encourage people to visit, but the right number of people to visit in the right way, especially when individuals' interpretations of "a quality recreation experience" vary so widely. "Backcountry managers assume that [the backpacker] seeks real solitude," Laura and Guy Waterman observe. "Yet the tendency of so many to head for so few choice wilderness meccas, to hike the same trails, climb the same summits . . . makes one wonder how much solitude they really want."[17]

Pete Nelson may write, "I climbed Cascade on Labor Day morning with 200 other visitors and we all had a wonderful time."[18] But having spent my share of days trying to control crowds atop Cascade, I can't say I find two hundred visitors all that wonderful. What about those "social and psychological aspects" of the land—in particular, the solitude—that the APSLMP strives to keep from being degraded?

I can't begrudge Nelson's sentiment, though: "I wanted every one of those people to experience and value this place. And they did."[19]

Or, at least, they experienced it. Whether they valued it is a different matter.

Heart Lake became my sanctuary. Although located next to one of the busiest trailheads in full view of the highest and thus highly popular High Peaks, it was a center of calm. Swimming out to the center of its cool, deep waters and floating amid the mirrored mountains, my body became weightless and my mind almost free. After long, busy days stewarding,

I'd return to the yurt, drop my pack, swap my uniform out for a swimsuit, then dash over to my bench, unwrap my towel and unstrap my sandals, and step into the water. With one step, I could feel the tranquility radiating up from my ankles, muck squishing satisfyingly under my toes. Another, and I'd be shin-deep. Another, water at the knees. Pause—always a bit of a pause, a glance toward the ridgelines—then dive, coolness radiating throughout my body. A few kicks forward, spin onto my back, float, and let the world fall away. Suspended, bathing in sky.

When it was sunny, I'd stay in the shadows, splashing to remove the day's perspiration and angst. If clouds were drifting along, I'd drift with them, poised between their reality and their reflections. But I liked swimming in the rain best—the times when the sky's heavy blanket of gray began to lose definition, a few droplets sent out concentric ripples on the water, more drops overlapped, then sheets roiled the entire surface as rain and lake merged. I could have been duck, fish, or mermaid for all the difference it made. These absolute downpours rarely lasted more than a minute or two at a time, though. All too soon, drops would separate into patters, then single droplets; the clouds would have dimension again. Mt. Jo would emerge from the curtains of rain, then the MacIntyres. I'd whirl around, watching the freshly washed world reappear.

On days off, I also took to swimming at sunrise. By midsummer, the water was warmer than the crisp dawn air; there was almost always mist. I'd strip off my outer layers, shivering, then dive in and stroke to the center of the lake. Sometimes, the loons would be there. They didn't frighten easily nor seem terribly curious about the large, flappy-limbed thing that invaded their space. They just kept to their lives—floating, diving, calling out into the dawn. If I timed it right, I'd have a few moments' rest before sunlight began to make the mist glow, then struck the treetops on the far edge of the lake. As the light crept across the water, I'd swim to the line of illumination, then turn, eyes closed, to soak in the glow. Baptized by sunlight and mountain water, I'd almost feel ready to try to appreciate the Adirondacks again.

Mid-July, I finally found Lake Arnold. Turns out I'd actually missed it twice the previous year—not seen the turn when I was racing to make it back to the Loj, and not noticed the lake itself when I was skipping down from Colden after Trap Dike. After another exhausting week on Marcy, I decided to take the longer, less trafficked route to the Loj again.

This time, though, I left early enough to dawdle along the way—soak in the views from the south side of Marcy, pause to appreciate still-lovely Lake Tear of the Clouds, and bob carefully across the still-floating bog "bridges" past Feldspar before beginning the ascent toward Colden. Moving patiently and attentively, I took note when the trail leveled off and looked for the yellow-on-brown sign announcing Lake Arnold. How could I have missed it? (Aside from the fact that it was tucked back in the trees and facing the wrong direction.)

There's nothing special about the lake—it's one of thousands found throughout the Adirondacks, ringed with rocks and spruce, cheery yellow lily pads resting on tannin-stained water. Not particularly spectacular or even that scenic. Not deep enough for loons, not even any ducks. Plenty of black flies, and probably its share of leeches. I barely stayed for two minutes, but for those two minutes Lake Arnold was all mine—a bright mountain pond center of tranquility, nestled in the heart of the High Peaks.

Mid-August, I sought a similar experience at the Wallface Ponds, destination for one of the more remote trails in the region, with little reason to venture out to it unless one's insistent on bushwhacking up MacNaughton to notch off all of the maybe-true four-thousand-foot peaks. Lists get complicated and a touch comical: when Bob and George Marshall looked for peaks above the tidy but arbitrary four-thousand-foot cutoff, they used maps from 1903 that listed MacNaughton as twenty-four feet too short. Surveys of 1953 put the summit at exactly four thousand feet, compelling some forty-sixers to become forty-seveners. Although re-surveys of 1980 knocked the elevation back down seventeen feet, some people climb MacNaughton just in case, or for the adventure of it: it's a practically trailless peak, with a mess of herd paths and logging tape marking the way to the summit.

I had little desire to climb MacNaughton (okay, the idea crossed my mind, briefly), but I was still looking for solitude. Easy solitude, that is. I could have wandered off into the woods and found it in spades, but brief attempts at bushwhacking reminded me how miserable, claustrophobic, and monotonous it is to fight through endless trees. The Wallface Ponds offered a name on the map and an objective.

The hike began well, following the familiar trail to Scott's Clearing, then turning to ascend the shoulder of Wallface—a thousand feet up, relatively gradual, with the typical rocks, roots, and puddles. And bogs. Just past a lovely little lake reminiscent of Arnold, I began mucking through the first of several marshes, trying to follow old muddy boot prints that wove around the waterlogged trail and alongside more shimmering pools—the series of ponds on Wallface. Each of the waters was charming—quiet, unassuming, calmly rippling reflections of green-standing forest and cloud-floating sky—but the path was submerged for long stretches. *Why bother calling this a trail*, I thought, as I clambered through brush and over logs, scouring the landscape and backtracking in search of markers. I'd have been better off navigating on my own, yet I felt obligated to try to stick to the designated corridor. Half through and half around another long, deep bog, I caught a glimpse of a much larger body of water gleaming through the trees—the final and surprisingly wide Wallface Pond itself. For a second, I believed that it would all prove worth it—the hike, the summer, this place. That Wallface Pond would be a gem of the wilderness. That I'd finally find the serenity I sought.

But as I emerged from the bog and started to cross the final few meters to the shore, I came around a large pine and found a bright orange tent, pitched smack-dab in the middle of the trail. Startled by the sight and furious with myself for getting my hopes up and letting my guard down—How could anyone dream that a trail in the High Peaks would be untraveled?—I stepped around it, muttering "In the middle of the trail, really?"

Someone coughed.

Oh, the tent was still occupied. When I heard the camper begin to unzip the rain fly, I dashed to the pond, snapped a photo, and ran away, embarrassed to be there and to be filled with deflated hopes and bitter intolerance, incapable of appreciation.

If one person ruined the illusion, two made it even worse. Racing back, blind to moss and mud, just wanting to be done with that place and all of the Adirondacks as quickly as possible, I plunged knee-deep into one of the bogs. As I was extricating myself, a dog came bounding through the swamp, splashing water and spraying mud. Its owner followed behind but made no move to control her pet. Both surprised to meet a fellow solo female hiker—I could count on one hand the total number I encountered during my entire time in the Adirondacks—and annoyed with the dog off-leash, I made no greeting. She spoke first: "Did you do MacNaughton?"

No hello, no lovely day for a hike. Just the assumption that the only reason anyone would be out here was for peak bagging, to "do" the deed of conquering a summit, checking off a name. Yeah right, Edwin Bernbaum, "many who hike and climb for sport and recreation are seeking an experience of spiritual awakening."[20] What sort of spiritual awakening can be reached via trampled trails, pointless lists, and treed-in summits? These mountains are trophies, not temples.[21]

I know Ketchledge would have chided me for "disparagingly refer[ing] to climbing as 'peak bagging'" and invited me to climb, intent on "demonstrat[ing] the deeper insights and rewards with the summit experience beyond the physical exertion that currently constitutes [my] limited horizon."[22] Guy and Laura Waterman write a whole chapter in *Backwoods Ethics* celebrating the stewardship of the Adirondack 46ers and rebuking anyone who would dismiss them as mere peak baggers.[23] My own friend and mentor Kevin Blake—one of the professors who'd taken me to the Bradford Washburn American Mountaineering Museum—would remind me that in the Adirondacks, as with the Colorado Fourteeners, "Peakbaggers are also some of the strongest advocates of protecting the [mountains], and their desire to climb every mountain does not mean that they ignore spiritual renewal."[24] But MacNaughton is nothing more than an increasingly popular "High Peak #47." "The mountain that is on everyone's list during or after they finish the 46 High Peaks"[25] is not a cherished destination for those who seek wilderness education or enlightenment.

"No thank you," my reply, laced with exhaustion and unwarranted judgment. "I just wanted to see the ponds." Unspoken: I hate your mountains, I hate your lists. I want to walk down a trail without having to make small talk with strangers. I want to skinny-dip in a lake without worrying that anyone might see. I want to stand on a mountain without having to tell people not to step on the plants. I want to head into the woods without encountering a pile of toilet paper or a mound of human waste. I want to believe that all of the rules, regulations, and attempts at education are working—that when people care *about* a place, they'll care *for* it—without witnessing so many people ignorant of Leave No Trace or ignoring their own impacts. I want to be somewhere with open horizons, old rocks, and no people. There are pockets of wildness, but there is no true wilderness here. I give up on this place.

CHAPTER 12

Interim

BLACK CANYON OF THE GUNNISON NATIONAL PARK, COLORADO

Four years after my first season at Black Canyon, my supervisor had funding for another season of paleontological surveying and wanted to rehire me. Rather than return to the Adirondacks for more rain, black flies, throngs of hikers, and occasional moments of beauty, I was happy to accept. Mid-May, I packed my car and made the weeklong drive from New York west to the glorious expanses of southwestern Kansas, the wide valleys and windy passes of Highway 50 in Colorado, the welcoming brown NPS sign, and the familiar twists up to the park entrance, quarters, and chasm itself.

As soon as I got there, late on a broken-altostratus afternoon, I dashed out along the Rim Trail, eager to reacquaint myself with as much as possible before night fell. Yes, same old scrub oak, same old sage. (Sage! How I'd missed sage!) Fork in the trail—did I want to go to the canyon, say hello to the juniper? No, that should wait until dawn; evenings were for Oak Flat. I turned onto the overland route, as familiar as if I'd been there the day before. When I reached the road crossing, though, I changed my mind. Instead of staying on the trail, I'd follow the pavement around to Pulpit Rock. I wasn't yet ready for the overlook.

Hurrying—it was more than a mile, nearly two, and dusk was seeping into the sky—I exalted in the fresh air, the rhythm of my footsteps, the sight of the snow-covered West Elks, and especially the knowledge that the canyon was there, falling off to my right, just beyond the oak and pines. How had it changed? Four years deeper. How had *I* changed?

Around the final curve to Pulpit Rock. There it was, Black Canyon. Before the view, even, the sound, the feel—the river, the space. Then the rock walls, cliffs, and crags. Shadows swallowing what was left of the

Dragon Point, Black Canyon. Back to hunger and absence.

light. Water snarling below, clouds soaring overhead, and *me*, still part of "that cosmology of restless hunger."[1] Oh, Black Canyon, I'm back!

It was entirely a mistake to return. The landscape was littered with memories. Instead of rejuvenating a sense of awe, the Oak Flat over-look opened old wounds. Instead of affording glimpses of the sublime, my morning walk became a desperate routine. Instead of promising any sort of solace, the Rim Trail juniper stood gnarled, uncaring. The shadows weren't deep enough, the river fierce enough; even the mist refused to rise. *Have I lost the eye for beauty*, I scrawled into my tattered old notebook, *the capacity for joy?*

The actual job was still enjoyable—even more so than before. What a relief, to be out reading outcrops again, trusty rock hammer in hand. I scaled the cliffs of the North Rim and sifted for multituberculate teeth on the shores of Curecanti. I meandered the ravines of Red Rocks and tangled with scrub oak on Green Mountain. I found impressive new leaf assemblages, lots of petrified wood fragments, and wasted several full days hiking across landscapes that were entirely non-fossiliferous but undeniably beautiful. It was even fun to be in the office on bad-weather days, database work enlivened by my supervisor, who was as good humored as ever.

But the vegetation technician—my closest friend from the first sea-son—wasn't there. The mountain lion didn't reappear. And, of course, the bio tech from Fossil Butte. He'd long ago moved on. Absences, all absences. Carve deeper, river.

I took to prowling the road at night. Or, rather, very early morning. As astronomers packed up their telescopes and long before birds began to sing, I'd wake to a 3:00 a.m. alarm, step out into the cool, predawn darkness, and walk for hours under an inky-black sky peppered with planets and stars.

Located far from any large city and shielded from the glow of Mon-trose, Black Canyon boasts remarkably dark nighttime skies. That sum-mer, the park was in the process of being certified as an International Dark Sky Park—one of the few places left in America where it's possible to see the full Milky Way arc across the universe. Night skies aren't a natural resource that most people think of as needing protection (heav-ens aren't seen as a fixed part of the scenery; darkness isn't a natural or historic object, much less a living thing), but with the continued proliferation of light pollution, people and wildlife are now are more likely to experience an orange glow overhead at night than a shooting star. In recent decades, the NPS has developed a Night Skies Team to inventory, monitor, protect, and celebrate the "vanishing resource" of darkness, mainly by minimizing use of and shielding artificial lighting and collaborating with nearby communities to do the same.[2] "Night sky protection enhances qualities of solitude and undeveloped wilder-ness character that animals depend on for survival, [and] park visitors seek for connections," the NPS attests; darkness "is part of a complex ecosystem that supports both natural and cultural resources."[3]

To celebrate and make use of its pristinely starry skies, Black Canyon hosts an annual astronomy festival and weekly telescope observations, at which astronomers from all around the region share their knowledge and passion with visitors (and employees). By joining in their star parties, I gradually learned a new vocabulary (they bandied about familiar terms like "galaxy" and "nebula" alongside "star cluster," "M-3," "M-51," all sorts of "Messier numbers"), new geography (turns out, the familiar Mercury, Cassiopeia, and Dippers are surrounded by infinite planets, constellations, and asterisms I'd never seen), and new sense of appreciation for and kinship with what I'll call the astro-paleontological scale. When astronomers spoke of stars located thirty-seven million light years away, I thought, *The Eocene!* When that light was emitted, tiny anthropoids were still scrambling around the forests of Asia, and early camelids were just beginning to coevolve with American grasslands. The Andromeda Galaxy, two million light years away? Why, that light has been traveling for the same amount of time that the Gunnison River has been carving the inner canyon. Stars let us peek back millions of years across thousands of trillions of miles, through the fabric of space-time.

Under that infinity, it was refreshingly easy to forget how unmoored I felt, in a place that I'd come to expecting to feel whole again but that offered no solace.

In the darkness, my feet had no trouble feeling out the crunch of pavement down the park road, leaving my eyes free to follow the Milky Way. The sight of it streaming across the sky, "Silver, / changeless—the Star River,"[4] was so psychophysically moving that I could almost agree with the eighteenth-century German physician Franz Anton Mesmer (eponym of "mesmerize"), who believed that humans are affected by the gravitational force of the planets and other heavenly bodies.

While I marveled at the enormity of the universe, the rest of my senses simultaneously hyper-attuned to my immediate surroundings: a warm patch of air, a whiff of water, every rustle from the brush. "Hey, bear?" I called nervously into the night, "Just me, bear. Passing by." A handful of times, my skin prickled with primordial fear. I unhooked the straps of my backpack and hunched it up over my neck, figuring that if the mountain lion was crouching nearby, watching me with its golden eyes and preparing to leap onto my back, its claws and teeth would dig into my snacks and extra layers first.

I usually rounded Pulpit Rock at the darkest, deepest predawn interlude. There, the earth opened up into Black Canyon, the purest black I'd ever known, a black hole. Starlight didn't seem capable of shining down into the chasm. Sight was useless, but I could *feel* the space, could hear it in the echoes of the river reverberating up. Space yawning into the abyss, so deep and dark and old, eroding down; even more space opening through the sky, so deep and star filled and even older, expanding out.

So short lived and entirely inconsequential, little me. All of human history.

All too soon, early birds would begin to sing, their calls deafening to ears attuned to the slightest variation in the shape of the sound from the canyon. At about the same time, my eyes could start to pick out shapes, then colors; make out the stripes on the road, then distinguish yellow from white. Finally, the canyon. Rock walls solidified out of the air between them. In anticipation of sunrise, wind would begin to stir. If I'd timed it just right, I could be on the last stretch to High Point when the sun popped quietly over the horizon, scattering warm rays across the landscape, seeking the upper edge of the chasm.

With that, the spell would break. Mind no longer out in the stars or deep in the earth, I'd be back in the present, feet on the ground, having to trudge seven miles back to quarters, alone and tired.

When summit stewarding, I was forced to stand on a mountaintop all day—stay put, occasionally pause, watch the world change around me instead of striving to stay a step ahead. But at Black Canyon, I never stopped moving—working and walking, driving and hiking, trying to find new fossils and outpace my ossified memories at an increasingly frenetic rate. Hiking down and back up East Portal Road. Skirting sandstone ledges below Dillon Pinnacles. Weekends bumping down distant Forest Service roads to access less popular wilderness areas. Two- and three-day solo backpacking treks through the San Juans, more a matter of grit than actual pleasure. Day after day, walking and looking and alone with the wild. The more I sought joy, the harder it was to find.

One night, mid-August, the full moon was so bright that three o'clock in the morning seemed more like midday. My dark, starry walk was ruined. (Even more so than it had been on the morning a month earlier when the sky had been overcast. With cloud cover, the darkness had been darker; with humidity, sounds were both muffled and amplified. Just before daybreak, a thunderstorm had put on a spectacular show over the West Elks.) In the glare of the moonlight, the universe faded, making it impossible to forget that I was tethered to the earth, surrounded by tangle-shadowed scrub oak. There was no mystery, no space for wonder, just mile after mile. My soul felt heavy. Oh, Mary Oliver,

> Wherever I am, the world comes after me.
> It offers me its busyness. It does not believe
> that I do not want it. Now I understand
> why the old poets of China went so far and high
> into the mountains, then crept into the pale mist.[5]

Rock Point. In hindsight, it was a stupidly dangerous thing to do, to try navigating a precipitously sided path to the overlook in the dark. But the moon was so very bright. And I was so very tired. I didn't want to walk the road any farther, didn't want any more backpacking or fossil hunting or summit stewarding or anything-ing. I found my way to the edge of the abyss and, for what seemed like the first time since I'd left four years earlier, sat.

Rock.

Cold, gritty. More than a billion years old.

River.

Insistent, churning. Two thousand-odd feet below.

Air.

Soft, swirling. Here, now.

The summer hasn't been that bad, I tried to convince myself. I'd seen some spectacular new places—alpine lakes, mesa tops, more of the steep cliffs of Morrison on the North Rim. Work had been an unqualified success—monitoring bats with the wildlife crew, scouting for archaeological sites with my supervisor, documenting a gorgeous assemblage of plant impressions distributed across a jumble of giant-sized boulders. No multituberculate teeth, but on one of my first returns to Red Rocks, at the end a long, hot day, I turned on a whim into a side ravine and there discovered, its splayed toes popping out perfectly in the late afternoon sunlight, the long-desired dinosaur track.

I found a dinosaur track! The first person ever to see it! The first ever recorded in the park!

And yet.

I know, I know: no expectations, no desires. Just space. So empty. Alone.

Not entirely alone—the canyon was there, and the river, of course. A few bushes and the skeleton of a long-dead juniper, ghostly white in the moonlight. As the world tilted toward dawn, I started to hear cliff swallows whooshing past, their chirrupy calls. Then a rustle of wings as a raven alit on the branches of the juniper, its feathers gleaming in the pale light. *Iridescence*, my mind registered; *little dinosaur.* (By studying the shape and structure of melanosomes in fossil feathers, paleontologists can determine pigmentation. Corvid-like iridescence has been documented in species dating back to the Cretaceous.[6])

Caw! it screamed, the sound reverberating between the walls of rock, the millions of years between then and now.

Caw, I replied, without its conviction and resonance, mired hopelessly in memories and dreams.

Caw! it rebuked me, then launched into a string of garbles that mimicked both the sound of water tumbling over boulders and the sound of a string of stones plunking into water. *Is this how the world sounds to a raven?* I wondered. *Or how the world expresses itself?* I resolved to stay there, sitting at Rock Point, until I figured it out. Weeks, months, years. Millennia, if need be.

The raven fell silent. We sat together, surrounded by the whisper of real water from far below. A breeze rustled the leaves of small shrubs, air flowed around rock pillars, the sky lifted toward dawn. Slight inhale with the rising sun. Brightness poured through the valleys on either side of Grizzly Ridge and began to warm the southeast-facing canyon walls, the junipers, the raven, and me, blinded by the onslaught of sight.

We all sat together, timeless, until the bird had had enough. Away, leaving only water, air, sun, rock; a great gap in the earth. Echoes:

Caw.

Caw.

CHAPTER 13
Self

I couldn't decide whether to punch him or burst into tears.

No, I still didn't love the Adirondacks and I wasn't sure why I was back for yet another season—my fourth, by then; a record for summit stewards, whose knees tend to wear out or whose minds get bored with the same trails and same mountaintops, day after day. But I still cared about wilderness, even if only an ideal or illusion. And this guy—this skinny-jeans-and-flannel-shirt-wearing, hipster-mustachioed, and thick-rimmed-round-glasses-clad, wholly dismissive and supercilious *guy* (actually, I have no idea what he was wearing and don't really remember what he looked like, but that's how I envision him)—dared suggest that it's fine for people to trample a few flowers as long as they're out enjoying the mountains. Of all people to be saying something so outrageous—to insist that summit stewards are ineffective and insinuate that human desires trump ecological integrity—he himself was a summit steward! Albeit for the Green Mountain Club (GMC), but that almost made it worse; the GMC had originated the idea of alpine protectors.

I should have been more respectful. He was a guest of the ADK, there to participate in preseason training and share stewarding strategies. That day's botany hike up Algonquin had been rather fun; perhaps "exhilarating" would be a better word. Noting that thick lenticular clouds were engulfing Algonquin, our group of summit stewards in training, DEC rangers, and the bryophyte expert shifted our aim to the shorter, lower-elevation Wright Peak. True to reputation, the weather on Wright was terrible. (As the first big mountain catching and channeling northwesterly winds, Wright is especially hard hit. Its arctic-alpine zone starts a good five hundred feet lower than other peaks'.) Above tree line, we were buffeted by forty-five-mile-per-hour wind gusts (verifiable—we carried an anemometer) and drenched by sideways-falling rain pellets, yet still fought up to the first patch of diapensia to discuss its niche and adaptations. The hike felt like a rite of passage, proof of our resolve—no matter the conditions, we were there for the plants. As if to reward us for our effort, on the descent the sky began to glow, then pockets of blue appeared between breaking clouds. Sunbeams settled on Heart Lake.

Afterward, ADK and GMC stewards in training headed to a brew pub in Lake Placid to celebrate the day and continue sharing stories and perspectives. More content to observe than to participate in group discussions, I nestled in at the far end of the bar, intending to silently sip my beer and listen. But somewhere along the way, the conversation waded into issues of effectiveness, and this GMC guy remarked that he didn't do anything when he saw people stepping on plants; it was better to let them just enjoy the mountains.

Just enjoy the mountains! *Stepping on plants!* Granted, the ADK approach can be a bit overzealous—we speak with every hiker on the summits, whether they want to hear from us or not—but to do *nothing* when rare, fragile species were being squashed? How would people ever learn? How would the plants ever grow? I couldn't hold my tongue. "But it's *not* worth it," I interjected, to the surprise and probably the amusement of my ADK friends, "for people to enjoy the mountains if they're going to destroy them." If I didn't mutter it out loud, I was at least thinking, *And people probably aren't enjoying the actual mountains if they're stomping all over taking selfies.*

From there, it escalated into an argument about the very definition of wilderness. Its purpose. Do we say we'll keep places forever wild for people—so that we can enjoy ourselves, recreate, re-create primitive and unconfined experiences—or for the wild beasts, the wilderness itself, free from human trails and trammels? He believed people need to enjoy the mountains, and I believed people need to learn from the mountains, without leaving an impact on them. Rather than acknowledge mutual interests, we eventually worked ourselves into extremes, the GMC guy saying that it'd be better to have crowds of people out climbing even if that meant they trampled all the vegetation to death; me saying that it'd be better to entirely ban people from wilderness areas if we prove oblivious to wildness. *Do you even know what wilderness is?* (This is when I was halfway between punching him and bursting into tears.) *There's so very little of it; we can't lose it.* We are, in fact, letting it erode right in front of our supposedly watchful eyes.

"The idea of wilderness needs no defense," I should have quoted Ed Abbey at him. "It only needs more defenders."[1] "Do something for wildness"—how could I have failed to invoke John Muir? Damn it, "make the mountains glad." By Aldo Leopold's standards—"a thing is right when it tends to preserve the integrity, stability, and beauty of the biotic community. It is wrong when it tends otherwise"[2]—the GMC guy's approach was wholly in the wrong.

Mostly in the wrong.

Of course, it's not an either-or. Stewardship itself is predicated upon the idea that people want to and will care for places that we know and love. The countless hours that volunteer stewards spend standing atop the High Peaks, the money and labor that Adirondack 46ers donate to trail construction, all of the clean-up days and lean-to adoptions—these are done out of love for the Adirondacks. The Adirondack Mountain Club organized around the idea that people can recreate responsibly and will give back to the forest, ponds, and peaks in whatever ways they can.

But what does that mean for all of the places that we won't ever go to—that we don't know about and don't love? Distant deserts and tundra, boring old sagebrush steppe? Why should anyone care about the barren Red Rocks Wilderness or windswept Primrose Ridge, much less the ATV trails weaving through the Mancos Shale outside Black Canyon or the wolf killed when it ventured outside the borders of Denali? Who's ever going to visit the Arctic National Wildlife Refuge or the National Petroleum Reserve-Alaska; why protect them? Is it really enough, Wallace Stegner, to hinge our hopes on a wilderness *idea*, to have places available to us if we're not ever even going to get the chance to "drive to [their] edge[s] and look in"?[3] Ed Abbey, why do we "need wilderness whether or not we ever set foot in it"? What is it about a refuge that we need "even though we may not ever need to go there"?[4]

And what does that mean for the places that we visit and know but do not love? Can we—can *I*—still be good stewards if our heart's not in it?

Same thing, season three (the summer after Black Canyon) and again season four: settling back in to Marcy, Algonquin, and Wright, more begrudgingly to Cascade; familiar returns to Avalanche Pass, Indian Pass, Skylight; happy jaunts up Jo and Van Ho. Wilderness first aid as cautionary as ever; Leave No Trace more enlightening. Hikers more numerous. Black flies, equally so. Rain and wind and not infrequent snow or hail. Sun dogs, sun haloes. Cirrus, stratocumulus. Fog, fog, fog.

But something new, the third time around. I caught the peak-bagging bug. (Hypocrite.) Mid-June, while hiking to Johns Brook Lodge, I decided to swing by Big Slide. With its mossy brooks, boreal traverse, and wide panorama, it instantly became my new favorite hike in the Adirondacks. A week later, after work on Marcy, I took advantage of the long daylight hours to dash down and up to Gray Peak, its forest-choked scramble decidedly *not* my favorite. Mid-July, during a long weekend that I was supposed to spend resting, I danced up Giant, ignoring thunder and lightning to touch the socked-in summit, unwise but invigorating. Phelps next, also in the pouring rain. (Thus two of what are supposedly the most scenic summits are, in my mind, nothing but walls of gray.) Mid-August, I made a long loop out of Marshall, opting for the unmaintained route up Cold Brook Pass and getting gleefully lost, tired, and muddy along the way. *You'd be glad to know*, I mentally addressed Bob Marshall while wandering around cliffs and bogs on his namesake, looking for the herd path or any semblance of a game trail, *that there are still pockets of wildness here.*

Even more so the fourth season. The first weekend out, I joined a troupe of ADK employees setting out to climb a slide on Lower Wolfjaw. For years, I'd regretted not attempting Lower Wolfjaw during my first season, when I'd been assessing trail conditions atop Gothics and managed to bob up and down to Saddleback, Armstrong, and Upper Wolfjaw but had been too worn out to finish the lower Great Range. Now, I was glad I'd saved it—the weather was perfect, the slide far less nerve wracking than the Trap Dike, the views new and spectacular, and the group hilarious to hike with, a comedy act all day.

The next weekend, I accompanied the ADK backcountry trips leader as he scouted the Seward Range. We'd been warned that it was all mud and no views, so we were pleasantly surprised to find a few overlooks triangulating back toward the MacIntyres and Marcy. But we were not so pleasantly unsurprised by the elevation loss and gain between each of the summits, and should have known better than to take advice to make it a loop, ascending via the col below Donaldson and descending the absurdly steep north side of Seward—yet another Adirondack "trail" that careens straight down a creek bed. Near the bottom, we encountered a solo hiker in an alarming state—stumbling and mumbling, with torn pants and a gash across his forehead. Our first thought was that he'd hit his head; our second, that he was dehydrated. A bit of both—he was tired and lost, unable to find the spot where the trail turned onto an old truck road and unequipped to navigate "trailless" peaks. Although unlikely to make it far in that condition and unprepared to spend the night out, he'd been trying to go all the way up and over Seward, back to the more obvious trail. Instead, we offered to walk him to the truck road. For the next mile, he proceeded to talk ceaselessly of his quest to be a forty-sixer, listing all the peaks that he'd already checked off but obviously hadn't learned a thing from.

Thus I lost my newfound desire to earn the green, red, and gold patch of the Adirondack 46ers.

Still, new mountains meant new adventures. And I was remembering what fun it can be to share the experiences with other people. Esther and Whiteface with a DEC assistant forest ranger on a remarkably sunny day—typical Adirondack ascent, all rocks, roots, and trees, but a lovely walk down via the Memorial Highway, drinking in the expansive views at every turn. Cliff and Redfield with the Loj chef—or actually, only Cliff, as we lingered too long at Lake Arnold, got hilariously mired in knee-deep mud, and saved time for a refreshing dip in the frigid Opalescent River. (True to its name, the bedrock contains huge labradorite crystals, which shimmer with iridescence in the afternoon sun.) Team stewarding on Cascade with a dedicated volunteer. Vegetation surveys on Algonquin with an academic colleague and a former student. Rock packing on Gothics with a fellow steward in perfectly terrible weather; laughing together into the mist and sideways-falling rain.

Perhaps it all would have been okay. I felt renewed purpose the fourth season, thanks to a great crew, new duties, and in no small part the provocation of the GMC guy. I was determined to defend the wilderness, and that meant returning to my original intent: to think like a mountain, no?

But hikers were becoming more numerous, some clueless and bor-
derline belligerent. While many people—most, actually—were friendly
and curious, happy to talk to me and do the "rock walk" once they learned
about arctic-alpine flora, all it took was a few uncooperative and even
aggressive people each day to squash the plants as well as my resolve.
This was the summer when the couple refused to leave a sheltered patch
of sedges and gentians on Algonquin, insisting that they were more
important than plants. This was also the summer when a camp group
on Wright agreed to return to bedrock, then went right back to their
original picnic spot in the vegetation as soon as I turned my back. A tent
pitched atop Marcy. A taco stand on Marcy Plateau. (?!) Innumerable
people who read and proceeded to entirely ignore the signs on Cascade,
stepping over the string fence to cross a battered stretch of sandwort.
The week after walking the aspiring forty-sixer out of the Sewards, I was
racing down from Algonquin as a storm was about to break. A dark wall
of rain had already erased the Santanonis, and rumbles of thunder were
too close for comfort. I'd shooed everyone off, collected all my gear, and
turned the corner from the summit rock when I ran into—literally ran
into—a man staring at his phone. "What are you doing?" I shouted at
him, trying to make myself heard over the sudden roar of rain-scented
wind. "There's a thunderstorm; it's not safe up here!"

"Oh, I'm checking the weather," his reply.

He was still trying to pull up a weather app when it began to hail.

Rain. Rain all through June into July, reminiscent of my first season.
Sections of trail that I'd never seen flood before became flowing
streams. Spots that were always a bit muddy were ankle-deep. Heading
up to Marcy one day, I decided not to go far past the Hopkins Junction.
The trail was already a foot under running water, and it was continuing to pour; if the water rose much more, I'd have trouble getting back
down the steeper sections. I found a rock to sit on, wrapped myself in a
poncho, and proceeded to spend the next five hours watching rain pour
down from the formless clouds, a sky cataract.

Another day, while aiming for Algonquin via an unmaintained
shortcut, I found that I couldn't cross a minor creek. Overnight, storms
had turned what was usually an easy rock hop into a dangerous, roiling river. I had to backtrack all the way to the Loj, slosh up the first

Sky-world for weeks atop Mt. Marcy.

two miles of regular trail, and negotiate the borderline-treacherous MacIntyre Falls, only to find another usually minor creek crossing impassable. Again, hours sitting in the rain.

Then a week on Marcy that saw four straight days of cold, wet clouds. Four days of waking each morning to dark, heavy skies and fumbling to light a soggy camp stove. Trudging up the increasingly muddy trail, pausing to brush in paths forming around the deepest of puddles. Emerging above tree line into the colorless, shadowless cloud ceiling and tucking in under the summit plaque or behind erratics, depending on wind direction. Studying the way droplets pooled on the vegetation or flowed off the rocks. Tuning the radio to the weather forecast—an automated voice continuously announcing "Northern Adirondacks: showers, and summits obscured in clouds." Confirming: yes, showers, summits obscured, all morning and afternoon, until it was time to pack up and slosh back down. Four days of replying to hikers that I had no idea when the views would clear. Four days in my own little mountain-top sky world.

All worth it for day five, when the fog lifted and the world reappeared.

David Hinton warns, "You can't live like a mountain and still be human."[5] But I was sinking into stone. Rain washed, lichen encrusted. Clouds rolled in, clouds rolled out.

After long stretches—hours or days—of being socked in, the mist sometimes cleared from above, starting with a glow, then patches of blue, the color incandescent after so much monotone gray. When that happened, fog might stay nestled in valleys for hours, churning through as rivers of white vapor, or rise and roll over low passes like a standing wave.

More often, the mist broke from beneath—the cloud ceiling lifted or the mountains shrunk, bit by bit, to reveal the landscape below. Instead of a glow, this process began with shadows—glimpses of dark forest, slopes of lesser peaks. Then more distinguishable features would solidify, as if being conjured from the clouds. From Marcy, Panther Gorge's broad hollow, Haystack's craggy profile, and, of course, Skylight's open dome. From Algonquin, the slides on Colden and the outcrops on Wright. From Wright, the huge mass of Algonquin looming overhead.

Below the summits, the land blended together in one thick carpet of forest, punctuated by shimmering lakes and pools. The darker the sky stayed, the brighter the waterbodies seemed. Wright has a perfect view down to South Meadows and Heart Lake. Algonquin overlooks Lake Colden and the streams of the Flowed Lands—like Marcy Dam, a former dam site, slowly being reclaimed by natural marshes. By rock hopping south from Marcy's summit, I could reach a spot from which I could see Lake Tear of the Clouds, a silver bead amid a bed of moss, as well as a bald patch on Redfield labeled as "Moss Pond"—one of dozens in the Adirondacks.

Directly from Marcy's summit, a series of large lakes are visible farther to the south. Beyond Skylight, behind Allen, the last feature before the horizon ripples away into infinite lower peaks. "Are those the Ausable Lakes?" hikers often asked, referring to popular and photogenic lakes hidden in the fjord-like valley between Haystack and Colvin, directly east of Marcy. Or "Is that Elk Lake?"—a sizeable body of water sitting behind Blake to the southeast. Sometimes: "That must be Lake Placid!" in which case I'd gently turn them around to face the waterbody and city, in the exact opposite direction.

"No, Boreas Ponds," I'd reply, relishing the toponym and its origin—Boreas, as in the Greek god of the north wind, known to fly on his purple wings "down from the cold mountains . . ., chilling the air with his icy breath."[6] What a perfect name for these lakes, some seven miles south of and three thousand feet below Mt. Marcy. Fierce winter winds must sweep down from the rime-coated summit and through the open valley, unobstructed by any peaks or ridges. "Boreas Ponds?" Most hikers had never heard of them and didn't care to hear the mythology. (One of Boreas's daughters was the goddess of snow.) The ponds and the land around them were privately owned, part of the unique public/private patchwork making up Adirondack Park. Maps didn't indicate who owned the tracts, but they didn't grant access like the Ausable Club, a private group that allows the public to cross their land, much less the ADK with their trailheads and information center. Because visitors weren't allowed at Boreas, few people knew or cared much about the ponds. But I'd spent so many hours standing atop Marcy, studying maps and looking out across the landscape, that I couldn't help but notice and dream about them, tucked quietly away in what seemed like lush wilderness. I remember looking down at the lakes and imagining what an impressive view it must be, looking *up* toward Allen, Skylight, Marcy, and the other High Peaks from their shores.

Then, in spring 2016, New York State acquired the Boreas Ponds Tract. Turns out, the land had been owned by Finch, Pruyn—a paper manufacturing company operating in the Adirondacks for more than a century. The Nature Conservancy bought the 20,000-acre parcel—part of 161,000 acres in the Adirondacks formerly owned by the company—in 2007 and, having identified it as an ecologically sensitive area not suitable for logging, worked with the DEC to transfer it into the public domain. The Adirondack Park Agency still had to classify it—Would it be "Wild Forest," with limited motorized access? Or "Wilderness," undeveloped and unimpaired?—but for all intents and purposes, it was under "forever wild" protection.

The following summer—my third season stewarding—whenever anyone asked about the bodies of water gleaming to the south, I'd exclaim, "Boreas Ponds!" Then, instead of discussing Greek gods, I would proudly announce the newest part of the forest preserve. I loved gazing at them. I loved the very *idea* of them. All across the state, from all angles—conservation, preservation, stewardship—people were continuing to add to a long legacy of land acquisition and ecological protection in the Adirondacks. The Finch, Pruyn purchase was one of the biggest land exchanges in state history and involved not just acreage for the forest preserve but also tracts managed for sustainable silviculture. *This* is what happens when so many people care about a place, I thought, buoyed by hope and beauty, watching the ponds glint in early morning light and gleam under late afternoon storms, emerge from the mist and stay hidden in the rain. Forever kept as wild.

Midway through the fourth season, I injured my right ankle. There wasn't a specific incident; it just began to swell and pierced with pain any time I stepped slightly off-kilter. (Impossible not to step off-kilter in the Adirondacks.) To any rational onlooker, the injury was an accumulation of years of navigating those steep, uneven trails, ankles constantly twisting, knees constantly pounding, shoulders and back aching with the weight of the packs and the work building cairns or moving rocks. To me, though, it felt like the place had had enough of me. This was its way of telling me to go away, move on.

As soon as my supervisor found out, she sent me to the local health clinic and made me take time off. I begrudgingly sat in the Loj staff kitchen for a few days, applying ice and feeling useless, scrapping weekend plans to explore Seymour or Rocky Peak Ridge. Then, *Boreas!*, the idea came to me. Supposedly, the ponds were accessible via a primitive but drivable dirt road, followed by a few miles on foot down an overgrown old logging road. The walking should be relatively flat and easy. *I can handle it*, I rationalized. *I'll take ibuprofen and lean on trekking poles*. I needed to stretch my legs. I really wanted to experience Boreas firsthand.

Of course, it was pouring the morning I set off to see Boreas, accompanied by the assistant forest ranger with whom I'd hiked Whiteface as well as several other non–High Peaks trails. First, we navigated a bumpy, deep-potholed access road, then parked in a small gravel-strewn lot, donned raingear, and strode/limped forth. The walk was unremarkable—wide dirt path; trees and more trees; throbbing ankle. Really, I don't remember any of it. It may have seemed short, at a mere three and a half miles. Or, more likely, it seemed interminable, with the occasional misstep causing me to collapse in pain. All I remember was reaching the edge of the ponds, where I shouldn't have been surprised to find a dam. Turns out, the gloriously large body of water was, like so many others in the Adirondacks, man-made or man-modified, created when an original series of multiple ponds was flooded for logging. I also shouldn't have been surprised to find that, looking north, none of the High Peaks were visible through the wall of rain. Just another pond, pocked with raindrops and fringed with white pine.

It crossed my mind to jump in and swim out into the grayness. Perhaps that would have changed my impression of the ponds—the feel of the water on my skin; the sound, the smell, in my ears, my nose; the freedom of floating in a lake in the rain. But as we arrived, a flock of ducks startled at our appearance and flapped quackily away. Followed by a great blue heron, who silently and somewhat reproachfully lifted from the shore, spreading its wings and soaring off into the mist. Usually, the sight of a heron strikes me as auspicious: their primordial grace, their fierce gaze, their stillness, even in flight—*especially* in flight. But, in this instance, I couldn't help feeling abashed with every deliberate stroke of its wings. What right did I have to be there, intruding on its solitude? And the ducks—this was *their* pond; how offensive, for me to scare them away. I was invading their home, trespassing on their lives, for what? A scenic view? A need to walk? A bit of boredom? *Do something for wildness, don't just ogle it.* I hobbled back to the car.

Two years after they acquired it, the Adirondack Park Agency (APA) finalized the classification of the Boreas Ponds Tract: 11,412 acres of designated wilderness in the northern part of the parcel, including the entire ponds; 9,118 acres of designated wild forest to the south, including the road. It seemed like a great win for preservation. With the designation, the tract connected the High Peaks and Dix Mountain Wildernesses, forming the third-largest contiguous wilderness area in the eastern United States. Making the shoreline off limits to motor vehicles—including motorized watercraft—minimized impacts to the sensitive high-elevation aquatic and semiaquatic ecosystems. And as a journalist from the local news magazine *Adirondack Explorer* writes, it means that "paddlers can delight in magnificent views from Boreas Ponds."[7] Paddlers, skiers, snowshoers, hikers, and campers, especially as the DEC plans to construct several new trails and campsites. Bicyclists, down most of the road. Drivers and snowmobilers in the wild forest, up to within a tenth of a mile of the ponds, with a permit.

The APA decision was not unanimous. Chad Dawson (remember Chad Dawson, the *Wilderness Management* expert?), who sits on the board, was "the lone dissenter . . . [H]e wanted a classification that included more wilderness acreage and cited thousands of public comments that support greater wilderness areas."[8] The classification process had proved contentious, with factions forming not just between those who wanted more motorized access and conservation groups eager to add to wilderness, but *among* conservation groups, which disagreed on just how much wilderness should be designated, and where. The biggest, most established organizations acknowledged that public land management in the Adirondacks (and world) has, in the words of a spokesperson for the nonprofit Adirondack Council, "always been a political process, and it will always be."[9] The deal to create both wilderness and wild forest from the Boreas Ponds Tract was thus "pragmatic" and "a compromise."[10] "Sometimes *compromise* is a dirty word," Neil Woodworth, executive director of the ADK, rationalized. "In this case, it's not."[11] In approving the classification, Governor Andrew Cuomo issued a statement reading, "this classification package . . . strikes the right balance between preservation and access," continuing on to "encourage visitors from around the world to explore and enjoy the Adirondack Park."[12] "Any time land is added to the Forest Preserve the Adirondacks grows wilder," executive director of Protect the Adirondacks Peter Bauer reminds supporters.[13]

But then there were those who saw "compromise" as compromising the ecological integrity and recreation potential of the entire tract; "balance" as a precarious teeter-totter. "Looks good, but it's not," the Adirondack Council insisted, noting that plans for a motorized corridor reaching so close to the water limited the APA's best options to "False Wilderness" and "Faux Wilderness."[14] (Interestingly, the Adirondack Council went on to champion the compromise.) A new nonprofit, Adirondack Wilderness Advocates, formed specifically to call for more wilderness at Boreas and, in broader terms, to "promot[e] the knowledge, enjoyment, expansion, and protection of the Adirondack Park's wildest places."[15] A sea of people wearing green t-shirts with the slogan "I Want Wilderness!" turned out at every public meeting during the classification process, and individual after individual spoke or wrote to the APA calling for more wilderness. Of the thousands of comments, eighty-four percent expressed desire for more wilderness than the proposals considered.[16] (Confession: my comment, illustrated with sketches of Boreas from Marcy, was among them. I also wrote and illustrated an essay for the Adirondack Wilderness Advocates website.) "You can put a road up every mountain to every pond, but you have to consider what do we lose when we put a road to every pond," said ADK employee and activist Tyler Socash, channeling Bob Marshall as he explained to a reporter why he was dissatisfied with the wild forest corridor. "We lose a sense of wilderness."[17]

Yet, the decision was made—a road nearly to the water's edge. Parking lots. Space for twenty vehicles where I'd parked, three and a half miles from the shore. Space for fifteen to seventeen more only a mile away. Spots for a half dozen special-permit vehicles within a few hundred feet. At full capacity, forty cars—eighty, a hundred or more people? Snowmobiles in winter, traffic in the summer. Already, the road and lake are filling with boaters, bikers, horseback riders.[18] What do the ducks and herons think of that? Not to mention the moose, the bears, the marten—all of the animals hidden deep on those previously privately owned lands that hadn't been bothered by people for perhaps their whole lives?

In his brilliant *Encounters with the Archdruid*, journalist John McPhee invites "Archdruid" David Brower—then the executive director of the Sierra Club—to go on field trips with his late 1960s contemporaries, all of whom have different perspectives on conservation and preservation. Out hiking in the mineral-rich Glacier Peak Wilderness in Washington with geologist Charles Park and rafting the Colorado River in Arizona with Bureau of Reclamation commissioner and big-dam builder Floyd Dominy, Brower and his supposed archnemeses all show some level of appreciation if not affection for the places and processes they see, but they vary wildly in terms of the purpose and appropriate uses of natural landscapes and resources.

In the second section, Brower visits Cumberland Island, Georgia, with developer Charles Fraser to discuss their preferences for its relatively intact, forested southern shoreline. Fraser envisions homes and golf courses, carefully planned to preserve trees, shorelines, and a semblance of naturalness. Brower, of course, wants wilderness.

The island, which had been privately owned by generations of Rockefellers, is now managed by the NPS as a national seashore, featuring "pristine maritime forests, undeveloped beaches, and wide marshes [that] whisper the stories of both man and nature."[19] Although McPhee, a consummate journalist, rarely injects his own presence, much less opinions, into the "encounters," he can't help but slip a poignant commentary into the section's conclusion:

> In the battle for Cumberland Island, there could be human winners here or there, but—no matter what might happen—there could be no victory for Cumberland Island. The Frasers of the world might create their blended landscapes, the Park Service its Yosemites. Either way, or both ways, no one was ever to be as free on that wild beach in the future as we had been.[20]

Poor Boreas Ponds, there could be no victory for you. As such an accessible spot in such a popular place, you can never be truly wild and free, unregulated and untrammeled. Perhaps you would have been better off unknown.

The season limped on.

Like David Hinton, "each time I walk here on [any] Mountain, I wander it a little more deeply."[21]

Yet, like Peter Matthiessen, "I am still beset by the same old lusts and ego and emotions, the endless nagging details and irritations—that aching gap between what I know and what I am."[22]

Oh, Lao Tzu: "Sometimes you are stifled / Sometimes you breathe easy / Sometimes you are strong / Sometimes you are weak." "If you want to grab the world and run it / I can see that you will not succeed."[23]

My penultimate day stewarding was marked by a partial solar eclipse. It was bright, clear mid-August weather—perfect for hiking into the woods and standing atop Algonquin Peak. I hiked quickly, arrived early, and sat alone on one of the erratics near the summit to ruminate on the landscape and my place in it. As usual, others began arriving midmorning. People tend to linger longer when it's warm and sunny, but this was special—a few dozen eclipse watchers came intending to stay for the event, at least a few hours. We chatted and watched and waited, then waited some more, unsure of if or how the eclipse would proceed. Almost imperceptibly at first, then with more of a pronounced effect, the formerly bright sky started to become noticeably dusky, as if thick clouds were passing overhead, but without a puff in sight. We stopped chatting and fell silent. Even the breeze seemed to still, the cottongrass stop rustling. As the darkness grew more pronounced, we passed around a pair of paper-framed safety glasses, held them up to the sun, and gasped, "Wow!" in turn. Moon shadow.

I think we all felt a touch of reverence, if not gratitude for a natural world that still has the capacity to surprise and awe us. Moreover, in sharing the experience, I think we all felt kinship with one another—our little eclipse family, briefly united by the remarkable celestial event and our shared decision to witness it from a mountaintop.

But in their eagerness to see the event or their general joy for being on Algonquin Peak on such an extraordinary day, at least a quarter of those people walked through patches of alpine vegetation.[24]

The final day—also Algonquin—was more typical: clouds, rain, wind; brief moments of sunglow and long stretches of solitude. I spent the morning huddling under the usual summit boulder, joined only by a rowdy college orientation group who'd gotten turned around during their ascent from Lake Colden and thought they were on Iroquois Peak. Around lunchtime, I relocated to a slightly more sheltered spot lower on the trail and waited there until midafternoon, when a father and two sons stumbled to the top and had me take photos of them leaning into the wind and rain. "Please stay on rock surfaces!" I had to shout so that they could hear me over the weather. "Plants in the alpine zone are rare and fragile!" They nodded, then proceeded to aim for a clump of sedges on the leeward side of the summit. "Please stay on rock surfaces!" I iterated, pointing at a spot that was vegetation-free but not quite as sheltered. Cold, hard, wet rock. They did not seem pleased.

I commiserated—I *really* commiserated, having already spent some four or five hours that day, some four summers total sitting on cold, hard, wet rock. Having slogged up and down those trails seventy-odd times each for Algonquin and Wright, and Marcy nearly a hundred; having stood on those mountaintops in rain, hail, snow, sunshine, fog; having gotten bruised, bloody, bug bitten, sunburnt, wind burnt, nearly hypothermic; having done all of that in some absurd, futile quest to protect plants, understand mountains, and appreciate wilderness, only to find myself more exhausted and more disheartened than before.

As the trio left the summit and began their descent, the father stepped outside the stone-lined path to walk in the soft, rain-soaked alpine meadows. Maybe he just wasn't paying attention; maybe he hadn't really heard me on the summit. "I want to believe it was out of ignorance or inattentiveness, not malice," read my last notes from the Adirondacks. "But his intent matters little to the squished sandwort, flattened deer's hair, and broken-stalked Bigelow's sedge."[25]

In her quiet masterpiece *The Living Mountain*, British novelist and poet Nan Shepherd recognizes a transition she made during her lifetime of trekking around northeast Scotland's Cairngorm Mountains. "At first," she admits, "I was seeking only sensuous gratification—the sensation of height, the sensation of movement, the sensation of speed, the sensation of distance, the sensation of effort, the sensation of ease: the lust of the flesh, the lust of the eyes, the pride of life. I was not interested in the mountain for itself, but for its effect upon me."[26] Me, I. My, self.

"But as I grew older," she continues, "I began to discover the mountain in itself . . . its contours, its colours, its water and rock, flowers and birds."[27]

Thus *The Living Mountain* begins not with Shepherd's story, but with the Plateau, its "essential nature."[28] The Plateau; then the Recesses; the Group ("peaks piled on peaks"[29]); Water (that "wells from the rock, and flows away . . . It does nothing, absolutely nothing, but be itself"[30]); Frost and Snow; Air and Light; Plants; Birds, Animals, Insects. Man— "many forceful and gnarled personalities, bred of the bone of the mountain"[31]—doesn't appear until the ninth chapter, merely a subset of "Life." From there, Sleep, Senses, and Being—our muscles and bones, brains and minds, our dreams, desires, joys, losses, and loneliness, all part of the landscape.[32] "All are aspects of one entity, the living mountain. The disintegrating rock, the nurturing rain, the quickening sun,

Ravens taunting me as I huddle under an erratic on Algonquin, trying to stay dry(ish) and warm(ish), melding into rock.

the seed, the root, the bird—all are one . . . part of the mountain's wholeness."[33]

Shepherd didn't go to the Cairngorms for personal glory or to conquer, tame, or cultivate their wildness. She went "out merely to be with the mountain": "the mountain gives itself most completely when I have no destination, when I reach nowhere in particular."[34] Similarly, she doesn't write about the Cairngorms for any discernible purpose—to celebrate them, yes, and describe the slow process of building a sense of self in place, but not to insist others make similar conversions, and certainly not to encourage tourists to come visit. In fact, she worries that the Cairngorms are already overrun, "the very heather tatty from the scrape of boots (too many boots, too much commotion)." "But then" (she couldn't possibly agree with the GMC guy?), "how much uplift for how many hearts."[35]

After decades of trekking and writing, living with and for and about the plateau, Shepherd arrives at the conclusion: "As I penetrate more deeply into the mountain's life, I penetrate also into my own." The

Cairngorms taught her, changed her. But also, from the very first page, "one never quite knows the mountain, nor oneself in relation to it."[36]

To think like a mountain—or to think like a lake filling with mountain water; or a forested hollow, a tundra-carpeted ridge, a river entombed in its canyon—would be to think in terms of systems, wholes, centuries. Rock and water and sky and life. Eons. We may go to the mountains to try to extend our understandings further back in time or beyond our human selves. But in so doing—in venturing forth, seeking adventure or perspective or just the sheer joy of being alive in this magnificent world—as humans, we're trapped in our own short lives, our own fleeting desires. "But behind [matters that involve man]," Shepherd realizes, "is the mountain itself, its substance, its strength, its structure, its weathers. It is fundamental."[37]

Just be, Skylight. Just be, Marcy, Wright, Algonquin. I went to you wanting to love you, wanting to care for you, wanting you to teach me something, I don't know what. Rock-ness? Height, mass, grace? Erosion, resilience, acceptance? I should have known better. Just as wilderness isn't a playground or photo background, it also isn't a setting for on-demand awe. It doesn't think or teach or endlessly ponder what meanings we ascribe to it. Will I never learn what Peter Matthiessen calls the "secret of the mountains"? That "the mountains simply exist, as I do myself: the mountains exist simply, which I do not. The mountains have no 'meaning,' they are meaning; the mountains are."[38]

Just be, Adirondacks. Heart Lake, Boreas Ponds, beaver dams at Wallface Ponds. Go ahead and rain, and snow, and hail. Let storms engulf summits and mist roil up through the valleys. Let the sun beam down and the black flies bite. Diapensia bloom, sparrows sing, creeks run, rocks crumble and fall. May your anorthosite heart persist for another billion years. I won't ask anything more of you. I'm not a part of you. I'll go.

In the process of trying to learn to think like a mountain, I became less mountain than cloud.

Mountains the Gate, Rivers the Door

ARCTIC ALASKA

Headwaters of the Anaktuvuk River near the Arctic Divide, Brooks Range, Alaska. "Vast and majestic, mountains embrace your shadow; / Broad and deep, rivers harbor your voice" —T'ao Ch'ien (translation by David Hinton 2005, 1).

Space, solitude, wilderness—is this what I thought I wanted? Fine, I had it. Eight and a half million acres of it, where I could feel alone and terrified, open and exposed to transcendent beauty and life-threatening danger.

It was, hands-down, the stupidest thing I've ever done: an eleven-day solo backpacking trip in Gates of the Arctic National Park and Preserve, traversing the spine of the Brooks Range—the northernmost and arguably most remote mountains in the country, arcing high above the Arctic Circle. No roads. No trails. Nobody else. Just me and my much-too-heavy pack, facing the steep, snow-filled passes, the rain-swollen rivers, the ankle-twisting tussocks, the unexpected ravines, the recent landslides, and however many bears lurking in the mist.

What a thoroughly stupid thing to do.

Glorious, too. But only in hindsight. Only because I survived.

I have no excuse or explanation for why I did it. I suppose I had the same nebulous reasons as anyone who does these sorts of things. Adventure. Hope. Desperation. After spending five years floundering along in New York, feeling lost, lonely, and wholly out of place, I needed recalibration and a reminder of what it's like to feel alive. Nothing makes you feel more acutely alive than being close to disaster—a misplaced step here, a shift of the rocks there, a chance encounter with a big, angry animal. Over and over again, an inch from injury, in a place where any injury could prove fatal.

How admittedly, absolutely *absurd*, to expose myself to such danger willingly, naively; almost eagerly. I got what I deserved.

It began with the backcountry ranger from Denali. We'd stayed in touch over the years, sending sporadic emails, usually about our travels, academia, or references to Thoreau. While I was up and down the same mountains in New York, he was in the Andes, the Rockies, back in Alaska; packrafting the entirety of the Susitna River from the Alaska Range south across south-central Alaska, then the Jago from the Eastern Brooks Range north through the Arctic National Wildlife Refuge. For years, he'd had his eye on the remote, relatively unknown Anaktuvuk River—floating it all the way from the Arctic Divide in the Central Brooks Range to its confluence with the Colville River, then along the edge of the National Petroleum Reserve-Alaska to the Arctic Ocean, across some two-hundred-odd miles of pure wild space: Alaska's North Slope.

The year after my final season in the Adirondacks, everything aligned: he needed to go to the village of Anaktuvuk Pass near the headwaters of the Anaktuvuk River to finish a research project and might try making the float trip, early July; all of my short- and long-term plans to get out of New York were crumbling, and I found myself, mid-May, with nothing to do and nothing I wanted to do for the summer. And, for that matter, for years ahead, empty. "Let me know if you need a research assistant," I emailed him, half joking, half wistful. "It could be good to have you on the float, but you'd have to be prepared for serious bugs, a lot of paddling, etc.," his practical reply.

"Unraveling a bit," began my next message, a week later, after my plans and hopes had entirely shattered, emptiness tugging on my soul. Followed by some rambling explanation. Then, tossed in at the end, about forty percent joking, maybe ten percent serious and the rest flinging for any small dream: "(How do you get to Anaktuvuk? Small plane from Fairbanks?)"

Again, a straightforward response: "Yes, a small plane." Followed by a reference to the North Slope as "the Great Plains of the North" and links to information about paleontology on the lower Colville.

"Tony Fiorillo!!!" My exclamation-point-filled follow-up. *The* Tony Fiorillo, from both Black Canyon and Denali. The Alaska dinosaur expert. Of course, he'd done work along the Colville; of course, he'd discovered a tiny tyrannosaur in the bone-filled bluffs. "You should have led with the fossils."

From the backcountry ranger, a long list of realities and deterrents. Expensive equipment and flights. Also "10–12 days of continuous paddling in a small, confined boat," including a stretch of estimated Class II rapids. Terrible and terribly unpredictable weather. Extreme remoteness. Bugs—"just imagine the worst you can imagine." Aggressive and unpredictable polar bears. (Polar bears?)

From me: "Right now, the thought of mountains and rivers and great swaths of tundra is the only thing that brings me joy. How serious are you about letting me join the float?"

In trying to research the potential trip, I made the mistake of looking up the only online report regarding the Anaktuvuk—an "Expedition Arguk" from 2013, whose four members note "the only record we can find of someone running the Anaktuvuk River dates back to 1901, when it was surveyed in a bark canoe."[1] They write of violent, tent-crushing storms, cold wind and thick fog, a "chaotic" braided river, encounters with a grizzly and, yes, a polar bear. They also write of "wilderness on a stupefying and humbling scale." They even recognize:

When judging the value of landscapes, we're drawn to the superlative. We admire and praise the deepest canyons, the loftiest peaks, the longest arches, and the tallest waterfalls . . . Much of the Brooks Range Mountains are protected as wildlife reserve and national parkland, but the park ends, predictably, at the foothills. We just don't tend to value places without extraordinary topographical relief, which is too bad because the North Slope is, without a doubt, one of America's great unknown national treasures.[2]

I was sold.

Problem was, their trip had had two stages. Before rafting, they backpacked across part of the Brooks Range, to Anaktuvuk Pass from the Dalton Highway. An idea seeded in my sleep-deprived and depression-steeped brain. "Would it be entirely crazy and/or impossible of me consider backpacking in?" I emailed the backcountry ranger. He called to dissuade me, and we began making plans.

"There's a reason people don't do these things." I should have read Expedition Arguk's report more closely. "These are not things people want to do."

"Too late now. It's happening."[3]

As soon as the shuttle van dropped me off, deep in the Brooks Range near the headwaters of the Dietrich River and cusp of the Arctic Divide, I realized the enormity of my mistake. During the flights to Fairbanks and the long, bumpy drive up the Dalton—less a "highway" than a pot-holed strip of dirt—I'd felt a healthy, growing mix of excitement and trepidation. I was as prepared as I could be: route planned, maps outlined, meals carefully measured; pack overladen with everything from dry-suit pants (for the rafting trip, but also crucial for river crossings) to a personal locator beacon (my only concession to modern technology) to a copy of the *Tao Te Ching* (dead weight). But there's no way to really prepare. Left alone among the sharp, snow-striped mountains on the banks of a turgid river, wolf prints the size of my hand fresh in the mud at my feet, excitement dissipated and pure fear remained. The peaks were taller and steeper than I'd imagined, the water stronger than expected. I had to cross *that*?

I thought I'd planned a relatively easy route—fording rivers near their headwaters, cresting passes at their widest, too far north for brush that would harbor moose—but there's no such thing as "easy" in a place like Gates of the Arctic. I realized this right off the bat, as I fought my way across the Dietrich, using every ounce of strength to shuffle one leg at a time sideways against the nearly overpowering current, trying to use my trekking poles for balance but barely able to keep them—and myself—from being swept away. Safe on the other side, once my legs stopped trembling and heart stopped pounding, I crashed through dense willows, discovered an anonymous side drainage I also had to cross—even wider, deeper, and stronger than the Dietrich—then scrambled up a mud-coated cliff, staggered over a half mile of uneven sedges and grasses, reached an impassably deep ravine that didn't show up between the lines on my map, and, in the attempt to contour up around it, felt something pop in the same ankle I'd injured the previous year. The only somewhat flat patch upon which I could stake my tent was a yard from the edge of a cliff. It was perfect habitat for bears.

That was just the first evening—the first few hours, in perfect weather, still in sight of the road. The Dalton Highway—more accurately, the "Haul Road," the only road in northern Alaska, connecting Fairbanks to Prudhoe Bay—was laboriously carved across the North Slope in the 1970s to enable construction of the Trans-Alaska Pipeline, not to drop foolish tourists off at the edge of one of the biggest, wildest parks in the country. At that point, though, I didn't think I'd be able to re-cross the Dietrich, much less the other drainage, so I knew my only way was forward, through land protected as Wilderness, over high mountain passes, back and forth across the Arctic Divide, through snow and ice and fog and what turned out to be much (much, much) deeper, stronger drainages, seventy-odd miles to Anaktuvuk Pass. If I'd known then what lay before me, would I have turned back? I should have turned back.

Blame it on Bob Marshall—his romantic notions of wildness, his romanticized descriptions of Alaska, his work with the Wilderness Society to protect places such as Gates of the Arctic. The same Bob Marshall of 46er fame. After his adventures in the Adirondacks, Marshall went on to explore ever bigger, wilder terrain, finally reaching interior

Alaska—"what seemed on the map to be the most unknown section of Alaska"—in 1929.[4] A collection of essays and letters he wrote about his several expeditions to the region were published posthumously in 1956, under the title *Arctic Wilderness* (now *Alaska Wilderness: Exploring the Central Brooks Range*).

In preparation for my harebrained backpacking expedition, I purchased a copy of *Alaska Wilderness* and underlined and dog-eared every inspiring sentence: "As I walked for hours beneath the stupendous grandeur of these colossal mountains, I felt humble and insignificant."[5] "We felt a genuine exultation in seeing the flawless white of those summits and the flawless blue of the sky, and the razor-edge sharpness with which the two came together."[6] "Man may be taming nature, but no one standing on the bank of the North Fork of the Koyukuk on this gray morning would have claimed that nature is conquered."[7] "I got soaked and saw little."[8]

With the hope of experiencing the same stupendous grandeur, genuine exultation, and unconquerable nature, I planned my route to follow and allow side forays to see features Marshall first named and described—Grizzly Creek, Boreal Mountain, Frigid Crags (the very "Gates of the Arctic," Marshall dubbed them), and Mt. Doonerak (a word meaning "spirit or . . . devil"[9])—"mountains everywhere under the blue sky."[10] I intended to climb the same ridges, tangle with the same tussocks, ford the same creeks, marvel at the same glorious sky. To rediscover a world where everything is sharp and bright, where the sun "shin[es] brilliantly on countless lofty peaks without name and beyond the scope of human knowledge" and where "[a]ll [i]s peace and strength and immensity and coordination and freedom."[11]

But once I was actually out *in* the arctic wilderness—a true wilderness, not just one labeled as such on a map—all of the mountains seemed like Dooneraks, and all the creeks inhabited by grizzlies. Alone in that big, wild place, I felt no peace and freedom, only weakness and fear. "To be honest, I don't even care," I scribbled in my little notebook, midday on day seven, while sprawled on the soggy, lumpy tundra, too exhausted to even swat the mosquitoes away from my eyes and ears. "I'm sure it's beautiful—the photographs will attest to that, belatedly—but right now, I have neither the energy nor the inclination to appreciate it. Why am I here?"

That's what I wanted, right? As authentic a "wilderness experience" as possible in the twenty-first century? To be far from people and roads and trails and technology, to be on my own in a big, real place? Oh, I'd had no idea what that meant, what I was longing for.

Although park regulations, LNT principles, and common sense allow for some concessions to modern technology—a bear canister, camp stove, water filter, a camera—when packing for the trip, I'd absolutely refused to carry a GPS and only conceded to a personal locator beacon after much convincing. "So this is where my wilderness purism has gotten me," I wrote on the afternoon of the fourth day: "staring at a ridge of mountains half-lost in rain, wondering if I'm reading the map correctly and aiming for the right pass." If I'd had a GPS, I could have always known where I was and where I needed to be. Instead, I had to pull out my compass and maps at least once an hour, squint at the landscape, and try to translate it into topographic squiggles. I was never quite sure whether I was navigating correctly, and to make a mistake could have cost me hours' or days' worth of grueling travel over treacherous terrain. Moreover, the map and compass were almost entirely useless in the fog. It didn't matter what direction I was facing when I couldn't see any features and couldn't tell how far I'd traveled. Bob Marshall seemed to think it a great lark to be lost, but the perpetual uncertainty gnawed at me.

The personal locator beacon, though. That magnificent little collection of plastics, minerals, and metals became a talisman of hope. Of prayer. Should anything happen (or, in my mind, it was "*when* something happens")—should I be swept away by any of the raging streams, should I be crushed in a rockslide, should I slip or trip or twist off a tussock and snap a leg—I could press a few buttons to activate the beacon. Then my life would no longer be in my hands. I'd be able to simply wait and hope that help would come. "Between the weather and the terrain," a ranger at the Interagency Visitor Center in Coldfoot had warned me, "it's not always possible to mount rescues." Even though I'd nearly rather die than use it, and even though safety wasn't guaranteed, it was *something*. I don't know how I could have gone on without it.

Except that I had to go on. Once I'd started—once I'd crossed the Dietrich and, the next day, once I'd straggled across a rock- and

Undulatus over Limestack Mountain, headwaters of Grizzly Creek, just over the Arctic Divide.

tundra-barren saddle; once I'd crossed over the Arctic Divide for the first time, skirting an ice-filled, snow-rimmed lake and hiding from a hailstorm; once I'd spent another day fighting tussocks, traversing rockslides, fearing crossing the Oolah River, and, finally, struggling across the mid-thigh-deep and ice-cold Oolah River, crawling out into the willows on the far bank, sprawling on the mud, and spending a good half hour crying with terror and relief—well, there was no going back. Onward. More icy passes, more rock falls, more rivers. Rain. Thunder. Mile upon mile upon mile of bogs, not a single flat step. Fog.

I needed everything I'd ever learned about and from wilderness to keep me alive. Those eleven days were a summation and examination of all of my previous experience: being alone in backcountry Black Canyon, mountain lions lurking in the brush; navigating the rivers and rocks of Denali, discovering the truths of the tundra and techniques for travel in bear country; and, especially, the Adirondacks. I would not have survived the Arctic had I not spent four full seasons in the Adirondacks, carrying a heavy pack through uneven terrain, using trekking poles as extensions of my own limbs, wrapping myself in a bug net and poncho and sitting patiently through squalls. Waking to the sound of rain on the tent on day five, day six, day seven, not wanting to hike, not wanting to go anywhere *at all*, but then sighing, pulling on my wet socks, repacking my wet tent, and setting off again. The Adirondacks taught me something, after all—perseverance.

Of the week and a half in Gates, there was only one storm- or drizzle-free stretch, night eight. I left the rainfly off my tent and sat, protected from mosquitoes, for hours, watching the pale arctic sun drift round from mountaintop to mountaintop, a pinkish orb pausing to examine each peak. By that point, I'd made it to a wide valley near the headwaters of the Anaktuvuk River—the same water I'd be rafting down in a few days, if everything worked out. The river's braids gleamed in the long light, the brightest feature in an otherwise dusky landscape: sky the color of perpetual sunset, shark-fin mountains shadowed purple, tundra speckled with eager wildflowers, whites, pinks, golds, greens. Sitting there, soaking in the first and only moments of tranquility in the Brooks Range, something about the colors and calm reminded me of Skylight—the sense of serenity and belonging, the curious slant of the light. (And here, I didn't have to worry about any other hiker showing up and ruining the magic.)

Then there was the afternoon, day six, I found myself staring at a snowbank that filled a wide ravine and separated me from where I wanted to be: safely on solid ground in the headwaters of Grizzly Creek. I'd just completed a strenuous, precarious slog up and over Peregrine Pass—what I'd thought, judging from maps and Google Earth, would be the crux of the trip (and the most important test of my map-reading skills/guesses.) After spending the previous afternoon and evening tent bound, deep in a cirque near the headwaters of the North Fork of the Koyukuk River, listening to rain patter on the fabric and rocks crumble and crash off surrounding cliffs, I'd woken that morning to find a weak blue sky, a skin of ice in my water bottle, and a glorious fog-bow arcing across the boulder-strewn tundra. I ought to have given the sun time to melt the ice and evaporate the fog, but I didn't want to delay my attempt at the pass, so I packed and stumbled, with numb toes, across a mile of shifting, moss-coated and ice-glazed old rockslides. Praying I was navigating correctly, aiming for what looked like a saddle that was slightly lower than nearby ridges, I turned into a south-facing valley and picked my way up its steepening slopes, eventually coming to a wall of loose slabs of shale. Nothing to do but mountain-goat up. Step, step, slide; step, step, slide. I wasn't sure if I was actually gaining ground. Step, step, slide, for hours. I earned every inch. Finally: success! I peeked over the crest, flush with exertion and triumph, only to see . . . snow. A huge wave of snow, clinging to the north-facing side of the ridge—remnants of what I'd been warned had a been a harsh winter and late, wet spring. Not just snow but steep, crusty snow. If I slipped on that, there'd be no self-arrest; I'd slide over the last visible ledge into who knows where. As I stood and stared, I had a flashback to the return from Fang in Denali: crossing the snow patch in the mist, kicking each foot in to create little steps, slowly all the way across the nothingness. So that's what I did, again. (Main difference: the other paleontology intern wasn't here to share the experience, or to help if I fell.)

On the second-to-last day, I had one final drainage to cross, and knew it was going to be a big one—biggest of the trip, judging from the size of the watershed upstream, plus the snowmelt, plus days of rain. As soon as I noticed it on the map (when planning the route, it hadn't even registered as something to worry about, just a single blue line), a knot of fear formed in my stomach. By that point, I'd crossed a half dozen waterways, each progressively deeper and stronger; me progressively weaker. At some point, I was sure, my luck would run out. But onward. The night before meeting it, I lay awake for hours, clinging to the personal locator beacon like a security blanket, imagining what I'd do if I couldn't cross the drainage or if I was swept away trying. Nothing I *could* do. The land dominated here. Forces of nature. Man a visitor who does not remain. Why hadn't I believed Bob Marshall when he'd described "barely manag[ing] to get across" swollen creeks, even when "using . . . horses as support"[12]? (Probably because "freed from our nerve-wracking plight [he] felt coz[y] and joll[y]," giddily dismissive of the "hardships ahead."[13]) Why on earth had I come? Was this what I thought I wanted? I had no choice; the drainage would decide.

That morning, I couldn't eat. It took forever to get going—to force my fingers to lace my boots and tighten the final straps on my pack. Once I started moving, though, I wanted to get it over with. For once, the terrain cooperated—mostly solid, well-drained tundra, with only a few boggy stretches and the occasional black-bellied plover popping up to protest my presence. The weather wasn't too bad, either—overcast skies and occasional showers, but not pouring and not too cold. The only problem was the drainage, farther away than I'd thought. (Darn it, why hadn't I brought a GPS?) I kept squinting at the horizon, looking for any sign of the ravine that it must cut through, but there was nothing there—the same undulating hills in the same broad valley, still the upper Anaktuvuk, which I'd been in forever, it felt like. Endless tundra, rain, only the slightest of shifts in perspective. Now, this drainage.

I heard it before I saw it. Snarling fury emanating from the earth. I walked on to meet it. Churning gray-brown mass, racing over boulders and smashing into banks. Cutting into the land, leaving a sheer cliff on one side—my side; that's why I hadn't been able to see it—and swallowing shrubs on the other, at least a foot if not two higher than usual, judging by how it engulfed the vegetation. As I stood on the bank above it, my fear melted away and I entered a state of deep calm. For a moment, I thought, *Black Canyon—the Gunnison*. The sound of the water, the desperation in my heart—I'd been here before. I knew this world, and my place in it.

Then I stepped out into the drainage, and all the terror of the present came rushing back. My right foot slipped, and the water whipped it away.

I remember each moment of that hike vividly, almost traumatically, and could recount them in real time. But that's not the point. No, it's that I survived. And journeyed on to a place where I finally felt at peace: the North Slope—everything unfurling from the Brooks Range to the shores of the Arctic Ocean. Sixty million acres, eighteen and a half of which are in the Arctic National Wildlife Refuge to the east, twenty-three million of which are in the National Petroleum Reserve-Alaska to the west, the rest a mix of state and Iñupiat lands, so much *space*.

When I dragged myself, exhausted and exhilarated to be alive, into the village of Anaktuvuk Pass on day eleven, a cool, fog-thick afternoon, I wasn't at all sure I still wanted to do the raft trip. Backpacking had shown me how much I'd underestimated the landscape and overestimated my own adventurousness. The plans the ranger and I had loosely gathered took us through even more remote, almost unknown terrain, at the middle of which we'd be nearly a hundred miles from any sign of civilization and help, should we need it. What if the raft overturned? What if it ripped? What if a bear attacked? What if the river proved impassable—could I walk another fifty or seventy miles back or forward, with a re-injured ankle? (I'd *really* re-sprained it partway through that final drainage but had managed to hang on somehow, barely, and crawled and cried and limped on.) Was it worth it—was all of this worth it? What was the point? Still some insatiable search for self?

Of course, there would be two of us in the raft, and the ranger was far more competent than me. I wouldn't have to walk or climb. I didn't even have to steer, really. He'd do that; he knew how to read the water. I could sit, paddle, and just let the river carry us to wherever it wanted to go. Plus, we'd be on "the Great Plains of the North," as he'd characterized the landscape. I was done with mountains. No more mountains, no more canyons; just an open horizon and an infinite sky.

We put in at a little rill, barely wide enough for the raft. I didn't trust that it would carry us to the river, but it continued to weave through rushes and reeds, picking up momentum as it gurgled happily down from the Arctic Divide, carrying us across a wind-rippled lake, past the first of hundreds of ducks we'd send flapping over the course of the next two weeks, and into a deeper, slightly less narrow, shrub-lined, clear-watered, pebble-bottomed channel. That channel, in turn, grew deeper and wider as tributaries flowed in and out, or as the tributaries we followed left and joined the larger channels. There were a dozen rivers, all thinning and dividing and weaving back together, carrying us north, toward the vast slope, toward the ocean, toward the edge of the world. Late afternoon transitioned into early evening, but human time doesn't matter to the arctic summer. Rain showers alternated with whispers of rainbows.

The first night, we camped on a gravel bar between five-thousand-foot-high peaks that the ranger wanted to climb and I wanted to get away from. By the second night, the mountains had receded to the horizon, a jagged blue-gray backdrop to rolling green foothills. By the third night, the Brooks Range was gone and I could breathe again. Even the hills flattened out. Aside from the occasional odd geologic twist—including one particularly narrow set of sandstone cliffs that we saw on the maps and worried would constrict the water and churn it into rapids, but instead welcomed and swirled us pleasantly along—there was little topographic relief. The river meandered between four- to five-foot-high river bluffs and wide gravel bars. The tundra was textured with shrubs, mosses, puddles, and pools. The sky collided with clouds from the west, the north, the land, the sea. While the ranger watched the water, steering toward deeper channels and sometimes toward boulders for the slight thrill, I stared at the sky: colors and birds and glorious nothingness.

We reached the confluence with the Colville River on the sixth day, leaving the Anaktuvuk's haphazard rapids, riffles, and meanders for the Colville's wide, smooth channel. We'd worried that the Colville wouldn't have much of a current; over a distance of about a hundred miles from the confluence to the ocean, it drops only two hundred feet in elevation. But we hadn't accounted for the volume of water flowing from upstream, gathering momentum from across the entire central Brooks Range. The Colville was a muddy mass, carrying us along at a good three to four miles per hour—the same pace at which I walk, but instead I was sitting, letting my ankle and soul heal, soothed by the wildness flowing by.

According to the map, everything north and west of the Colville is part of the National Petroleum Reserve-Alaska (NPRA)—the largest single unit of public land in the country and an odd man out, with no comparable designations or management protocols. Upon its transfer from the US Navy to the Bureau of Land Management in 1976, the tract had been evaluated for both energy resources and ecological significance. The BLM opened some regions to oil and gas leasing and elsewhere acknowledged the presence of important ecological and cultural resources, creating five somewhat nebulously defined and legislatively unprotected "Special Areas." We were skirting the Colville River Special Area—a 2.4-million-acre stretch containing "unique bluff and riparian habitats," including a high density of nests of peregrine falcons, gyrfalcons, and rough-legged hawks.[14] We certainly saw our share of raptors. They became our chaperones, a pair of peregrines following and screaming at us for miles, then passing off the duties to the next pair, day after day. But we found no fence or sign or any sort of indication that the special area (or, for that matter, the NPRA) existed. Tundra, rock, river, raptor, sky as far as the eye could see.

While the Colville is free to wander along its eastern shoreline, its western edge—the NPRA side—is constrained by a set of two- to three-hundred-foot-high cliffs—layers of tawny sandstones and mudstones, dark shales, and black coal seams that make up the Late Cretaceous Prince Creek Formation. Erosional forces were well at work on them. Water trickled and gushed down every ravine, adding sediment to the turbid river below. Occasionally, huge chunks of rock, mud, and melting snow gave way and crashed into the channel below, sending out waves large enough to bobble the raft.

Who knows what remarkable traces of Cretaceous life were being exposed and lost. As soon as I saw the cliffs, my paleontologist brain reengaged, wanting to hop ashore to investigate the sandstones and mudstones for ancient wonders. The sheerness of the bluffs kept us constrained to the river, though. We only had a handful of opportunities to land, in which cases the ranger would scramble up the cliffs while I slowly peered at and under every outcrop, looking for fossils (numerous plant impressions and near-ubiquitous coalified wood). For the most part, we just drifted past the dinosaurs, letting the snow and rock crumble and peregrines scream at us from the cliffs.

As we got closer to the ocean, floating and looking, looking and sometimes talking, the bluffs gradually melted away. The farther north we went, the flatter and bigger the horizon. The land was marked by hundreds of abandoned meanders, thousands of pools in the permafrost. Polygons. Pingoes. One great swath of tundra, blooming with flowers and buzzing with mosquitoes on its surface, bulging and cracking with ice underneath. But the *sky*. The *light*. Its clear, insistent color, blue or gray midday, tinged with pinks and golds at midnight. Even in the middle of the summer in the Arctic, with twenty-four hours of sun, the sky retains some quality of the midwinter night—a luminosity, a brilliance, the shimmering echoes of aurorae.

Plus the *clouds*. Layer upon layer of cumulus, altocumulus, cirrus, cirrostratus, stratocumulus; undulatus, floccus, fibratus, translucidus. Halos. Virga. Rain. Everything all at once, sweeping in from a dozen different directions, flowing away. I was dizzy with looking. I was dizzy with delight.

Looking south, a halo over the Colville bluff.

Not that rafting across the North Slope was a wholly wondrous—or even comfortable—experience. My ankle throbbed. My back and arms stiffened, sitting in the same position in the same little red boat hour after hour, day after day. I shivered into near-hypothermia on the cold, rainy fifth day, and spent the eighth through eleventh swatting at mosquitoes. Good god, the mosquitoes.

A moose nearly trampled my tent on night one. We camped by too-fresh grizzly tracks on night nine. We were buffeted by the wind, always. We constantly ran aground. We argued. Oh, did we argue—about how to use a sail properly, about whether birds are dinosaurs, about art and music and phenomenology and reality and the implications of me letting a plastic bag blow away. Not infrequently, I wished I was on my own again, with no one else there to see me cry or laugh or sing or seethe. Nothing lonelier than feeling alone with another person present. When it was over, we shared flights from the village of Nuiqsut to Utqiagvik to Anchorage to Fairbanks, then parted ways.

But from the confluence with the Colville all the way to the Arctic Ocean—really, from the time we floated away from the Brooks Range and onto the vast northern plain—I felt at peace, at rest, a building "sense of expansiveness, of deep exhilaration . . . summed up in a single Eskimo word: *quviannikumut*, 'to feel deeply happy.'"[15]

On a brilliantly sunny day, a week and a half after putting in at the clear little rill just below the Arctic Divide, we veered into the Nigliq Channel on the western side of the Colville Delta, floated past the village of Nuiqsut—rows of colorful metal buildings, gravel roads, and electrical wires nestled atop the tundra, air buzzing with the sound of ATVs, motorboats, and barking dogs—then floated past a tangle of energy infrastructure—phallic orange drilling rigs, pipelines, a shiny new bridge, and more oil pads under construction, all absurdly out of place on the harsh, distant edge of the continent. (Though we must have seemed out of place, too. Truck drivers paused partway across the bridge to stop and stare at our little red raft bobbing along, and Nuiqsut residents steered their fishing boats over to chat with us: *You came from <u>where</u>?*) A few miles before reaching the coast (and hopefully not yet in polar bear habitat), we found the perfect spot to camp: a small island, rising no more than ten feet out of the channel, maybe a few hundred yards long and half as wide, its flat top carpeted with moss and wildflowers. By the time we'd landed, deflated the raft, pitched our tents, and begun to boil water for dinner, it was nine or ten at night and the sun-infused sky was beginning to soften, taking on a warm, coppery sheen. A gentle but persistent breeze kept the wildflowers bobbing and mosquitoes at bay. The air smelled of salt.

After dinner, we circumambulated the shoreline, counterclockwise, discovering all sorts of feathers, tracks, and flowers. Gulls and bears. (Grizzly? Polar?) I'd never seen so many mountain avens in one place— a full colony of *Dryas octopetala*, eight-petaled arctic-alpine nymphs, turning their happy, heliotropic faces to follow the sun. We lingered at a little mud-smoothed beach at the northern tip of the island, squinting out across the rippled water of the channel and cirrostratus-speckled sky, as if we could see the Beaufort Sea, the North Pole, the whole world over the curvature of the earth. The *ocean*! We were almost there! I could feel its pull, as if I'd been spending not just weeks but years looking forward to reaching it. But at the same time, I didn't want the journey to end. I could have stayed on that island forever, standing tall on the soft moss, staring at the flat horizon, the infinite possibilities, until the summer ended and storms swept in, until I was coated with ice and buried in snow, until I was scoured as cleanly as the caribou skull sitting twenty yards away.

Onward. We continued along the western shore, crumpled with frost heaves and riddled with ground squirrel burrows, then paused again, this time at the rocky southern shore, overlooking the space we'd come from—the Nigliq Channel, a partially constructed drilling pad, lots of tundra. Tomorrow, we'd be rafting back through, fighting the wind and current to get to Nuiqsut in time to catch our flight to Utqiagvik the following day. I'd see a red-throated loon. But for that moment we were *there*, on a little island in the middle of a channel in part of a delta on the edge of the ocean, the sediment of the Brooks Range and a million acres of mountain, rain, and melted snow and ice flowing past, the color of arctic non-night flooding the sky overhead.

The ranger, tired of looking, headed back to his tent. I stood alone, feet on the ground, head in the clouds, where I belong.

For a decade, I'd been lugging around a beloved and now rather tattered copy of Barry Lopez's *Arctic Dreams*, filling it with lines and notes and sketches, absorbing the words and thinking I understood them. But now, I was actually experiencing them—the "Corridors of Breath," the "Ice and Light," the "Country of the Mind," the colors so rich that I could *feel* them. I could feel everything. "The beauty here is a beauty you feel in your flesh," Lopez observes. "You feel it physically, and that is why it is sometimes terrifying to approach. Other beauty takes only the heart, or the mind."[16]

Eight years earlier, I'd been reading *Arctic Dreams* while out for an evening walk at Fossil Butte. The third of July, according to the note I'd scribbled at the bottom of the page, "air warm and sage-scented, heart light" (having just met the bio tech). I remember reaching this sentence in the book and stopping in my tracks. Stopping to box it in, to dog-ear the page, to whisper it out loud, to look up at the butte and across the marvelous sagebrush-steppe and even more marvelous emptiness above it, and to recite Lopez's words again: "In the reprieve at the end of a day, in the stillness of a summer evening, the world sheds

Island, Nigliq Channel, three miles from the Arctic Ocean, mid-July, near midnight.

its categories, the insistence of its future, and is suspended solely in the lilt of its desire."[17]

Two years later, my handwriting at the bottom of the same page: "Desire, desire, beauty and desire, beauty and despair. Sitting by an unnamed creek, one ridge from Fang Mtn. Denali NPP, 05 July."

Squeezed in on July 12, three years after that: "Loneliness, longing. Walking E. Portal Road, Black Canyon."

Adirondacks, June of the following year: "Deep sorrow, always. Sorrow and joy."

Now, having carried the book with me back and forth across the Arctic Divide and all the way across the North Slope, to the ocean—nearly there!—I stood alone on that little island under the great northern sky, "in the reprieve at the end of a day, in the stillness of a summer evening," the world suspended. Lilting. All desire, all presence.

While waiting for the ranger to wake the next morning, I walked back around the island, clockwise this time, more slowly than the night before, trying to internalize every inch of it. The day was already miraculously warm and sunny—entire sky a deep blue, layered with high white wisps and lower puffs. Had it been only two weeks since I'd been scrambling through snowdrifts and shivering in rainstorms, skirting ravines and surrounded by mountains? A year since Boreas? Three since Black Canyon? Lifetimes ago.

By the time he got up, we made breakfast, folded up our tents, reinflated and repacked the raft—experts at it, by now—it was past noon. Had I been on my own, I would have left hours earlier. (Had I been on my own, I never would have been there.) But then the timing wouldn't have worked so perfectly. We reached the ocean just as the tide was finishing flowing out, slowing, pausing. Wind calming. Channel widening and land melting away, from moss to mud to mirror-calm water. Mirages shimmered in the distance. Distance became meaningless. Impossible to tell what was near or far, land or sky, true or false. None of that mattered.

We ran aground in the muck of low tide, the channel no longer separate from the ocean, distant edge of sea ice indistinguishable from clouds. We ventured out to stand on the blurry end of the continent, legs wobbly on the ambiguous ground. Not knowing where to go or what to do when there was no land left, we began picking our way across the tidal mudflats, only barely remembering to bring pepper spray should a polar bear mistake one of us for a seal (as if that would stop it). My senses continued to work—smell of the sea, feel of warm sun and cold water, sound of muck pulling at my feet and mosquitoes buzzing at my ears, every shade of blue, blue, blue—but my brain failed to process them. I was standing, but not upright. I was walking, but not moving. I was breathing, but was my heart still beating? Maybe the earth had stopped spinning.

Then I realized, with a dreamy awareness, that the mudflats were filling with little rills and pools. Time was indeed passing—the tide had turned and was beginning to flow back in. We dashed back across an infinity of muck to catch the raft just as it was about to float away.

I was only at that place—that mud-laced, pool-pocked, cirrus-swept, land-water-sky spot—for a few moments, and will likely never be there again. But for a brief, shining pause, I stood suspended in time and space—no canyons, no mountains, no fossils or flowers; no roads, no trails; no things, no thoughts, no one. Empty horizon, distant ice.

Yes, Barry Lopez, "The ethereal and timeless power of the land, that union of what is beautiful with what is terrifying, is insistent . . . The land gets inside us; and we must decide one way or another what this means, what we will do about it."[18]

The land got inside me. I am part canyon, part mountain, part cloud. The merging of land, water, and sky; the boundary between the human and the wild; a vast blueness. I have decided, this is who I want to be.

Tiny red raft at the confluence of land, water, ice, and sky. The End.

Acknowledgments

Although this work sometimes questions and critiques our relationships with American parks and protected areas, underneath it all is a deep, abiding love of and gratitude for public lands and the people who help preserve and steward them. Special thanks to the dedicated and inspiring individuals who have worked and continue to work to protect Black Canyon of the Gunnison National Park, Denali National Park and Preserve, Adirondack State Park, and Gates of the Arctic National Park and Preserve.

And while this work focuses more on relationships with wild places than with people, people are, of course, integral to anyone's experience of place. In particular, to the biology technician from Fossil Butte, my supervisor at Black Canyon, the backcountry ranger at Denali, my fellow GeoCorps intern at Denali, Sylvie the sled dog (even if she wasn't technically a person), both of my supervisors / summit steward coordinators at the Adirondack Mountain Club, fellow summit stewards and ADK staff, the New York State Department of Environmental Conservation assistant forest ranger, and everyone I've had a chance to hike with and learn from over the years: a heartfelt thank-you for sharing your time and perspectives with me, and for helping me see and think about places and myself differently.

Lastly, as always, I couldn't have written this book or lived the experiences described in its pages without the support of my parents, Jon C. Olstad and Jane L. Olstad, who may sometimes question my interpretations of what's "interesting," "fun," or "mostly safe" but always encourage me to live life to the fullest and to bring extra socks.

Notes

PREFACE

1 Snyder (1965, 400).
2 Snyder (1990, 182).
3 Lopez (1986, 228).
4 Lopez (1986, 368).
5 Hinton (2012).

CHAPTER 1

1 145 Cong. Rec. H22, 821–26 (1999).
2 Translation by J. P. Seaton in Hamill and Seaton (2004, 32).
3 Northern Colorado Plateau Inventory and Monitoring Network (2004).
4 Appleton (1975, vii).
5 Appleton (1975, vii).
6 Appleton (1975, 69).
7 Kaplan (1979; 1987; 1995).
8 Carr (1999).
9 Bureau of Land Management (1986).
10 Ross (1979, 668).
11 Gussow (1979, 6).
12 Gussow (1979, 9).
13 Leopold (1969, 40).
14 Leopold (1969, 2–3).
15 Leopold (1969, 10–11).
16 Gussow (1979, 10).
17 Bernbaum (1990, 208).
18 Fudge (2001, 275).
19 Saito (1998, 101).
20 Pyne (1998).
21 Grand Canyon National Park (2016).
22 Powell (1909, 29).
23 Dutton quoted in Jenkins (2018).
24 US Department of the Interior (1903).
25 Muir (1918, 348).
26 Muir (1918, 349).
27 Muir (1918, 349).
28 Lopez (1981, 51–52).
29 Herzog (1987).
30 Herzog (1987, 150).
31 Burmil et al. (1999, 99 and 100).
32 Burmil et al. (1999, 100).
33 Stephen Pyne, quoted in Aton and McPherson (2000, 50).
34 Brown and Daniel (1991).
35 Diaz et al. (1996).
36 Black Canyon of the Gunnison National Park (2015b).
37 Powell (1909, 29).
38 Lopez (1981, 51).
39 Lopez (1981, 53 and 51).
40 Stiger and Carpenter (1980, 6).
41 Stiger and Carpenter (1980, 6).
42 Black Canyon of the Gunnison National Park (2015a).
43 Vandenbusche (2009, 7 and 55).
44 Vandenbusche (2009, 39).
45 Black Canyon of the Gunnison National Park (2015a).
46 Local rancher Douglass Lytle in 1934, quoted in Beidleman (1963, 163).
47 Quoted in Beidleman (1963, 167).
48 Official report to NPS Director Horace Albright, 1932, quoted in Beidleman (1963, 170).
49 Beidleman (1963).
50 Han Shan as translated in Hamill and Seaton (2004, 32).

51 Tuan (1977, 6).
52 Buttimer (1976, 279).
53 Casey (2001).
54 Bunkše (2007).
55 Cheng et al. (2003); Olstad (2014, 78).
56 de Wit (2003, 6).
57 Lopez (1986, xxi).
58 Williams et al. (1992, 31).
59 Tuan (1974, 4).
60 Schroeder (1991, 232); Altman and Low (1992).
61 Tuan (2001).

CHAPTER 2

1 Fiorillo and May (1995; 1996).
2 Koch et al. (2006, 35).
3 Trujillo (2001).
4 Koch et al. (2006, 35).
5 Koch et al. (2006).
6 Pub. L. No. 106–76, 113 Stat. 1126 (October 21, 1999), and H.R. 6493, 111th Cong. (December 2, 2010).
7 Carlson (1998).
8 Carlson (1979, 272).
9 Tuan (1989, 234).
10 Black Canyon of the Gunnison (2006).
11 Kellogg et al. (2004).

CHAPTER 3

1 Bass (1997, 6).
2 Resource Systems Group (2017).
3 Resource Systems Group (2017, 322).
4 Snyder (1990, 16).
5 Black Canyon of the Gunnison (2016).
6 Holmes et al. (2010).
7 Holmes et al. (2010).
8 Holmes et al. (2010).
9 Warner (1934).
10 Warner (1934).
11 Lopez (1981, 53).
12 Lopez (1981, 53).

CHAPTER 4

1 Sahney and Benton (2008, 759).

CHAPTER 5

1 Service (1907).
2 Lopez (1986, 181).
3 Lopez (1986, xxv).
4 Lopez (1986, xviv).
5 Lopez (1986, xviv).
6 Lopez (1986, 370).
7 Brown (1991).
8 Brown (1991).
9 Brown (1991).
10 Brown (1991).
11 Act to Establish the Mount McKinley National Park in the Territory of Alaska, Pub. Act No. 353, 39 Stat. 938 (February 26, 1917).
12 Brown (1991).
13 Murie (1944).
14 National Park Service (2017).
15 Murie (1944).
16 Leopold et al. (1963).
17 National Park System Advisory Board Science Committee (2012, i).
18 National Park System Advisory Board Science Committee (2012, 11).
19 Abbey (1968, 46).
20 National Park System Advisory Board Science Committee (2012).
21 Murie (1944).
22 National Park Service (2017).
23 Abbey (1968, 51).
24 Abbey (1968, xiv).
25 Denali National Park and Preserve (2017c).
26 Denali National Park and Preserve (2017c).
27 Denali National Park and Preserve (2017c; emphasis original).
28 Matthiessen (1978, 249).
29 Denali National Park and Preserve (2020).
30 Denali National Park and Preserve (2018a).

31 Olstad (2012b).
32 Olstad (2012b).
33 Manni et al. (2012).
34 Manni et al. (2012, 93).
35 Manni et al. (2012, 93–97).
36 Manni et al. (2012, 32).
37 Denali National Park and Preserve (2018c).
38 Echtner and Ritchie (2003).
39 Wycoff and Dilsaver (1997, 6).
40 Garrod (2009, 346).
41 Garrod (2009, 347).
42 San Martín and Rodríguez del Bosque (2008, 266).
43 Manni et al. (2012, 84).
44 Manni et al. (2012, 52).
45 Manni et al. (2012, 86).
46 National Park Service (2020a).
47 Fitzgerald et al. (2014).
48 Fitzgerald (2014); National Park Service (2016c).
49 National Park Service (2016c; 2020a); Denali National Park and Preserve (2018a).
50 See National Park Service (2016a) and National Park Service (2020a), respectively.
51 Denali National Park and Preserve (2016e); National Park Service (2016a).
52 National Park Service (2016d).
53 National Park Service (2016a).

CHAPTER 6

1 Washburn (1991, 20).
2 Washburn (1991, 20).
3 Denali National Park and Preserve (2017b).
4 Washburn (1991, 20).
5 Denali National Park and Preserve (2016f).
6 Denali National Park and Preserve (2019).
7 George Leigh Mallory, quoted in Lowe-Anker (2008, 107).
8 Mallory, quoted in "Climbing Mount Everest Is Work for Supermen" (1923).
9 MacFarlane (2003, 19).
10 Veenstra et al. (2006).
11 Gates (2006, 138).
12 MacFarlane (2003, 19).
13 Mallory, quoted in "Climbing Mount Everest Is Work for Supermen" (1923).
14 Krakauer (1997, 270).
15 MacFarlane (2003, 18).
16 Thoreau (1864, 65).
17 MacFarlane (2003, 157).
18 Quoted in Heil (2008, 55).
19 Fickling (2003)
20 Naess (1970, 55).
21 Naess (1992, 53).
22 Quoted in Lowe-Anker (2008, 219).
23 Bernbaum (1990, xiii).
24 Bernbaum (1990, xv).
25 Bernbaum (1990, xvii).
26 Bernbaum (1990, xviii).
27 Bernbaum (1990, xviii).
28 Bernbaum (1990, xiii).
29 Bernbaum (1990, 213; emphasis added).
30 Bernbaum (1990, 144–45).
31 Bernbaum (1990, 144–45).
32 Bernbaum (1990, 20).
33 Bernbaum (1990, 7).
34 Daumal (2004, 32; emphasis original).

CHAPTER 7

1 Denali National Park and Preserve (2017a).
2 Tomsich et al. (2010).
3 Siber (2017).
4 Denali National Park and Preserve (2017a).
5 Denali National Park and Preserve (2016b).
6 Fiorillo and Adams (2012); Denali National Park and Preserve (2016b).
7 Denali National Park and Preserve (2016d).
8 Tomsich et al. (2010, 389); Sousanes (2016).
9 Norris (2020).

10 Denali National Park and Preserve (2016a).
11 Fiorillo et al. (2006).
12 Quoted in Siber (2017).
13 Denali National Park and Preserve (2016c).
14 Dillard (1974, 218).
15 Snyder (1965, 400).
16 Thoreau (1864, 71).
17 BrianSchmidt (2012).
18 Fiorillo et al. (2009).

CHAPTER 8

1 Abbey (1975, 389).
2 Long and Averill (2003, 22).
3 Burger (1995).
4 Burger (1995, 105).
5 Long and Averill (2003, 30).
6 Korpela and Staats (2014, 356).
7 Korpela and Staats (2014, 358).
8 Korpela and Staats (2014, 358).
9 Olstad (2012b).
10 Hinton (2012, 78).
11 Hinton (2012, 79).
12 Olstad (2012a).
13 Hinton (2012, 59).
14 Shepherd (2011, xvii).
15 Hinton (2012, 4).
16 Matthiessen (1978, 43).

CHAPTER 9

1 Muir (1917).
2 Snyder (1974, 148).
3 Dr. Seuss (1971).
4 Leopold (1949).
5 N.Y. Const. art. XIV (emphasis added).
6 Adirondack Wild (2020).
7 Adirondack 46ers (2020).
8 Adirondack 46ers (2020).
9 Adirondack Mountain Club (2020).
10 Terrie (2008).
11 Dawson (2012, 7).
12 Dawson (2012, 7).
13 Waterman and Waterman (1979, 214).

14 Waterman and Waterman (19, 215).
15 Quoted in Waterman and Waterman (1979, 153).
16 Yang Wan-li, translation by Hinton (2005, 258).
17 Hinton (2012, 78).
18 MacKenzie (2016).
19 Ketchledge et al. (1985, 5).
20 Ketchledge et al. (1985, 6).
21 Waterman and Waterman (1993, 204).
22 Goren and Jones (2020).
23 Slack (1993).
24 Wright (1947, 3).
25 Baylor (1978).
26 Baylor (1978).
27 George Marshall, quoted in Riley (2014).
28 Plaque affixed to the summit rock of Mt. Marcy.
29 Quoted in Groom (2012).
30 Thomas Cole in 1836, quoted in Nash (2001, 80–81).
31 Hinton (2012, 95).
32 Mobley (2008, 382).
33 The Leave No Trace Seven Principles have been reprinted with permission from the Leave No Trace Center for Outdoor Ethics.
34 See the website of the Leave No Trace Center for Outdoor Ethics, accessed September 30, 2020, www. lnt.org.
35 New York State Department of Environmental Conservation (2020).
36 Bernbaum (1990, 247).
37 Waterman and Waterman (1993, 79).
38 Waterman and Waterman (1993, xi).
39 Whiteface (2020).
40 Roosevelt (1935).
41 Johnson (2015, 27).
42 Warren (2015).
43 Brown (2017).
44 Wiltse (2020).
45 Schwab et al. (2016, 827).

46 Schwab et al. (2016, 827).

CHAPTER 10

1 Cousineau (2012, 395).
2 Quoted in Weber (2011).
3 Weber (2011).
4 Hinton (2012, 68).
5 Translation by Hinton (2005, 140).
6 Quoted in Boyle (1969, 68).
7 Bernbaum (1990, xvii).
8 Dawson (2012, 4).
9 Dawson (2007).
10 Dawson (2007; 2012).
11 Frederickson (2002).
12 Dawson (2007; 2012).
13 Frederickson (2002).
14 Frederickson (2002).
15 Frederickson (2002, 351).
16 Graefe et al. (2010).
17 Williams et al. (1992, 31).
18 Kyle et al. (2005).
19 Williams et al. (1992, 32); Mitchell et al. (1993, 34).
20 Ketchledge (1993).
21 Mitchell et al. (1993, 34).
22 Kittle (2016).
23 Kittle (2016).
24 Dawson (2007; 2012).
25 Frederickson (2002).
26 Frederickson (2002).
27 Ketchledge (1993).
28 Bernbaum (1990, xiii and 127).
29 Daumal (2004, 107).

CHAPTER 11

1 Daumal (2004, 107).
2 Olstad (2017a).
3 Olstad (2017a).
4 Laura Waterman, in Waterman and Waterman (1993, xi).
5 Dawson and Hendee (2009, 12).
6 Landres et al. (2012, 7).
7 Zahniser (1963).
8 Rowland (2019).
9 Nagle (2015).
10 Brandborg (2015).

11 Adirondack Park Agency (2019, 22; emphasis added).
12 Adirondack Park Agency (2019, 1; emphasis added).
13 Waterman and Waterman (1979, 23).
14 Nelson (2019).
15 Nelson (2019).
16 *Adirondack Almanack* Editorial Staff (2019).
17 Waterman and Waterman (1979, 23).
18 Nelson (2019).
19 Nelson (2019).
20 Bernbaum (1990, xiii).
21 Bernbaum (1990, 213).
22 Ketchledge (1993).
23 Waterman and Waterman (1979, 145–53).
24 Blake (2002, 165).
25 Morrisey (2015).

CHAPTER 12

1 Hinton (2012, 4).
2 National Park Service (2016b).
3 National Park Service (2019).
4 Tu Fu, translated by Hinton (2005, 13).
5 Oliver (2004, 59).
6 Li et al. (2012).

CHAPTER 13

1 Abbey (1977, 223).
2 Leopold (1949, 225).
3 Stegner (1960).
4 Abbey (1968, 116).
5 Hinton (2012, 114).
6 Atsma (2020).
7 Brown (2018a).
8 Matson (2018b).
9 Matson (2018b).
10 Bauer (2018).
11 Brown (2018b).
12 *Adirondack Explorer* (2018).
13 Bauer (2018).
14 Adirondack Council (2020).

15 Adirondack Wilderness Advocates (2020).

16 Adirondack Wilderness Advocates (2017).

17 Matson (2018a).

18 Levine (2019).

19 National Park Service (2020b).

20 McPhee (1971, 150).

21 Hinton (2012, 307).

22 Matthiessen (1978, 97).

23 Lao Tzu (2005, 29).

24 Olstad (2017b).

25 Olstad (2017b).

26 Shepherd (2011, 107).

27 Shepherd (2011, 108).

28 Shepherd (2011, 1).

29 Shepherd (2011, 20).

30 Shepherd (2011, 23).

31 Shepherd (2011, 85).

32 Olstad (2017b).

33 Shepherd (2011, 48).

34 Shepherd (2011, 15).

35 Shepherd (2011, xli).

36 Shepherd (2011, 1).

37 Shepherd (2011, xliii).

38 Matthiessen (1978, 218).

EPILOGUE

1 Woelber (2020).

2 Woelber (2020).

3 Woelber (2020).

4 Marshall (2005, 3).

5 Marshall (2005, 22).

6 Marshall (2005, 38).

7 Marshall (2005, 26).

8 Marshall (2005, 19).

9 Marshall (2005, 22).

10 Marshall (2005, 152).

11 Marshall (2005, 164).

12 Marshall (2005, 29).

13 Marshall (2005, 29).

14 Kostohrys et al. (2003).

15 Lopez (1986, 122).

16 Lopez (1986, 361).

17 Lopez (1986, 66).

18 Lopez (1986, 368).

References

Abbey, Edward. *Desert Solitaire: A Season in the Wilderness*. New York: Simon & Schuster, 1968.

——. *The Monkey Wrench Gang*. New York: Perennial Classics, 1975.

——. *The Journey Home: Some Words in Defense of the American West*. New York: Plume, 1977.

Adirondack Almanack Editorial Staff. "High Peaks Public Use Planning Announced, Advisory Group Named." *Adirondack Almanack*, November 7, 2019. https://www.adirondackalmanack.com/2019/11/high-peaks-public-use-planning-announced-advisory-group-named.html.

Adirondack Council. "Boreas Ponds Classification Proposals." Accessed October 3, 2020. https://www.adirondackcouncil.org/page/boreas-ponds-classification-proposals-200.html.

Adirondack Explorer. "Cuomo Approves Boreas Ponds Classification," March 20, 2018. https://www.adirondackexplorer.org/news_releases/boreas-ponds-classification.

Adirondack 46ers. "Grace Leach Hudowalski, #9." Accessed September 30, 2020. http://www.adk46er.org/grace-things/gracebio.pdf.

Adirondack Mountain Club (ADK). "Employment Opportunities." Accessed September 30, 2020. https://www.adk.org/job-board/#summit-steward.

Adirondack Park Agency. *Adirondack State Land Master Plan*. Raybrook, NY: Adirondack Park Agency, 2019.

Adirondack Wild. "Our History." Accessed September 30, 2020. http://adirondackwild.org/who-we-are/history.html.

Adirondack Wilderness Advocates. "Comments Show Wide Public Support in Favor of Wilderness for Boreas Ponds," January 23, 2017. https://adirondackwilderness.org/comments-show-wide-public-support-in-favor-of-wilderness-for-boreas-ponds/.

——. "A Call for an Expanded High Peaks Wilderness at Boreas Ponds." Accessed October 3, 2020. https://adirondackwilderness.org/boreas-ponds/.

Altman, Irwin, and Setha M. Low, eds. *Place Attachment*. New York: Plenum Press, 1992.

Appleton, Jay. *The Experience of Landscape*. New York: John Wiley and Sons, 1975.

Aton, James M., and Robert S. McPherson. *River Flowing from the Sunrise: An Environmental History of the Lower San Juan*. Logan: Utah State University Press, 2000.

Atsma, Aaron. "Boreas." Theoi Greek Mythology. Accessed October 5, 2020. https://www.theoi.com/Titan/AnemosBoreas.html.

Bass, Rick. *The Book of Yaak*. New York: Houghton Mifflin, 1997.

Bauer, Peter. "Bauer: Making The Boreas Ponds Compromise." *Adirondack Almanack*, January 28, 2018. https://www.adirondackalmanack.com/2018/01/bauer-making-boreas-ponds-compromise.html.

Baylor, Byrd. *The Other Way to Listen*. New York: Aladdin, 1978.

Beidleman, Richard G. "The Black Canyon of the Gunnison National Monument." *Colorado Magazine* 40, no. 3 (1963): 161–78.

Bernbaum, Edwin. *Sacred Mountains of the World.* San Francisco: Sierra Club Books, 1990.

Black Canyon of the Gunnison National Park. "People." Last updated February 24, 2015a. https://www.nps.gov/blca/learn/historyculture/people.htm.

———. "Inner Canyon." Accessed February 24, 2015b. https://www.nps.gov/blca/planyourvisit/innercanyon.htm.

———. "Hiking Trails." Last updated November 4, 2016. https://www.nps.gov/blca/planyourvisit/hikingtrails.htm.

Blake, Kevin. "Colorado Fourteeners and the Nature of Place Identity." *Geographical Review* 92, no. 2 (2002): 155–79.

Boyle, Robert H. *The Hudson River: A Natural and Unnatural History.* New York: Norton, 1969.

Brandborg, Stewart. "Wilderness, Wildness, and Wilderness Character." *International Journal of Wilderness* 21, no. 3 (2015): 4–5.

BrianSchmidt. "Fang Mountain Trip Report." Peakware, October 1, 2012. https://www.peakware.com/peaks.php?pk=2579&view=logs&log=22347. (Site no longer accessible.)

Brown, Phil. "The Map of Adirondack Remoteness and Boreas Ponds." *Adirondack Almanack*, January 25, 2017. https://www.adirondackalmanack.com/2017/01/boreas-ponds-map-remoteness.html.

———. "Big Plans Proposed for Boreas Ponds." Adirondack Explorer, June 28, 2018a. https://www.adirondackexplorer.org/stories/boreas-ponds-ump.

———. "APA Approves Boreas Ponds Classification." Adirondack Explorer, February 2, 2018b. https://www.adirondackexplorer.org/outtakes/apa-approves-boreas-ponds-classification.

Brown, Thomas C., and Terry C. Daniel. "Landscape Aesthetics of Riparian Environments: Relationship of Flow Quantity to Scenic Quality along a Wild and Scenic River." *Water Resources Research* 27, no. 8 (1991): 1787–95.

Brown, William E. *A History of the Denali-Mount McKinley Region, Alaska: Historic Resource Study of Denali National Park and Preserve.* Santa Fe, NM: US Department of the Interior National Park Service Southwest Regional Office, 1991.

Bunkše, Edmunds. "Feeling Is Believing, or Landscape as a Way of Being in the World." *Geografiska Annaler* 89B, no. 3 (2007): 219–31.

Bureau of Land Management. *Manual H-8410-1: Visual Resource Inventory.* Washington, DC: Department of the Interior, 1986.

Burger, Jerry M. "Individual Differences in Preference for Solitude." *Journal of Research in Personality* 29 (1995): 85–108.

Burmil, Shmuel, Terry C. Daniel, and John D. Hetherington. "Human Values and Perceptions of Water in Arid Landscapes." *Landscape and Urban Planning* 44 (1999): 99–109.

Buttimer, Anne. "Grasping the Dynamism of Lifeworld." *Annals of the Association of American Geographers* 66, no. 2 (1976): 277–92.

Carlson, Allen. "Appreciation and the Natural Environment." *Journal of Aesthetics and Art Criticism* 37 (1979): 267–76.

———. "Aesthetic Appreciation of the Natural Environment." In *Environmental Ethics: Divergence and Convergence*, 2nd ed., ed. R. G. Botzler and S. J. Armstrong. Boston: McGraw-Hill, 1998.

Carr, Ethan. *Wilderness by Design: Landscape Architecture and the National Park Service.* Lincoln: University of Nebraska Press, 1999.

Casey, Edward S. "Between Geography and Philosophy: What Does It Mean to Be in the Place-World?" *Annals of the Association of American Geographers* 91, no. 4 (2001): 683–93.

Cheng, Antony, Linda Kruger, and Steven Daniels. "'Place' as an Integrating Concept in Natural Resource Politics: Propositions for a Social Science Research Agenda." *Society and Natural Resources* 16 (2003): 87–104.

"Climbing Mount Everest Is Work for Supermen." *New York Times*, March 18, 1923.

Cousineau, Phil. *The Painted Word: A Treasure Chest of Remarkable Words and Their Origins.* Berkeley: Viva Editions, 2012.

Daumal, Rene. *Mount Analogue: A Novel of Symbolically Authentic Non-Euclidean Adventures in Mountain Climbing.* Translated by Carol Cosman. New York: Overlook Press, 2004.

Dawson, Chad P. "Wilderness as a Place: Human Dimensions of the Wilderness Experience." In *Proceedings of the 2006 Northeastern Recreation Research Symposium*, ed. Robert Burns and Karen Robinson, 57–62. Washington, DC: US Department of Agriculture, 2007.

———. "Adirondack Forest Preserve Visitor Study Summary." March 15, 2012. https://apa.ny.gov/Mailing/2012/06/StateLand/Visitor-study-summary.pdf.

Dawson, Chad P., and John C. Hendee. *Wilderness Management: Stewardship and Protection of Resources and Values*, 4th ed. Golden, CO: Fulcrum Publishing, 2009.

Denali National Park and Preserve. "Cretaceous Climate." Last updated August 18, 2016a. https://www.nps.gov/dena/learn/nature/cretaceous-climate.htm.

———. "Dinosaur and Plant Fossils." Last updated June 29, 2016b. https://www.nps.gov/dena/learn/nature/3d-tracks.htm.

———. "Edmontosaurus." Last updated July 7, 2016c. https://www.nps.gov/dena/learn/nature/edmontosaur.htm.

———. "Fossil Bird Diversity." Last updated May 18, 2016d. https://www.nps.gov/articles/denali-fossil-bird-diversity.htm.

———. "Glaciers/Glacial Features." Last updated May 26, 2016e. https://www.nps.gov/dena/learn/nature/glaciers.htm.

———. "Historical Timeline." Last updated March 9, 2016f. https://www.nps.gov/dena/planyourvisit/climbinghistory.htm.

———. "Discovery of Dinosaur Tracks in Denali." Last updated September 19, 2017a. https://www.nps.gov/articles/denali-dino-discovery.htm.

———. "FAQ's about Mountaineering in Denali National Park." Last updated September 26, 2017b. https://www.nps.gov/dena/planyourvisit/mountainfaqs.htm.

———. "Protecting Wildlife and Visitor Experience along the Denali Park Road." Last updated September 18, 2017c. https://www.nps.gov/articles/denali-ecosystem-interactions.htm.

———. "Park Statistics." Last updated March 21, 2018a. https://www.nps.gov/dena/learn/management/statistics.htm.

———. "Transit Buses." Last updated April 30, 2018b. https://www.nps.gov/dena/planyourvisit/shuttles.htm.

———. "Where to See and Photograph Denali and Wildlife." Last updated May 22, 2018c. https://www.nps.gov/dena/planyourvisit/photography.htm.

———. "2018 Annual Mountaineering Summary." Last updated December 18, 2019. https://www.nps.gov/dena/planyourvisit/ams2018.htm.

———. "Wildlife Viewing." Last updated August 7, 2020. https://www.nps.gov/dena/planyourvisit/wildlife-viewing.htm.

de Wit, Cary W. "Field Methods for Investigating Sense of Place." *North American Geographer* 5, no. 1–2 (2003): 5–30.

Diaz, Gustavo E., Jose D. Salas, and Gregg E. Farris. *Impact of Diversions and River Regulation on the Flows of the Gunnison River at Black Canyon, Colorado*. Fort Collins, CO: Computing Hydrology Laboratory Hydrologic Science and Engineering Program Engineering Research Center, 1996.

Echtner, Charlotte M., and J. R. Brent Ritchie. "The Meaning and Measurement of Destination Image." *Journal of Tourism Studies* 14, no. 1 (May 2003): 37–48. [Reprint of original article published in *Journal of Tourism Studies* 2, no. 2 (1991): 2–12.]

Feld, Steven, and Keith H. Basso, eds. *Senses of Place*. Santa Fe: School of American Research, 1996.

Fickling, David. "'We Knocked the Bastard Off.'" *The Guardian*, March 13, 2003. https://www.theguardian.com/world/2003/mar/13/everest.nepal.

Fiorillo, Anthony R., and Thomas L. Adams. "A Therizinosaur Track from the Lower Cantwell Formation (Upper Cretaceous) of Denali National Park, Alaska." *PALAIOS* 27, no. 5/6 (2012): 395–400.

Fiorillo, Anthony R., and Cathleen L. May. "Depositional Environment of the First Dinosaur Remains from the Morrison Formation (Upper Jurassic) of Curecanti National Recreation Area (Southwest Colorado)." *Geological Society of America Programs with Abstracts, Rocky Mountain Section* 5 (1995): 11.

———."Preliminary Report on the Taphonomy and Depositional Setting of a New Dinosaur Locality in the Morrison Formation (Brushy Basin Member) of Curecanti National Recreation Area, Colorado." *Continental Jurassic, Bulletin of the Museum of Northern Arizona* 60 (1996): 555–61.

Fiorillo, Anthony R., Stephen T. Hasiotis, Yoshitsugu Kobayashi, and Carla S. Tomsich. "A Pterosaur Manus Track from Denali National Park, Alaska Range, Alaska, United States." *PALAIOS* 24, no. 7 (2009): 466–72.

Fiorillo, Anthony R., Paul J. McCarthy, Brent H. Breithaupt, and Phil F. Brease. "Dinosauria and Fossil Aves Footprints from the Lower Cantwell Formation (Latest Cretaceous), Denali National Park and Preserve." In *Alaska Park Science: Crossing Boundaries in a Changing Environment, Proceedings of the Central Alaska Park Science Symposium September 12–14, 2006*, 41–43. Anchorage: National Park Service, US Department of the Interior, Alaska Regional Office, 2006.

Fitzgerald, Paul G., Sarah M. Roeske, Jeffery A. Benowitz, Steven J. Riccio, Stephanie E. Perry, and Phillip A. Armstrong. "Alternating Asymmetric Topography of the Alaska Range along the Strike-Slip Denali Fault: Strain Partitioning and Lithospheric Control across a Terrane Suture Zone." *Tectonics* 33, no. 8 (2014): 1519–33.

Fredrickson, Laura. "The Importance of Visitors' Knowledge of the Cultural and Natural History of the Adirondacks in Influencing Sense of Place in the High Peaks Region." In *Proceedings of the 2001 Northeastern Recreation Research Symposium*, ed. Sharon Todd, 346–55. Washington, DC: US Department of Agriculture, Forest Service, Northeastern Research Station, 2002.

Fudge, Robert S. "Imagination and the Science-Based Aesthetic Appreciation of Unscenic Nature." *Journal of Aesthetics and Art Criticism* 59, no. 3 (2001): 275–85.

Garrod, Brian. "Understanding the Relationship between Tourism Destination Imagery and Tourist Photography." *Journal of Travel Research* 47 (2009): 346–58.

Gates, Nancy. *The Alaska Almanac: Facts about Alaska*, 30th ed. Anchorage: Alaska Northwest Books, 2006.

Goren, Julia, and Seth Jones. "Photopoint Monitoring in the Adirondack Alpine Zone." Accessed October 5, 2020. https://nsrcforest.org/sites/default/files/uploads/gorenfull09.pdf.

Graefe, David A., Chad Dawson, and Rudolph M. Schuster. "Roadside Camping on Forest Preserve Lands in the Adirondack Park: A Qualitative Exploration of Place Attachment and Resource Substitutability." In *Proceedings of the 2010 Northeastern Recreation Research Symposium*, ed. Cherie LeBlanc Fisher and Clifton E. Watts Jr., 205–13. Washington, DC: US Department of Agriculture, Forest Service, Northern Research Station, 2010.

Grand Canyon National Park. "Explorers." Last updated July 5, 2016. https://www.nps.gov/grca/learn/historyculture/explorers.htm.

Groom, Debra. "First Reported Trek Up Mount Marcy Occurred 175 Years Ago." *Syracuse Post-Standard*, August 19, 2012. https://www.syracuse.com/news/index.ssf/2012/08/first_reported_trek_up_mount_m.html.

Gussow, Alan. "Conserving the Magnitude of Uselessness: A Philosophical Perspective." Presented at the National Conference on Applied Techniques for Analysis and Management of the Visual Resource, Incline Village, NV, April 23–25, 1979.

Hamill, Sam, and J. P. Seaton, trans. *The Poetry of Zen.* Boston: Shambhala, 2007.

Heil, Nick. *Dark Summit: The True Story of Everest's Most Controversial Season.* New York: Henry Holt, 2008.

Herzog, Thomas. "A Cognitive Analysis of Preference for Natural Environments: Mountains, Canyons, and Deserts." *Landscape Journal* 6, no. 2 (1987): 140–52.

Hinton, David. *Mountain Home: The Wilderness Poetry of Ancient China.* Washington, DC: New Directions, 2005.

——.*Hunger Mountain: A Field Guide to Mind and Landscape.* Boston: Shambhala, 2012.

Holmes, Nancy C., Ariel Blotkamp, and Steven J. Hollenhorst. 2010. *Black Canyon of the Gunnison National Park Visitor Study.* Natural Resource Report NPS/NRPC/SSD/NRR—2011/144/106894. Moscow: Visitor Services Project, Park Studies Unit, University of Idaho, 2010.

Jenkins, Mark Collins. "Clarence Dutton: Poet of the Grand Canyon." *National Geographic*, January 20, 2018. https://blog.nationalgeographic.org/2018/01/20/clarence-dutton-poet-of-the-grand-canyon/.

Johnson, Phil. "How New York Lost Its Marble." *Skiing History* (May-June 2015): 26–29.

Kaplan, Stephen. "Perception and Landscape: Conception and Misconception." In *Proceedings of Our National Landscape*. General Technical Report PSW-35, 241–48. Washington, DC: US Department of Agriculture, Forest Service, 1979.

——."Aesthetics, Affect, and Cognition: Environmental Preference from an Evolutionary Perspective." *Environment and Behavior* 19, no. 1 (1987): 3–32.

——."The Restorative Benefits of Nature: Toward an Integrative Framework." *Journal of Environmental Psychology* 15, no. 3 (1995): 169–82.

Kellogg, Karl, Wallace R. Hansen, Karen S. Tucker, and D. Paco Van Sistine. *Geologic Map of Gunnison Gorge National Conservation Area, Delta and Montrose Counties, Colorado.* Scientific Investigations Map 2825. Washington, DC: Bureau of Land Management, 2004.

Ketchledge, Edwin H. "Adirondack Insights #24: The Four Rewards of Visiting Alpine Summits." *Adirondac* (1993): 30–31.

Ketchledge, E. H., R. E. Leonard, N. A. Richards, P. F. Craul, and A. R. Eschner. *Rehabilitation of Alpine Vegetation in the Adirondack Mountains of New York State.* Research Paper NE-553. Washington, DC: US Forest Service, Northeastern Forest Experiment Station, 1985.

Kittle, Shaun. "Lessons, Laughter and Love: Peter Fish and the Adirondacks." Lake
    Placid Regional Office of Sustainable Tourism, January 19, 2016. https://www.
    lakeplacid.com/story/2016/01/peter-fish-adirondack-forest-ranger.

Koch, Alison L., Forest Frost, and Kelli C. Trujillo. "Paleontological Discoveries at
    Curecanti National Recreation Area and Black Canyon of the Gunnison National
    Park, Upper Jurassic Morrison Formation, Colorado." In *Paleontology and Geology
    of the Upper Jurassic Morrison Formation*, ed. John R. Foster and Spencer G.
    Lucas, 35–38. Albuquerque: New Mexico Museum of Natural History and
    Science, 2006.

Korpela, Kalevi, and Henk Staats. "The Restorative Qualities of Being Alone with
    Nature." In *The Handbook of Solitude: Psychological Perspectives on Social
    Isolation, Social Withdrawal, and Being Alone*, ed. Robert J. Coplan and Julie C.
    Bowker, 351–67. West Sussex: Wiley Blackwell, 2014.

Kostohrys, Jon, Kristine Kosnik, and Ethan Scott. *Water Resources of the Colville River
    Special Area*. Open File Report 96. Anchorage: Bureau of Land Management-
    Alaska, 2003.

Krakauer, Jon. *Into Thin Air: A Personal Account of the Mount Everest Disaster*. New
    York: Villard Books, 1997.

Kyle, Gerard, Alan Graefe, and Robert Manning. "Testing the Dimensionality of Place
    Attachment in Recreational Settings." *Environment and Behavior* 37, no. 2 (2005):
    153–77.

Landres, Peter, Wade M. Vagias, and Suzy Stutzman. "Using Wilderness Character to
    Improve Wilderness Stewardship." *Park Science* 28, no. 3 (2012).

Lao Tzu. *Tao Te Ching*. Translated by Charles Muller. New York: Barnes & Noble
    Classics, 2005.

Leopold, Aldo. *A Sand County Almanac, and Sketches Here and There*. New York:
    Oxford University Press, 1949.

Leopold, Aldo Starker, S. A. Cain, C. M. Cottam, I. N. Gabrielson, and T. L. Kimball.
    Wildlife Management in the National Parks: The Leopold Report. Washington, DC:
    National Park Service, March 4, 1963. https://www.nps.gov/parkhistory/online_
    books/leopold/leopold.htm.

Leopold, Luna. *Quantitative Comparison of Some Aesthetic Factors among Rivers*.
    Circular 620. Washington, DC: US Geological Survey, 1969.

Levine, Justin. "Boreas Ponds Tract Access Road Opens to the Public." *Post-Star*,
    September 17, 2019. https://poststar.com/news/local/boreas-ponds-tract-access-
    road-opens-to-the-public/article_6090bf6f-62c4-50c6-9aaa-ca03424b90f5.html.

Li, Quanguo, Ke-Qin Gao, Qingjin Meng, Julia A. Clarke, Matthew D. Shawkey, Liliana
    D'Alba, Rui Pei, Mick Ellison, Mark A. Norell, and Jakob Vinther. "Reconstruction
    of Microraptor and the Evolution of Iridescent Plumage." *Science* 335, no. 6073
    (2012): 1215–19.

Long, Christopher R., and James R. Averill. "Solitude: An Exploration of Benefits of
    Being Alone." *Journal for the Theory of Social Behavior* 33, no. 1 (2003): 21–44.

Lopez, Barry. *Arctic Dreams: Imagination and Desire in a Northern Landscape*. New
    York: Bantam Books, 1986.

———."Gone Back into the Earth." In *Crossing Open Ground*. New York: Vintage Books,
    1989.

Lowe-Anker, Jennifer. *Forget Me Not: A Memoir*. Seattle: Mountaineers Books, 2008.

MacFarlane, Robert. *Mountains of the Mind: Adventures in Reaching the Summit*. New
    York: Vintage Books, 2003.

MacKenzie, Kevin B. "Adirondack Landslides: History, Exposures, and Climbing."
    Adirondack Journal of Environmental Studies 21, no. 1 (2016): 167–83.

Manni, Marc, Yen Le, Gail Vander Stoep, and Steven J. Hollenhorst. *Denali National Park and Preserve Visitor Study, Summer 2011*. Natural Resource Report NPS/NRSS/EQD/NRR–2012/524. Washington, DC: National Park Service, 2012.

Marshall, Robert. *Alaska Wilderness: Exploring the Central Brooks Range*. Berkeley: University of California Press, 2005.

Matson, Zachary. "To Some Wilderness Advocates, Boreas Ponds Compromise Goes Too Far." *Daily Gazette (Schenectady)*, January 30, 2018a. https://dailygazette.com/article/2018/01/30/to-some-wilderness-advocates-boreas-ponds-compromise-goes-too-far.

———."Agency Board Adopts Boreas Ponds Classification, Growing High Peaks Wilderness." *Daily Gazette (Schenectady)*, February 2, 2018b. https://dailygazette.com/article/2018/02/02/apa-board-adopts-boreas-classificaiton-growing-high-peaks-wilderness.

Matthiessen, Peter. *The Snow Leopard*. New York: Bantam Books, 1978.

McPhee, John. *Encounters with the Archdruid*. New York: Farrar, Straus, and Giroux, 1971.

Mitchell, M. Y., J. E. Force, M. S. Carroll, and W. J. McLaughlin. "Forest Places of the Heart; Incorporating Special Places into Public Management." *Journal of Forestry* 91, no. 4 (1993): 32–37.

Mobley, Jason A. *Birds of the World*. New York: Marshall Cavendish, 2008.

Morrisey, Spencer. "High Peak #47." LakePlacid.com, September 3, 2015, https://www.lakeplacid.com/story/2015/09/macnaughton-or-macnaughty-you-decide.

Muir, John. "Letter to Henry Senger, May 22, 1892." *Sierra Club Bulletin* 10, no. 2 (1917): 138.

———.*Steep Trails*. New York: Houghton Mifflin, 1918.

Murie, Adolph. *The Wolves of Mount McKinley*. National Park Service Fauna Series No. 5. Washington, DC: Government Printing Office, 1944. https://www.nps.gov/parkhistory/online_books/fauna5/fauna.htm.

Naess, Arne. "The Conquest of Mountains: A Contradiction?" *The Trumpeter: Journal of Ecosophy* 21, no. 2 (2005): 55–56.

———."Mountains." *The Trumpeter: Journal of Ecosophy* 21, no. 2 (2005): 51–54. [Reprint of unpublished manuscript originally written in 1992.]

Nagle, John Copeland. "The Legal Meaning of Wilderness Character." *International Journal of Wilderness* 231, no. 3 (2015): 10–13.

Nash, Roderick. *Wilderness and the American Mind*, 4th ed. New Haven, CT: Yale University Press, 2001.

National Park Service. "New Fossil Preservation Law." Last updated April 24, 2015. http://web.archive.org/web/20151115094320/https://nature.nps.gov/geology/nationalfossilday/prpa.cfm.

———."Glacier Monitoring in Denali." Last updated April 21, 2016a. https://www.nps.gov/articles/denali-glacier-monitoring.htm.

———."Managing Lightscapes." Last updated September 14, 2016b. https://www.nps.gov/subjects/nightskies/management.htm.

———."Mountain Building in the Alaska Range." Last updated April 22, 2016c. https://www.nps.gov/articles/denali-mountain-building-ak-range.htm.

———."Rivers and Streams of Denali." Last updated April 21, 2016d. https://www.nps.gov/articles/rivers-and-streams-of-denali.htm.

———."Adolph Murie: Wildlife Biologist, Conservationist." Last updated August 15, 2017. https://www.nps.gov/articles/denali-adolph-murie.htm.

———."Protecting the Night." Last updated June 13, 2019. https://www.nps.gov/subjects/nightskies/index.htm.

———."The Alaska Range and Denali: Geology and Orogeny." Last updated January 7, 2020a. https://www.nps.gov/articles/denali.htm.

———."Cumberland Island National Seashore." Last updated July 15, 2020b. https://www.nps.gov/cuis/index.htm.

National Park System Advisory Board Science Committee. *Revisiting Leopold: Resource Stewardship in the National Parks.* Washington, DC: National Park Service, August 25, 2012. https://www.nps.gov/calltoaction/pdf/leopoldreport_2012.pdf.

Nelson, Pete. "We Need Visitor Management, Not Permits." *Adirondack Almanack,* October 22, 2019. https://www.adirondackalmanack.com/2019/10/pete-nelson-we-need-visitor-management-not-permits.html.

New York State Department of Environmental Conservation. "State Land Camping and Hiking Rules." Accessed September 30, 2020. https://www.dec.ny.gov/outdoor/7872.html.

Norris, Richard. "Cretaceous Thermal Maximum, ~85–90 Ma." Scripps Institute of Oceanography, accessed September 29, 2020. http://scrippsscholars.ucsd.edu/rnorris/book/cretaceous-thermal-maximum-85-90-ma.

Northern Colorado Plateau Inventory and Monitoring Network. "Biophysical Description of Black Canyon of the Gunnison National Park." Last updated June 7, 2018. https://www.nps.gov/im/ncpn/bpd-blca.htm.

Oliver, Mary. "The Old Poets of China." In *Why I Wake Early: New Poems.* Boston: Beacon Press, 2004.

Olstad, Tyra A. "The Mountain and Me." Best Made Projects, September 6, 2012a. http://www.bestmadeprojects.com/post/30993832662/the-mountain-and-me-by-tyra-olstad-three-and-a.

———."Making the Most of Denali." Best Made Projects, October 10, 2012b. http://www.bestmadeprojects.com/post/33160510379/making-the-most-of-denali-by-tyra-olstad-i-spent.

———.*Zen of the Plains: Experiencing Wild Western Places.* Denton: University of North Texas Press, 2014.

———."Of Mountains and [Too Many] Men." Blogspot, July 3, 2017a. http://taolstad.blogspot.com/2017/07/a-thing-is-right-when-it-tends-to.html.

———."The Living Mountain." Blogspot, August 28, 2017b. http://taolstad.blogspot.com/2017/08/the-living-mountain.html.

Powell, John Wesley. *The Grand Canyon of Arizona: Being a Book of Words from Many Pens, about the Grand Canyon of the Colorado River in Arizona.* Chicago: Atchison, Topeka, and Santa Fe Railway Co., 1909.

Pyne, Stephen. *How the Grand Canyon Became Grand: A Short History.* New York: Penguin Books, 1998.

Resource Systems Group, Inc. *Yellowstone National Park Visitor Use Study, Summer 2016.* White River Junction, VT: Resource Systems Group, 2017.

Riley, Howard. "First Ascent of Mt. Marcy." *Adirondack Daily Enterprise,* August 30, 2014. http://www.adirondackdailyenterprise.com/opinion/columns/you-know-what-local-history-by-howard-riley/2014/08/first-ascent-of-mt-marcy/.

Rodríguez del Bosque, Ignacio, and Hector San Martín. "Tourist Satisfaction: A Cognitive-Affective Model." *Annals of Tourism Research* 35, no. 2 (2008).

Roosevelt, Franklin D. "Remarks at the Dedication of the White Face Memorial Highway, Lake Placid, N.Y., September 14, 1935." Gerhard Peters and John T. Woolley, *The American Presidency Project.* https://www.presidency.ucsb.edu/documents/remarks-the-dedication-the-white-face-memorial-highway-lake-placid-ny.

Ross, Robert W., Jr. "The Bureau of Land Management and Visual Resource Management—An Overview." In *Proceedings of Our National Landscape: A Conference on Applied Techniques for Analysis and Management of the Visual Resource*, ed. Gary H. Elsner and Richard C. Smardon, 666–70. Berkeley, CA: Pacific Southwest Forest and Range Experiment Station, 1979.

Rowland, Tim. "Study: Young Adirondack Hikers Share Different Values." *Adirondack Explorer*, December 19, 2019. https://www.adirondackexplorer.org/stories/study-young-adirondack-hikers-share-different-values.

Sahney, Sarda, and Michael J. Benton. "Recovery from the Most Profound Mass Extinction of All Time." *Proceedings of the Royal Society B* 275, no. 1636 (2008): 759–65.

Saito, Yuriko. "The Aesthetics of Unscenic Nature." *Journal of Aesthetics and Art Criticism* 56, no. 2 (1998): 101–11.

San Martín, Hector, and Ignacio A. Rodríguez del Bosque. "Exploring the Cognitive–Affective Nature of Destination Image and the Role of Psychological Factors in Its Formation." *Tourism Management* 29 (2008): 263–77.

Schroeder, Herbert W. "Preference and Meaning of Arboretum Landscapes: Combining Quantitative and Qualitative Data." *Journal of Environmental Psychology* 11 (1991): 231–48.

Schwab, James J., Douglas Wolfe, Paul Casson, Richard Brandt, Kenneth L. Demerjian, Liquat Husain, Vincent A. Dutkiewicz, Kevin L. Civerolo, and Oliver V. Rattigan. "Atmospheric Science Research at Whiteface Mountain, NY: Site Description and History." *Aerosol and Air Quality Research* 16 (2016): 827–40.

Service, Robert. *The Spell of the Yukon and Other Verses.* New York: Barse & Hopkins, 1907.

Seuss, Dr. *The Lorax.* New York: Random House, 1971.

Shan, Han. In *The Poetry of Zen*, ed. Sam Hamill and J. P. Seaton, 30–35. Boston: Shambhala, 2007.

Shepherd, Nan. *The Living Mountain.* Edinburgh: Canongate Books, 2011.

Siber, Kate. "Where the Wild Things Were." *National Parks* (Summer 2017): https://www.npca.org/articles/1565-where-the-wild-things-were.

Slack, Nancy. *Adirondack Alpine Summits: An Ecological Field Guide.* Lake George, NY: Adirondack Mountain Club, 1993.

Snyder, Gary. *The Gary Snyder Reader.* Berkeley, CA: Counterpoint, 1965.

———. *Turtle Island.* New York: New Directions Books, 1974.

———. *The Practice of the Wild.* New York: North Point Press, 1990.

Sousanes, Pam. "Denali Climate and Weather Monitoring." Last updated April 2016. https://www.nps.gov/articles/denali-crp-climate-weather-monitoring.htm.

Stegner, Wallace. "Wilderness Letter to the Outdoor Recreation Resources Review Commission, December 3, 1960." The Wilderness Society. https://www.wilderness.org/articles/article/wallace-stegner.

Stiger, Mark A., and Scott L. Carpenter. *Archeological Survey of Black Canyon of the Gunnison National Monument*, Midwest Archeological Center Occasional Studies in Anthropology 7. Lincoln, NE: US Department of the Interior, National Park Service Midwest Archeological Center, 1980.

Terrie, Philip. 2008. *Contested Terrain: A New History of Nature and People in the Adirondacks.* Syracuse, NY: Syracuse University Press.

Thoreau, Henry David. *The Maine Woods.* Boston: Ticknor and Fields, 1864.

Tomsich, Carla, Paul J. McCarthy, Sarah J. Fowell, and David Sunderlin. "Paleofloristic and Paleoenvironmental Information from a Late Cretaceous (Maastrichtian) Flora of the Lower Cantwell Formation near Sable Mountain, Denali National

Park, Alaska." *Palaeogeography, Palaeoclimatology, Palaeoecology* 295, no. 3–4 (2010): 389–408.

Trujillo, Kelli C. *Report on Actual and Potential Fossil Resources in Curecanti National Recreation Area and Black Canyon of the Gunnison National Park.* Gunnison, CO: Curecanti National Recreation Area, 2001.

Tuan, Yi-Fu. *Topophilia: A Study of Environmental Perception, Attitudes, and Values.* New York: Columbia University Press, 1974.

———. *Space and Place: The Perspective of Experience.* Minneapolis: University of Minnesota Press, 1977.

———. "Surface Phenomena and the Aesthetic Experience." *Annals of the Association of American Geographers* 79, no. 2 (1989): 233–41.

———. "The Desert and I: A Study in Affinity." *Michigan Quarterly Review* 40, no. 1 (2001): 7–18.

US Department of the Interior. *Annual Report*, vol. 3, part 2. Washington, DC: US Department of the Interior, 1903.

Vandenbusche, Duane. *The Black Canyon of the Gunnison.* Charleston, SC: Arcadia Publishing, 2009.

Veenstra, Elizabeth, Douglas H. Christensen, Geoffrey A. Abers, and Aaron Ferris. "Crustal Thickness Variation in South-Central Alaska." *Geology* 34, no. 9 (2006): 781–84.

Warner, Mark T. "Through the Canyon." *Montrose Daily Press*, October 1, 1934.

Warren, John. "How the Adirondack Forest Preserve Was Motorized." *Adirondack Almanack*, September 22, 2015. https:// www.newyorkalmanack.com/2021/02/how-the-adirondack-forest-preserve-was-motorized

Washburn, Bradford, and David Roberts. *Mount McKinley: The Conquest of Denali.* New York: Harry N. Abrams, 1991.

Waterman, Laura, and Guy Waterman. *Backwoods Ethics: Environmental Issues for Hikers and Campers.* New York: Countryman Press, 1979.

———. *Wilderness Ethics: Preserving the Spirit of Wildness.* New York: Countryman Press, 1993.

Weber, Sandra. *Adirondack Roots: Stories of Hiking, History, and Women.* Charleston, SC: History Press, 2011.

"Whiteface Veterans Memorial Highway." Whiteface.com. Accessed September 30, 2020. https://www.whiteface.com/activities/whiteface-veterans-memorial -highway.

"The Wilderness Act." Public Law 88-577 (16 U.S.C. 1131-1136) 88th Congress, Second Session September 3, 1964.

Williams, Daniel R., Michael E. Patterson, Joseph W. Roggenbuck, and Alan E. Watson. "Beyond the Commodity Metaphor: Examining Emotional and Symbolic Attachment to Place." *Leisure Sciences* 14 (1992): 29–46.

Wiltse, Brendan. "Adirondacks within 1 Mile of a Road." Brendan Wiltse Adirondack Photography: ADK 1 Mile. Accessed September 30, 2020. https://www.brendanwiltse.com/Projects/1-Mile.

Woelber, Paxson. "To the Edge of the Top of the World." Expedition Arguk. Accessed October 5, 2020. https://expeditionarguk.com/ea-illustrated_trip_report.shtml#part_2.

Wright, John K. "Terrae Incognitae: The Place of Imagination in Geography." *Annals of the Association of American Geographers* 37 (1947): 1–15.

Wycoff, William, and Lary M. Dilsaver. "Promotional Imagery of Glacier National Park." *Geographical Review* 87, no. 1 (1997): 1–26.

Zahniser, Howard. "Guardians Not Gardeners." *Living Wilderness* 83 (1963): 2.

Index

A

Adirondack Forest Preserve, 132–133, 136, 148–149, 196–198
    aesthetics, 140, 144, 174, 177–178, 188, 189–190
    acid rain, 168
    Algonquin Peak, 150–152, 189–190, 224–225
    Avalanche Lake, 142
    Boreas Ponds, 219, 220–223, 224
    Cascade Mountain, 144–149
    Indian Pass, 159–161
    Lake Arnold, 200
    Lake Tear of the Clouds, 178
    Marcy Dam, 140–141
    Mt. Marcy, 159–160, 171–176, 179, 185–186
    overcrowding, 179, 184, 192–193, 197–198, 216
    Skylight Peak, 173, 177–178
    trail maintenance, 147
    Trap Dike, 187–188
    Wallface Ponds, 200–201
    weather, 168–170, 173–174, 176–177, 185–186, 189–190, 211–212,
        216–217, 225
    Whiteface Mountain, 167–169
    Wright Peak, 211–212
Adirondack 46ers, 132, 143, 146, 200–202, 213–215
Adirondack High Peaks Summit Steward Program, 146–147, 191, 197,
    211–212, 225–226
Adirondack Mountain Club (ADK), 134–135, 198
Adirondack Park Agency, 219, 221–222
Adirondack Park State Land Master Plan, 196–197
Adirondak Loj, 137. *See also* Mt. Jo; Heart Lake
alpine ecosystem, 146, 152–153, 153–156, 157–158
Anaktuvuk River, 232, 233, 242–243
Article XIV. *See* "forever wild"

B

Big Bend National Park, 50–51
backcountry travel, 94, 96, 98–101, 106–108, 111–112, 125, 180, 242
    solo, 16–19, 51–53, 85–86, 113, 114–118, 187–188, 231–232, 236–241
Black Canyon of the Gunnison National Park, 5, 16–18, 50–51, 58, 203–204
    aesthetics, 9, 45–46, 48
    dark skies, 205–208

history, 19–21
inner canyon, 17, 51
North Rim, 34–36, 51–53
paleontological resources, 26–27, 29, 35, 37–38
Red Rocks Wilderness Area, 28, 53
visitation, 47–48

C
Colville River, 232, 243
Curecanti National Recreation Area, 31–33
Blue Mesa Reservoir, 30–31
paleontological resources, 26–27, 31–32

D
Denali (Mountain), 66, 74–76, 80–81, 122
aesthetics, 86, 89–90
mountaineering, 84, 90
Denali National Park and Preserve, 63–65, 66–67, 71, 81, 85–86
aesthetics, 77, 79, 80, 96
Fang Mountain, 100–101
paleontological resources, 91–93, 94–95, 97, 103–105
road, 71, 118–123
tour busses, 71–72
visitation, 75–77
wildlife, 72–74, 125, 209
destination imagery, 77–80

E
environmental ethics. *See* landscape aesthetics: ethics; wilderness: ethics
ecological restoration, 155–156
environmental lapse rate, 169–170

F
Fiorillo, Anthony, 26–27, 92, 102–105, 233
"forever wild," 133
Fossil Butte National Monument, 55–56

G
Gates of the Arctic National Park and Preserve, 231–232, 234–235, 236–241
Grand Canyon of the Colorado, 11–13

H
Heart Lake, 141, 143–144, 162–163, 198–199
Hudowalski, Grace, 134, 191
Hudson River School, 159

I
International Dark Sky Park, 205

K

Ketchledge, Edwin, 154–156

L

landscape aesthetics, 7–9, 33, 87, 144, 188, 226–228, 249–250
 canyons, 8–11, 13–14, 207
 clouds, 45, 170, 176–177, 189–190, 218, 244
 ethics, 104, 108, 226
 lakes, 40–41, 144, 164, 199, 218
 mountains, 74–76, 85–90, 109, 176–177, 184
 night skies, 205–206
 plains, 6, 55, 83, 234, 244, 246
 rivers, 14, 242, 249
 wildlife, 54, 72–74, 162–163, 221
landscape perception, 65–66
Leave No Trace, 164–165, 193
Leopold, Aldo, 131
Leopold Report, 68–69
loons, 162–163, 164
Lopez, Barry, 65, 247–248

M

Marshall, Bob, 133, 235
mountaineering, 83, 85, 86–90, 108–109, 148, 181–182, 184, 224
 ethics, 88–90, 166–167, 186–187, 193, 202, 226–228
Mt. Jo, 140, 141
Murie, Adolph, 67–68, 70

N

National Park Service (NPS)
 Dual Mandate, 69
 resource science and stewardship, 26–27, 42, 68–69, 205. See also
  Leopold Report; paleontological resource management
 visitor expectations, 42, 46–47, 69–70, 71–72, 77
 visitor management, 42, 71
National Petroleum Reserve-Alaska, 232, 243–244, 246
New York State Department of Environmental Conservation, 134–135
North Slope (Alaska), 233, 234, 242–246

O

outdoor recreation. *See* backcountry travel

P

paleontological field work, 30, 37–38, 94–95, 97, 100–101, 103–105, 107,
 204–205
Paleontological Resources Preservation Act, 26
place attachment, 23, 50, 139, 143–144, 181–183, 188, 191, 220, 246–247
place creation, 16–19, 64, 148–150, 150–151, 163, 173–175, 184
place dependence, 43, 183

place identity, 6, 23, 50, 57–58, 126, 131, 183, 205, 208–209, 218, 226–228,
    242, 247, 250

R
recreation management, 71–72, 153–156, 181, 193, 195, 212–213. *See also*
    Leave No Trace; National Park Service: visitor management;
    overcrowding

S
sacred landscapes, 89
sense of place, 21–22, 49–50, 246
Sheldon, Charles, 67
Shepherd, Nan, 226–228
solitude, 113–114, 177, 195, 196, 247
solo hiking. *See* backcountry hiking
stewardship, 138–139, 196, 213, 225
sublime, 12, 13, 87, 131, 160, 225, 228, 236
summit steward. *See* Adirondack High Peaks Summit Steward Program

T
Tahawus, 175–176
Thoreau, Henry David, 99
tourist satisfaction, 42, 79–80, 182–183, 184

W
Washburn, Bradford, 84
wilderness, 17, 27, 29, 71, 74, 177–178, 182, 195, 196, 231, 236, 236–241
    ethics, 103–104, 147, 166–167, 194–195, 212–213, 221, 228, 237
    management, 195–196, 198, 212–213, 221–223, 224
    technology in, 107–108, 111, 148, 166, 216, 237, 241

Y
Yellowstone National Park, 41–42, 43–44

Z
Zahniser, Howard, 133–134